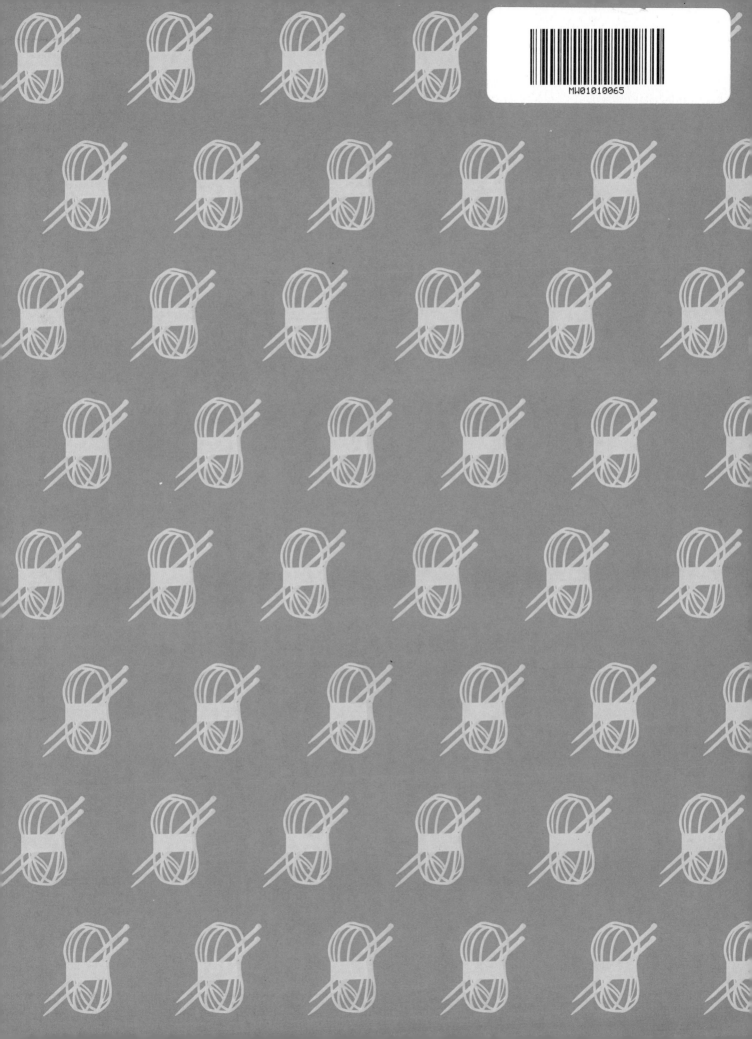

ultimate
knitting bible

ultimate knitting bible

A Complete Reference with Step-by-Step Techniques

Sharon Brant

COLLINS & BROWN

First published in the United Kingdom in 2008 by
Collins & Brown
10 Southcombe Street
London
W14 0RA

An imprint of Anova Books Company Ltd

Distributed in the United States and Canada by
Sterling Publishing Co, 387 Park Avenue South, New York, NY 10016, USA.

The moral right of the author has been asserted.

ISBN 978-1-84340-450-7

A CIP catalogue for this book is available from the British Library.

10 9 8 7 6 5 4 3 2 1

Reproduction by Rival Colour Ltd., UK
Printed and bound by Craft Print, Singapore

This book can be ordered direct from the publisher.
Contact the marketing department, but try your bookshop first.

www.anovabooks.com

contents

introduction

Welcome to the *Ultimate Knitting Bible*. If you are a novice knitter then this book will guide you step by step through everything you need to know in order to confidently knit any project that catches your eye, from the simplest scarf to the most gorgeously textured and embellished sweater. If you are already a member of the global knitting community, then I hope that you will find this book an invaluable treasure trove of techniques that you can dive into to look up and learn skills that have baffled you until now.

I have had the pleasure of working with Rowan for over 12 years, teaching beginners to knit and helping lots of keen knitters to improve their skills or to learn something completely new. So I dedicate this book to all of those ladies who have said to me over the years, 'Have you got all of these techniques written down?'. I've always had to say, 'No', but now I am pleased to be able to say a resounding 'Yes!'.

Many, many hours have gone into researching, illustrating and writing the myriad of techniques you will find in the 11 chapters that make up *Ultimate Knitting Bible*. The clear illustrations show you exactly how to manipulate the needles and yarn to achieve each technique and there are swatches so you can see just what the finished results should look like. The written descriptions of each step back up the illustrations with jargon-free explanations and there are lots of tips on how to obtain the best results and improve the appearance of your finished project. Look out for the samplers and stitch patterns that you can knit to practise the techniques you have studied in the chapters.

If you are picking up needles and yarn for the first time then I recommend that you start at the beginning of the book with the appropriately named 'Getting Started' chapter. Move on to 'Knitting Basics' for your first lessons in casting on, holding the needles and yarn, knitting, purling and casting off. Once these skills are mastered you can move from chapter to chapter as you wish, exploring the fascinating craft of knitting at your own pace. If textured knitting intrigues you, then turn to page 90 to see just how easy it really is to work cables, bobbles, twists, lace and other tactile techniques. Have the mysteries of colour knitting confounded you for years? Here, intarsia and Fair Isle are covered in depth with all the different ways of holding the yarns explained so that you can find a method you are comfortable with.

Whether you want to knit socks, use sequins and embroidery to embellish knitting, adapt a pattern to fit you beautifully or produce the perfect pocket, you can find out how to do it here. A comprehensive chapter on finishing your projects shows you how to get that really professional look and if you do make a mistake, just flip to the 'Troubleshooting' chapter to see how to fix it.

The world of knitting is contained in the 304 pages of this book and I hope that it inspires and teaches you to make many beautiful projects. I look forward to perhaps meeting you at a workshop one day and seeing some of the results of your work.

Sharon

Sharon Brant

getting started

From choosing the right needles to understanding your tension (gauge), on the following pages you will find useful information for all knitters, regardless of skill level.

equipment

Knitting always begins with a pair of needles and some yarn. However, there are some other items you will find useful.

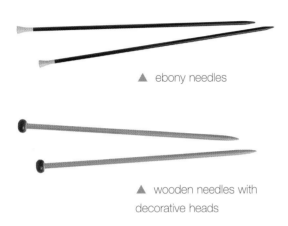

▲ ebony needles

▲ metal needles

▲ wooden needles with
decorative heads

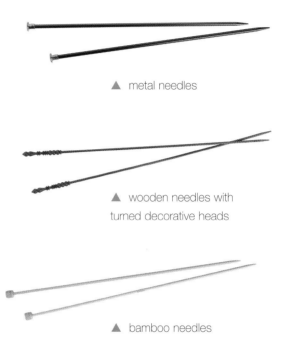

▲ wooden needles with
turned decorative heads

straight knitting needles

There is a huge choice of knitting needles available in different woods and materials. The key to good needles is for them to be flexible, smooth and have well-shaped points. Be careful, as lovely decorative tops can make the needles heavy and so give you wrist problems. However, they are beautiful for decorating your work room or office!

▲ bamboo needles

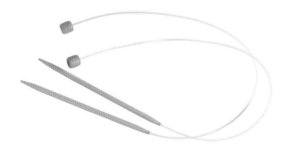

▲ straight needles with plastic extensions

These are my favourite needles for large projects. You knit backwards and forwards, as with normal straight needles, but the weight of the work slips onto the plastic extensions and can lie on your lap rather than having to be supported by your wrists. Great for travelling, these needles are available in bamboo, plastic and metal.

▲ double-pointed needles

These needles are used for working in a round (page 122) to make gloves, socks and neckbands. Always keep them tied together with an elastic band as it is so easy to lose one.

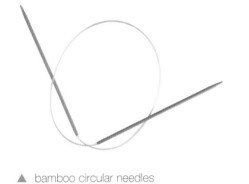

▲ bamboo circular needles

▲ ebony circular needles

circular needle

This is the needle to use when working in the round (page 120) on larger projects. They come in different lengths and it is important to use the correct length for the project as it will cause you problems if the needle is too long for the number of stitches. You can also work backwards and forwards on circular needles, which is useful for very large projects such as afghans and for front bands on cardigans (page 222).

▲ cranked cable needle

cable needles

Needles for working cables (page 92) come in different sizes and styles. Always try and match the size of the cable needle to the size of the knitting needles you are using. A cranked needle is a good choice when you are learning to cable, as it makes it almost impossible to drop a stitch while you are working the cable twist.

▲ straight cable needle

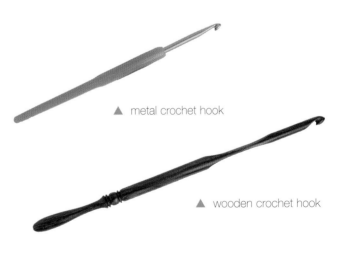

▲ metal crochet hook

▲ wooden crochet hook

crochet hooks

Hooks for crochet (pages 276–293), like knitting needles, are made in different materials – bamboo, wood, metal and plastic. I prefer metal hooks as the head glides through the stitch very easily. Look at the head of a hook before buying it and make sure it is smooth.

◀ bamboo crochet hook

▲ metal stitch holder

▲ plastic double-ended stitch holder

▲ safety pins

stitch holders

Stitch holders are used when you need to put a number of stitches to one side while knitting on the remaining stitches: for example, when working one side of a sweater neck. Have a variety of sizes of holder as sometimes you only need to hold two or three stitches (a safety pin is ideal in this case) and at other times it can be a lot. A large holder will just get in the way if you are holding only a few stitches. A double-ended holder allows you to knit straight off the holder rather than having to put the stitches onto a knitting needle first.

markers

Round markers are mostly used when working circular knitting (page 120). They are slipped onto a needle between stitches to mark the beginning of a round, or increase or decrease points. There are many decorative styles, but simple plastic versions can be bought. Stitch markers are looped through a knitted stitch to mark a point in the project that you need to refer back to later; for example, the point at which a sleeve is sewn to a sweater body.

▲ round markers

▲ stitch markers

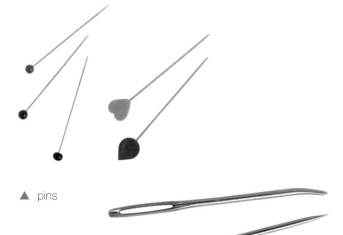

▲ pins

▲ needles

sewing up

When blocking (page 202) and then sewing up (pages 208–213) a project you will require pins. Long, thick pins with heads are best as they are less likely to split the yarn and are easy to see. Use a blunt-tipped tapestry or knitter's sewing needle for sewing up the seams. If you use mattress stitch you will find a sewing needle with a bent tip very useful as it makes it easy to see where it is coming through the knitted stitches.

colour knitting

When working with multiple colours (pages 146–175) you will need to use bobbins. You can buy bobbins or make your own (page 156). It is also advisable to make yourself a reference card with swatches of yarn on so you have a quick reference as to which colour refers to which letter or number in the pattern.

▲ plastic bobbin

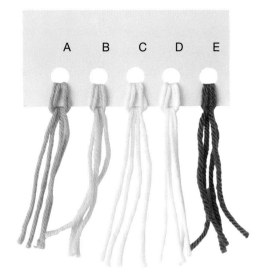
▲ yarn reference card

useful equipment

There is a variety of basic equipment that you will find useful. Use a tape measure that's not too old as they can stretch over time, which will give you an inaccurate measurement. A size gauge is needed if you are using old or foreign needles marked in a different measuring system (page 294). Point protectors stop stitches falling off the needle when you are not working on a project and stop needles punching holes in your knitting bag. Always cut yarn with scissors, don't try and break it by pulling; you might distort your work and hurt your hands. A row counter is useful with complex patterns to help you keep track of where you are, just don't forget to clock up the rows as you knit.

▲ tape measure

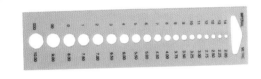
▲ needle size gauge

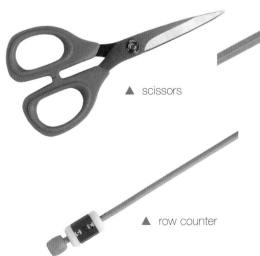
▲ scissors

▲ point protectors

▲ row counter

Buying equipment

There is a huge choice of lovely knitting equipment and it can be tempting to buy things that are pretty; just make sure they are practical as well. For example, overly ornate round markers can catch in the knitted fabric.

choosing yarn

Letting a knitter loose in a yarn shop to choose one yarn is like asking a child to pick out a toy in a wonderfully stocked toy shop. All those colours, textures and fibres: where do you start?

If you are buying the yarn recommended in a specific pattern then you just have to choose the colour, so it is a fairly simple operation. However, if you are substituting a pattern yarn for another yarn then not only do you have a wider choice, but there are some rules you must obey. Read the information on page 20 before buying a substitute yarn.

If you are buying yarn to knit a project you are designing yourself (pages 260–275), then it may be that you can buy anything, so bear the following in mind. Check the washing instructions on the ball band (see opposite) before you buy and be sure that you are happy to hand wash or dry clean the project if that is what the ball band states.

Look at how tightly twisted the yarn is. If it is very tight it will keep its shape when knitted up; if it is a loose twist and you can easily divide the plies (see below), this means it will change shape a little and could also split when you are knitting with it. Rub your hand over the ball of yarn a few times and make sure it isn't going to shed fibres too much, or that you are happy with how much it sheds. How chunky do you want your finished project to be? A thick yarn will make a lovely cosy scarf, but might not drape well if you are planning to make a sweater.

Structure of yarn

Yarns are made up of plies, thin strands of spun fibre that are then twisted together to make up the strand of yarn.
There are names for standard weights – or thicknesses – of yarn, such as double knitting (sport weight) and 4-ply (fingering) (page 296), but the number of plies twisted together to make up the yarn does not necessarily determine the weight of it. Thick yarns can be made from just one ply or thin yarns from four plies, and there are lots of yarns that do not fit into the standard categories.

Spinners use modern machinery these days and yarns can have very different appearances. A spiral yarn has a thin ply twisted around a thick one, while a slub is made up from one ply that varies in thickness along its length. Nub yarn has two or more plies that are twisted at different tensions so that bumps appear, while bouclé yarn also has two plies at different tensions, but a thinner binding ply means that loops of fibres appear.

Colour-fastness

Most commercially produced modern yarns are colourfast, but some eco-friendly yarns or yarns produced by traditional dying methods may not be.
You can check the colour-fastness of a yarn before you wash it or even knit with it, and this is a good idea if you are knitting a multi-coloured project and want to make sure a dark colour is not going to run into a pale colour. Simply wet a piece of the yarn and wrap it tightly around a piece of white paper kitchen towel. Allow it to dry, unwind the yarn and if the towel has changed colour then the yarn is not colourfast and may need to be dry cleaned.

Yarns can have special finishes to make them machine washable. A pure wool yarn, which you think would felt in the washing machine, might in fact be fine. You can test this by machine washing your tension (gauge) square (page 18) before washing the project.

Hanks

If your yarn comes in a hank, then you have to turn it into a ball before you can knit with it.
Untwist the hank and undo the ties at each end. Either ask a friend to hold the large loop of yarn over their wrists or hang it across the back of a chair. Start rolling up the ball with one of the loose ends, working in one direction until all the yarn is wound. Don't let your friend let go of the hank too early or you will be up very late at night undoing the large knot you have made.

If you want to make a ball that unwinds from the centre rather than the outside, start by making a bobbin (page 156). Wind the ball around the bobbin, making sure you keep the loose end free so that you can pull the yarn out from the centre of the ball. Do not wind too tightly at first or you may not be able to pull the yarn out easily.

ball bands

Ball bands are not only used for keeping the yarn in a ball, they also hold a lot of vital information that you may need, before and after knitting with it. It is always a good idea to keep one ball band from every project so you remember what you have used and know how to care for the project after it is finished. Always remember to give a ball band with the project if it is a gift.

Different manufacturers may have slightly different information on their ball bands and it might be set out in a different order, but a ball band should show you the following:

Country of origin This may be useful if you are trying to be more environmentally aware.

Average tension (gauge) and recommended needle sizes These may vary from what is stated in the pattern, in which case you must always go with the pattern information as the designer may have changed the needle size or tension (gauge) to get a certain look.

Name The manufacturer's brand name and the name the yarn is known by.

Weight The weight of the ball of yarn in grams or ounces.

Meterage (yardage) The approximate length of yarn in the ball. This is particularly important if you are substituting a yarn (page 20), or if you are designing your own project (pages 260–275).

Fibre What the yarn is made from (pages 16–17). As well as being important in how you care for the finished project, this may affect your choice of yarn. A wool yarn might not be suitable for a summer sweater.

Shade and dye lot numbers Sometimes a yarn may have a shade name as well as a number. The dye lot number is very important as balls of yarn with the same dye lot number were all dyed in the same batch of dye and so will be exactly the same colour. Even large commercial manufacturers rely on the batches of dyes being mixed to a precise specification, and that does not always happen. If a yarn is hand-dyed, then variations are even more likely. You need to make sure that all the yarn you buy for a project has the same dye lot number or else you may get a variation in shades, perhaps in the middle of the front of your sweater, which will look dreadful.

Care instruction symbols How to wash, press or dry clean the finished project.

country of origin

stitch tension
(gauge)

row tension
(gauge)

recommended
needle size

name of manufacturer

name of yarn

weight of ball

meterage/yardage of yarn in ball

fibre

shade name/number

dye lot number

care
instruction
symbols

different fibres

'Wool' is often used as a generic word for something to knit with, without reference to the fibre the ball is actually made from. It is better to use the word 'yarn' to describe knitting materials in general and think more carefully about which fibre you would like to work with. There is an ever-increasing range of yarns as new technologies allow different fibres to be spun and twisted into yarns. Fibres have varying properties and so the yarns made from them will be suitable for different types of project.

wool yarns

Wool is a warm fibre that can also breathe and is certainly the most popular knitting material in the world. It is made mainly from the fleeces of sheep, though some breeds of goats, llamas, camels and rabbits also have hair that is spun into wool yarns.

Merino, Shetland and Botany are just some of the types of sheep wool, the names referring either to the breed of sheep or where they originate from. Lambswool is made from the first shearing of a sheep and is the warmest and softest type of wool.

Angora yarn comes from the Angora rabbit while mohair comes from the Angora goat. Alpaca yarn comes from alpacas, an animal similar to a llama, and cashmere yarn is made from the finer fibres of the fleece of Kashmir goats.

Wool yarns are generally easy to knit with and if you are a beginner knitter you will find that their elasticity is quite forgiving if your tension (gauge) is a little uneven.

cotton yarns

Cotton is grown in many hot-climate countries and is available in different grades of softness, Egyptian cotton being the softest. Cotton is kind on the skin and so is usually suitable for people with skin allergies.

Though it is cool to wear, cotton fibre is heavier and less elastic than wool and so some spinners mix it with a synthetic fibre to make the yarn slightly more elastic and lighter in weight. Cotton takes dye very well and gives beautiful strong colours, as well as wearing and washing well.

Smooth, crisp cotton yarn shows stitch detail well and so is great for knitting textured patterns, though this quality also means that any unevenness in your knitting will show.

mixed fibre yarns

Spinners mix fibres to create yarns of different textures and weights. The addition of small amounts of synthetic fibre will make a yarn lighter and more elastic, though mixed fibres can still be natural; for example, cotton mixed with wool or cotton mixed with silk. If you find pure wool too itchy next to your skin, then try a wool and cotton mix yarn.

bamboo and soya yarns

As people become more aware of the environment, product content and what they are putting on their bodies, spinners have sourced new natural fibres that you would never have thought could be made into yarn. Bamboo from the centre of the bamboo stalk makes a soft, fine yarn that drapes beautifully and yarns made from the soya plant can be as fine as silk.

Silk yarns

Silk yarns come from the cocoon of various kinds of silk moths, most commonly the mulberry silk-worm. Collecting and spinning the silk fibres is a time-consuming job, hence the high cost of silk and the low availability of pure silk yarns. Look for silk-mix yarns if you want to knit with this fibre.

novelty yarns

Novelty yarns are mostly spun from man-made fibres and are often made up of several plies twisted together to make one yarn. These yarns are perfect for making a simple, plain garment into something more special. They are usually washable and durable, though many knitters are not keen on the feel of the finished knitted fabric.

tension (gauge)

Novice knitters sometimes ignore this aspect of a knitting pattern, but you really must pay attention to it or all the time you spend knitting a project could be time wasted.

Understanding a tension (gauge) instruction

Every knitting pattern will give a tension (gauge) instruction at the beginning of the pattern.

The tension (gauge) instruction will usually read something like: '20 stitches and 28 rows to 10cm (4in) square over stocking (stockinette) stitch using 4mm (US 6) knitting needles'. What this is telling you is that you must have 20 stitches across 10cm (4in) and 28 rows across 10cm (4in) of your knitted fabric.

These are the numbers of stitches and rows the designer has worked to and if your knitting doesn't match these then your finished project won't knit up to the correct measurements.

The ball band of a specific yarn (page 15) will also give a tension (gauge) and this is the manufacturer's tension (gauge), based on average use. This may be different to the designer's tension (gauge), in which case you must achieve the tension (gauge) given in the pattern rather than the one on the ball band.

Your first project

Tension (gauge) will often tighten as your skills improve, so consider knitting a scarf as your first project. It gives you a long, straight piece of knitting to practise your techniques and if your tension (gauge) does tighten up, it won't show very much.

How to do a tension (gauge) square

It can be tempting to skip knitting a tension (gauge) square and just rush on into the project, but it is much safer to spend the hour or so needed to knit the square than to have to unravel the project later on.

Using the yarn and needles given in the tension (gauge) instruction, cast on at least four stitches more than you need to achieve. Working in the stitch pattern stated, work at least four rows more than the number you need to achieve.

Do not cast (bind) off: leave the knitting on the needles while you measure it. The cast on edge and the row ends may be slightly tighter or looser than the middle of the knitting, so measure with the ruler centred on the fabric rather than touching the edges.

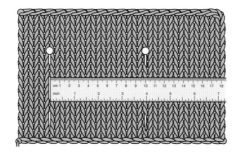

1. Lay the knitting flat, without stretching it. Lay a ruler across the stitches with the starting point a couple of stitches in from the edge. Put a pin in the knitting at the start of the ruler and at the 10cm (4in) mark. Count the number of stitches between the pins, including a half stitch if there is one.

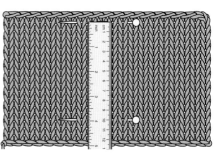

2. Measure 10cm (4in) across the rows in the same way and count the number of rows between the pins.

If you have too few stitches to 10cm (4in), then your tension (gauge) is too loose; if you have too many stitches, then your tension (gauge) is too tight. You may think it's not too bad if your tension (gauge) is out by one stitch, but those stitches add up.

If, for example, you are making a fitted sweater that is to be 50cm (20in) wide and the pattern tension (gauge) is 20 sts to 10cm (4in), but you have only been able to obtain 19 sts to 10cm (4in), then you may think that you are near enough. However, there are five lots of those 10cm (4in) across the sweater, so you are missing five stitches. Add the front and back together and you will have a difference of ten stitches. In measurements this will mean that your sweater will be 5cm (2in) larger than you want it to be. On a fitted sweater this will make quite a difference.

If you have a tension (gauge) of 21 sts to 10cm (4in) then the sweater could be 5cm (2in) too small: this could be the difference between wearing it and giving it away. These discrepancies are the result of being just one stitch away from the pattern tension (gauge), so it is vital achieve the correct tension (gauge).

Knitting accessories

Even if you are knitting an accessory, such as a bag, where the tension (gauge) isn't vital in terms of fit, then you should still do a tension (gauge) square. This is because the style and shape of the project will be affected by the tension (gauge). Also, the tension (gauge) you knit to determines how much yarn you use to work each stitch and if your tension (gauge) is too loose, you risk running out of yarn before finishing the project.

The swatches above all contain the same number of stitches and rows and were knitted with the same type of yarn on the same size needles. However, they were knitted by people who knit to different natural tensions (gauges) and you can see how different they are in size.

How to obtain the correct tension (gauge)

If you have knitted a tension (gauge) square and discovered you are out by one or two stitches, what should you do next? Never, ever just try to knit to a different tension (gauge). Everyone has a 'natural' tension – the tension (gauge) their knitting action and the way they hold their yarn creates – and if you try to knit to a different tension (gauge), you will just end up with an uneven piece of knitting.

Instead, you must change the size of the knitting needles you are using. The general rule is that one difference in needle size will create a difference of one stitch in the tension (gauge).

If you were aiming for 20 sts to 10cm (4in) using 4mm (US 6) needles but have obtained only 19 sts, then try again using 3.75mm (US 5) needles. Conversely, if you have obtained 21 sts, then try again with 4.5mm (US 7) needles.

If you are out by two stitches, then you would need to alter the needles by two sizes.

substituting a yarn

If you have found a pattern you love, but you don't like the yarn it uses, then it is possible to change it – you just need to follow a few simple rules.

Firstly, unless you are practiced at altering patterns (pages 270–273), choose a substitute yarn that is the same weight as the pattern yarn – trying to knit an Aran-weight pattern with a DK-weight yarn will cause you all sorts of problems. The yarns shown below are the same weights, though they look very different. This difference is another element you must consider when substituting a yarn: a jacket knitted in a smooth Aran-weight cotton yarn will have a very different look if it is made up in a knobbly tweed yarn.

However, you must be aware that yarns of the same weight do not always knit up to the same tension (gauge), so you really must do a tension (gauge) square. The ball band of the substitute yarn will provide an average tension (gauge), and as long as this doesn't differ by more than one stitch from that of the pattern yarn, you should be able to achieve the right tension (gauge) by changing needle size. More than one stitch difference could cause you a lot of problems; better to look for a different yarn.

The next step is to work out how much of the substitute yarn you need. You cannot just buy the number of balls given for the pattern yarn because, even though the balls may weigh the same amount as those of the pattern yarn, they will not necessarily contain the same number of metres (yards) of yarn, and it is this that is vital. This is particularly true if you are changing fibres – for example, from wool to cotton. Cotton is heavier than wool so there will be fewer metres (yards) of cotton yarn to a 50g (1¾oz) ball than there will be of wool yarn.

To work out how many balls of substitute yarn you need to buy, you must do the following sum.

Number of metres (yards) of yarn in one ball of pattern yarn multiplied by the number of balls needed to give you the total number of metres (yards) of yarn needed.
Total number of metres (yards) needed divided by the number of metres (yards) of yarn in one ball of the substitute yarn to give you the number of balls of substitute yarn you need to buy.

For example:
125 metres (yards) per ball of the pattern yarn and 15 balls are needed.
125 x 15 = 1875 metres (yards) in total of yarn needed.

95 metres (yards) per ball of the substitute yarn.
1875 by 95 = 19.73.

You will need to buy 20 balls of the substitute yarn.

Knitting a sweater

If you are using a substitute yarn it is always worth knitting first the back and then one sleeve. This is approximately half way through the sweater and you will be able to see whether you are going to have enough yarn to finish the project.

mixing fibres

Some knitwear designers use the technique of mixing different coloured yarns to increase their colour choices from 10 to sometimes 100 shades. This is called 'plying together' and it can be the gateway to a whole new world of yarns. You can use this technique to create a custom yarn of a specific weight, but one that is made up of more than one colour and texture.

You must always knit a tension (gauge) square in your plied yarns as these combinations will not always knit up perfectly, but as a general rule:
Two strands of 4-ply (fingering) knitted together will make a double-knit (sport weight).
One strand of 4-ply (fingering) and one strand of double knit (sport weight) will make an Aran (worsted) weight.
Two strands of double knit (sport weight) will make a chunky weight.

Therefore, if you were knitting a chunky garment you could put any of these combinations together:
One strand of chunky.
Two strands of 4-ply (fingering) and one strand of double knit (sport weight).
Four strands of 4-ply (fingering).
Two strands of double knit (sport weight).
One strand of Aran (worsted) and one strand of 4-ply (fingering).

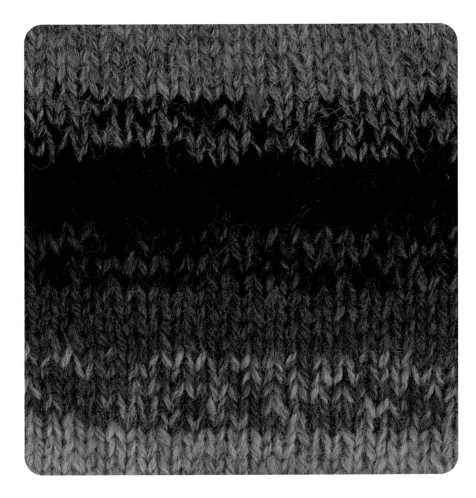

Blurred stripes can be achieved by plying yarns together. For the pattern for this swatch, turn to page 151. Bear in mind that if you will need to launder the project, the yarns must be compatible in that respect.

knitting basics

There isn't a lot to learn before you, too, are a knitter. Once you have mastered holding your needles, casting on, knitting, purling and casting (binding) off, you are a member of the worldwide knitting community.

what is knitting?

Knitting is a series of loops of yarn locked together to make a fabric. The loops are held on a needle then more loops are worked into them with the other needle, at the same time transferring the loops from one needle to the other. The loops are called stitches and when all the stitches are transferred from one needle to the other, this is called a row. The repeating of rows makes the knitted fabric.

The knitting stitches

There are just two stitches you need to master to be able to do all types of knitting: the knit stitch and the purl stitch. These stitches put together enable you to make a whole range of textures. Like anything new, you have to give it time, to practise, be patient and you will reap the rewards.

The most common knitted fabric is stocking (stockinette) stitch. This worked by knitting and purling alternate rows. These illustrations show both sides of stocking (stockinette) stitch, and if you look at them carefully you can see how the stitches are locked together to make the knitted fabric.

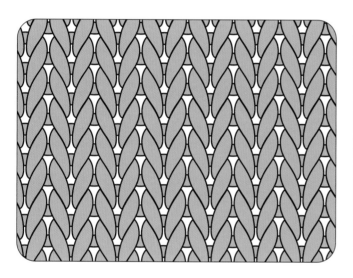

This is the right side of stocking (stockinette) stitch. This is also known as the knit side, as it is the knit stitches that form the interlocked V shapes.

This is the wrong side of stocking (stockinette) stitch; it is also a stitch in its own right, called reverse stocking (stockinette) stitch. This is sometimes called the purl side, as it is the purl stitches that form the bumps on the fabric.

casting on

To start knitting you need to get the required number of loops, or stitches, onto the needle – this is called casting on. There are many ways to cast on stitches, but here are five techniques useful to know. The technique you choose is either down to personal preference or the qualities of the specific cast on; you'll find notes on these qualities with each cast on technique. The tubular and invisible cast ons require you to be able to knit, so come back to these later on.

The slip knot

To cast on you need a starting point and this is the slip knot.
The slip knot will always count as the first cast on stitch.

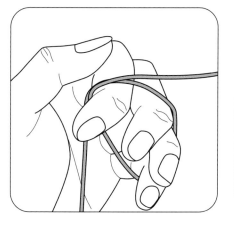

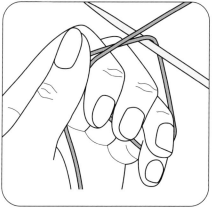

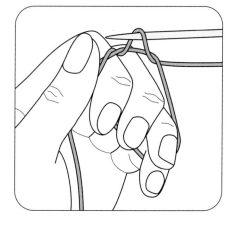

1 Hold the working (ball) end of the yarn in your right hand and wrap it around the fingers of your left hand.

2 Put the tip of a knitting needle, held in your right hand, through the loop around your fingers.

3 Wrap the working end of the yarn round the needle and pull the needle, and the yarn wrapped around it, through the loop around your left hand.

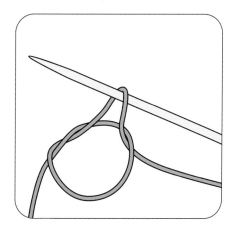

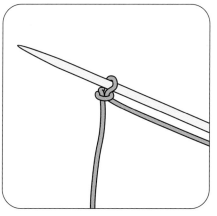

Tight cast on

With all cast on techniques, do not cast on too tightly. If your stitches are not moving freely along the needle, try using a larger needle.

4 Keeping the yarn on the needle, slip the loop off your left hand.

5 Pull gently on the ends of the yarn so that the loop tightens around the needle.

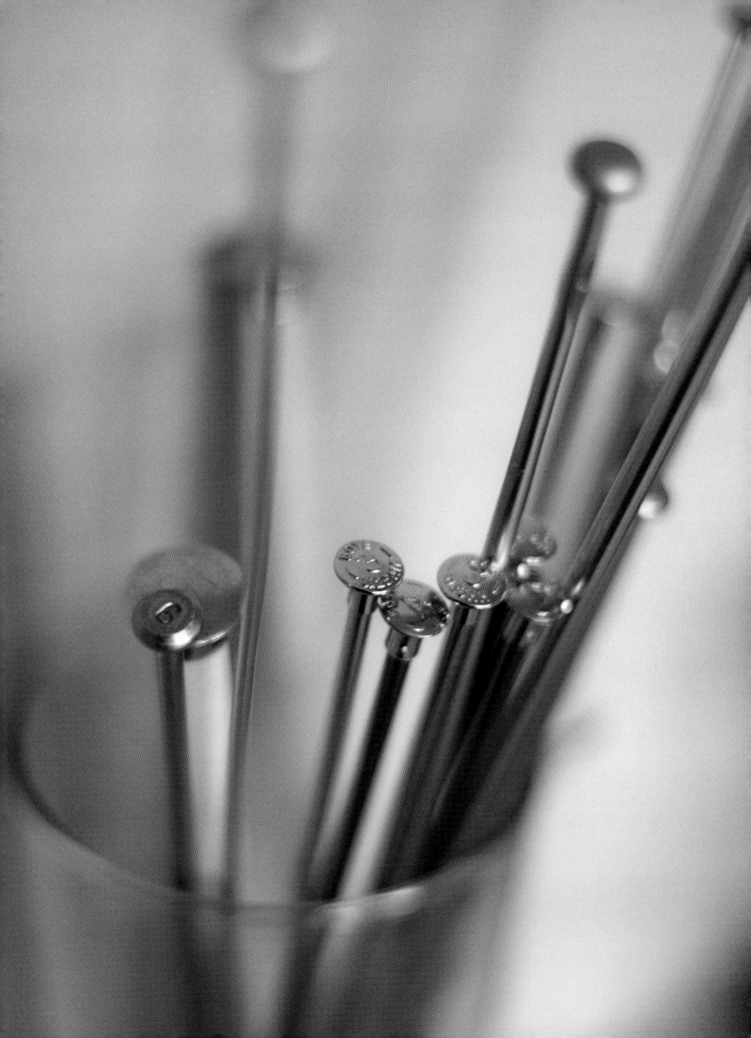

Cable cast on

This technique gives a firm edge that looks good with stocking (stockinette) stitch (page 24), and will keep its shape and not become baggy over time. It involves using both the knitting needles, so you may want to have a quick look at Holding the Needles and Yarn (pages 36–37).

Placing the needle

If you find it difficult to push the right-hand needle between the stitches in Step 6, try putting it through before you tighten the last stitch. With the needle in place, pull the last stitch tight, then work the next one.

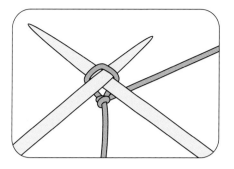

1 Make a slip knot about 15cm (6in) from the end of the yarn. Hold the needle with the slip knot in your left hand and the other needle in your right. With the working end of the yarn in your right hand, put the tip of the right-hand needle into the stitch on the left-hand needle.

2 Bring the yarn in your right hand under and around the point of the right-hand needle.

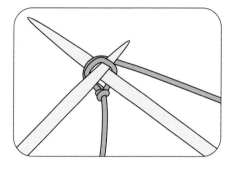

3 Pull the yarn taut so that it is wrapped around the tip of the right-hand needle.

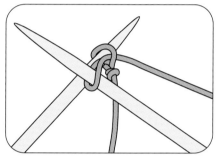

4 Bring the tip of the right-hand needle, and the yarn wrapped around it, through the stitch and towards you.

The smooth edge of a cable cast on.

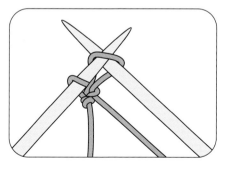

5 Pull gently until the loop is large enough to slip it over the tip of the left-hand needle. Take the right-hand needle out of the loop and pull the working end of the yarn so that the loop fits snugly around the left-hand needle.

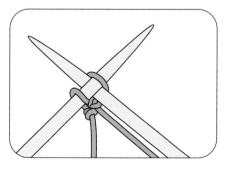

6 To cast on all the other stitches, put the tip of the right-hand needle between the last two stitches instead of through the last one. Then repeat Steps 2–6 until you have the required number of stitches on the left-hand needle.

Thumb cast on

The thumb technique produces an edge that has elasticity. This is very useful when working with yarns that don't have a lot of give, such as chenille or firm cotton, or when casting on for a ribbed edge (pages 46–47). It is also a cast on that looks good with garter stitch (page 44) and moss (seed) stitch (page 48).

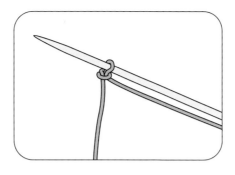

1 For this cast on you firstly need to pull enough yarn from the ball to make all the stitches; approximately 2cm (¾in) per stitch is needed. Measure out the correct amount of yarn then make a slip knot (page 26).

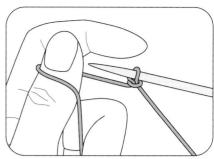

2 Hold the ball end of the yarn and the needle in your right hand. Hold the other end of the yarn (the measured length) in the palm of your left hand. Move your left thumb behind and under the yarn, so that the yarn is wrapped from front to back around your left thumb.

3 Insert the tip of the needle into the loop on your thumb

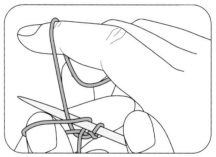

4 Wrap the yarn in your right hand under and around the tip of the knitting needle.

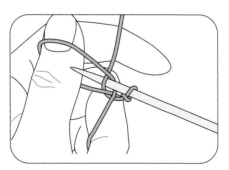

5 Bring the needle, and the yarn wrapped around it, through the loop around your thumb and towards you to make another stitch on the needle.

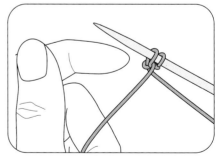

6 Slip your thumb out of the loop and pull the two ends of yarn away from the needle in opposite directions. Repeat Steps 2–6 until you have cast on the number of stitches required.

The ridged edge of a thumb cast on.

Continental cast on

If you hold the needles and knit in the Continental style (pages 36–37 and 40–41) try this cast on: it gives a similar end result to the thumb cast on (page 29). You need to calculate how much yarn you will use and it is best to allow 2cm (¾in) per stitch. Measure out the correct amount of yarn then make a slip knot.

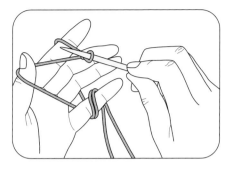

1 Wrap the ball end of the yarn around your left index finger and the measured end around your left thumb. Wrap both ends around your little finger to hold them in place.

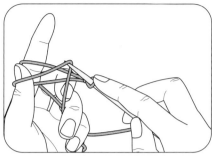

2 Holding the needle in your right hand, put the tip of it up through the loop around your thumb.

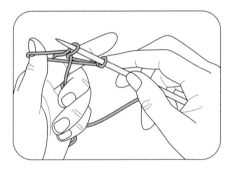

3 Now take it down through the loop around your index finger and then back under the loop on your thumb.

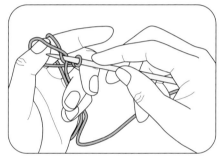

4 Slip your thumb out of its loop, making sure you don't drop the loop off the needle.

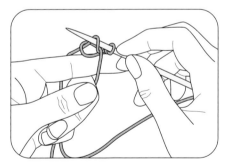

5 Using your left thumb, pull the new loop on the needle tight to compete the stitch. Repeat Steps 1–5 until you have cast on the number of stitches required.

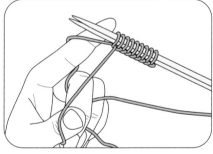

6 If your stitches are too tight, try casting on onto two needles held together. When you have cast on all the stitches, slip one needle out of them before knitting the first row.

Continental cast on edge.

Left-hand cast on

You may find this the easiest method if you are left-handed. It is a similar technique to the Continental cast on so you need to calculate how much yarn you will use; it is best to allow 2cm (¾in) per stitch. Measure out the correct amount of yarn then make a slip knot.

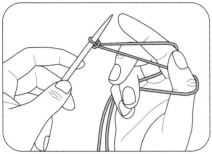  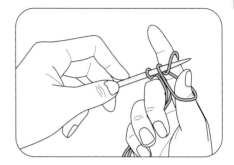

1 Hold the needle with the slip knot on in your left hand. Wrap the measured end of the yarn around your right thumb from back to front. Wrap the ball end over your right index finger and secure both ends between your palm and fingers.

2 Put the tip of the needle up into the loop on your thumb.

3 Insert the tip of the needle downwards into the loop around your index finger and draw it through the loop on your thumb. Pull the stitch tight. Continue until you have cast on the required number of stitches.

Holding the needles

Turn to page 37 to see how to hold the needles and yarn if you are left handed.

Left-handed knitting

Turn to pages 42–43 to see how to knit and purl if you are left handed.

Tubular cast on (first method)

This cast on produces a particularly neat edge that is ideal when working in rib (page 46). However, it is not recommended when using heavy-weight yarns.

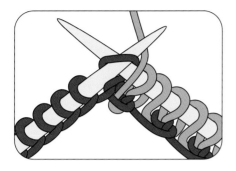 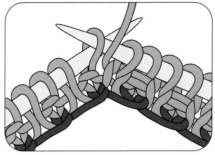 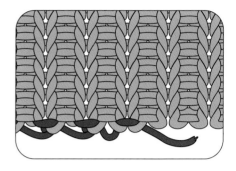

1 Using a contrast colour yarn and the cable method (page 28), cast on half the required number of stitches. This must be an even number, so if necessary add one extra stitch then work two stitches together when the rib is completed. Cut the yarn. Using the project yarn and holding it at the back, knit one, *bring the yarn forward, knit one with the yarn going over the needle to make an extra stitch (page 100). Repeat from * to end of row.

2 *Knit one, bring the yarn to the front between the needles, slip the next stitch purlwise, take the yarn to the back between the needles, repeat from * to the last stitch, slip this last stitch. On the following row, bring the yarn to the front, *slip one, take the yarn to the back, knit one, bring the yarn to the front, repeat from * to the last stitch.

3 Work these two rows once more then work in single rib (page 46). After you have completed the rib you can remove the contrast yarn at the bottom by carefully unpicking it.

Tubular cast on with half of the contrast yarn unpicked.

Tubular cast on (second method)

This is an alternative version of the tubular cast on. It is also ideal for rib (page 46) and produces a particularly neat edge.

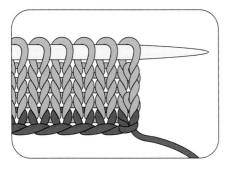

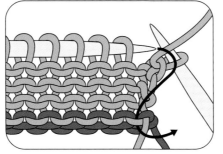

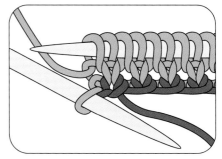

1 Using a contrast colour yarn and the cable method (page 28), cast on half the required number of stitches and then cut the yarn. Using the yarn needed for the project, purl one row and then knit one row. Repeat the last two rows once more. For the next row, the wrong side of the work will be facing you.

2 *Purl the first stitch, insert the tip of the left-hand needle into the back of the first stitch of the project yarn (which is between the first two contrast colour loops). Slip this stitch onto the left-hand needle and, with the yarn at the back, knit it through the back loop (page 51). Repeat from * to the last stitch.

3 Purl the last stitch, pick up the half loop in the main colour at the very edge of the row and knit it through the back loop. Remove the contrast yarn by carefully unpicking it. Continue working the project in rib.

Choosing contrast yarn

Use a yarn that is the same weight as the project yarn to work the contrast rows of a tubular cast on. The contrast colour makes it easy to see what needs unpicking once a few rows have been knitted.

Unpicking the contrast yarn reveals the neat cast on edge.

Invisible cast on

This technique gives a more rounded edge. It is strong and has great elasticity. You will need two pairs of needles – one pair in the size required for the pattern and another pair that is two sizes larger.

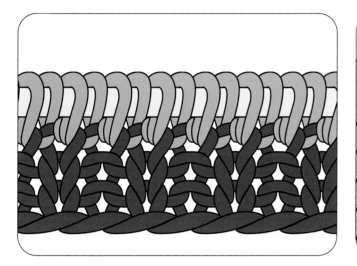

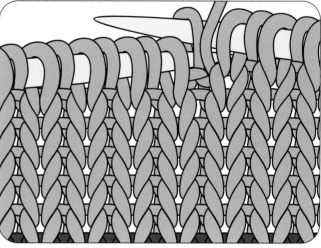

1 With the larger needles and contrast colour yarn, cast on half the required number of stitches. Work three rows of knit one, purl one rib then cut the yarn. Using the smaller needles and the yarn needed for the project, knit one and purl one into each stitch to double the number of stitches on the needle.

2 For the next four rows, knit the knit stitches and slip the purl stitches with the yarn at the front of the work. Then continue in single rib (page 46).

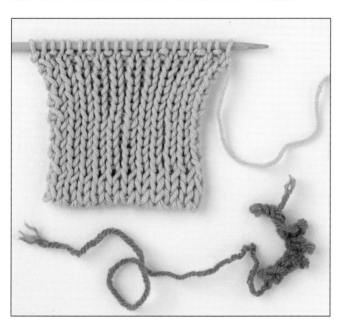

An invisible cast on edge with the contrast yarn completely unpicked.

Lace cast on

This is a more open cast on technique and is ideal when you are working a lace design (pages 100–107) or with very fine yarn that might need a little more stretch in the foundation row. It is very similar to the cable cast on, but you are working into the stitch each time rather than going between stitches. A common error is to use this cast on for all your knitting and then wonder why with stocking (stockinette) stitch the projects stretch and the edges look untidy.

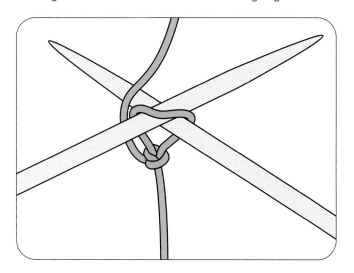

1 Make a slip knot about 15cm (6in) from the end of the yarn. Hold the needle with the slip knot in your left hand and the other needle in your right hand. Holding the working end of the yarn in your right hand, put the tip of the right-hand needle into the stitch on the left-hand needle.

2 Bring the yarn in your right hand under and around the point of the right-hand needle and pull it taut. Bring the tip of the right-hand needle, and the yarn wrapped around it, through the stitch and towards you. Pull gently until the loop is large enough to slip it over the tip of the left-hand needle. Take the right-hand needle out of the loop and pull the loop so that it fits snugly around the left-hand needle.

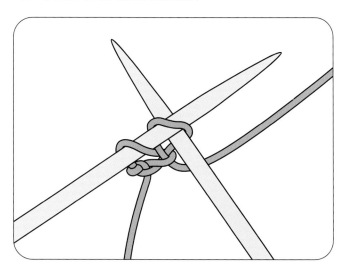

3 Put the tip of the right-hand needle into the stitch just made and repeat Steps 1–3 until you have cast on the required number of stitches.

A lace cast on edge with a simple lace pattern above it.

holding the needles and yarn

Holding the needles is one of the toughest things to master in knitting, so if you find it hard, don't be put off – it gets easier after this. How you hold the needles will depend on how you plan to knit, but you may not know that yet. You can hold the yarn in your right or left hand. If you hold it in your right hand, that is the English way; if hold it in your left hand then that is the Continental way of knitting. Though awkward at first, holding the needles either way becomes much more comfortable with practice. Have a go at both methods and you will quickly find out which one is most suitable for you.

The English method

This is the most commonly used method in the UK and USA. The needles are held differently in the right and left hands.

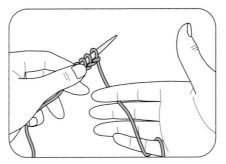

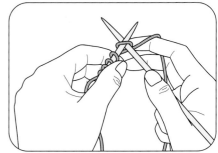

1 Hold the needle with the stitches on in your left hand. Wrap the yarn around the little finger of your right hand and then come up between your index and second fingers.

2 Hold the other needle in your right hand, placing it in the crook between the thumb and index finger, in the same way as you would hold a pencil. The right-hand index finger is going to control the tension (gauge) of the yarn, so it is important to keep the yarn slightly taut around this finger.

Perfecting your technique

Once you are able to control the needles, ignore them for a while and learn to knit. You can perfect your holding technique afterwards.

The Scottish method

As the name suggests, this way of holding the yarn and needles originated in the north of Britain. Some knitters tuck the end of the right-hand needle under their arm when using this method.

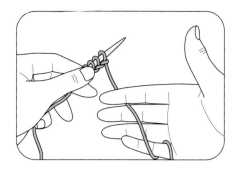

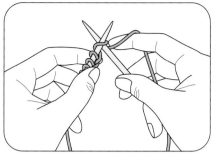

1 Hold the needle with the stitches on in your left hand. Wrap the yarn around the little finger of your right hand and then come up between your index and second fingers.

2 Hold the other needle into your right hand, placing your hand on top of the needle, in the same way as you would hold a knife. The right-hand index finger is going to control the tension (gauge) of the yarn, so it is important to keep the yarn around this finger slightly taut.

The Continental method

This method is the most popular in Continental Europe. It is also a technique that many left-handers find easy to use if they are knitting right-handed.

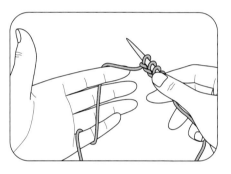

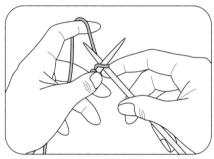

1 Hold the needle with the stitches on in your right hand. Wrap the yarn around the little finger and then around the index finger of your left hand. Then move the needle with the stitches on into your left hand.

2 Hold the other needle in your right hand, holding it from above. The tension (gauge) of the yarn will be controlled by your left-hand index finger, so it is important to keep the yarn around it slightly taut.

Left-handed method

Obviously this is probably the most suitable method if you are left-handed, though as all knitting techniques involve using both hands, many left-handers have no problem with right-handed techniques.

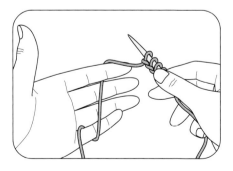

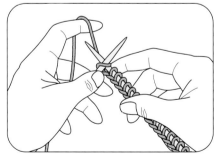

1 Hold the needle with the stitches on in your right hand. Wrap the yarn around the little finger and then around the index finger of your left hand.

2 Hold the other needle in your left hand, holding it from above. The tension (gauge) will be controlled by your left-hand index finger, so it is important to keep the yarn around it slightly taut.

the stitches

Once you have cast on the required number of stitches, you can start to make your knitted fabric. When you knit, you transfer stitches from the left-hand needle to the right-hand needle. When you come to the end of the row, you put the needle with the stitches on into your left hand and work on the reverse side of the project to knit, or purl, the next row. There are two main styles of knitting, English and Continental.

Knit stitch (English)

You can knit every stitch on every row and this will give you a texture called garter stitch (page 44).

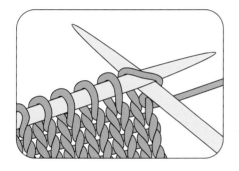

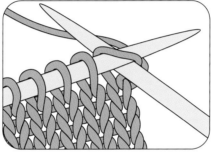

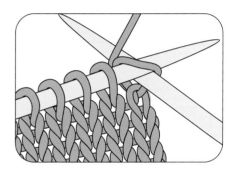

1 Hold the needles using either the English method (page 36) or the Scottish method (page 37). From front to back, insert the tip of the right-hand needle into the first stitch on the left-hand needle.

2 Bring the yarn you are holding in your right hand under the tip of the right-hand needle.

3 Wrap the yarn over the needle.

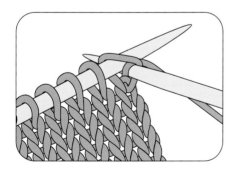

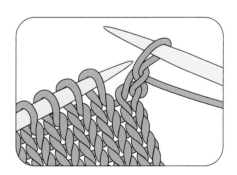

4 Bring the tip of the right-hand needle, and the yarn wrapped around it, through the stitch on the left-hand needle.

5 Pull the loop of yarn through to make a new stitch on the right-hand needle.

6 Slip the original stitch off of the left-hand needle. The knitted stitch is now complete.

Purl stitch (English)

Most knitting designs are made up of both knit and purl stitches. Once you have mastered the purl stitch you are able to go forward and try any design. It's best to practise the knit stitch until you are confident with it and then move on to purl stitch.

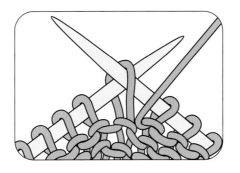

1 For purl stitch, you need the yarn at the front of the work as shown. From back to front, put the tip of the right-hand needle into the first stitch on the left-hand needle.

2 Bring the yarn forward and then take it over the tip of the right-hand needle.

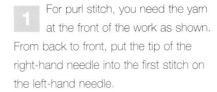

3 Wrap it under and around the tip of the needle.

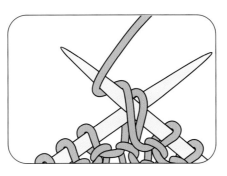

4 Bring the tip of the right-hand needle, and the yarn wrapped around it, backwards through the stitch on the left-hand needle, making sure that this stitch remains on the needle.

Incomplete stitches

A common problem when learning knit and purl is working incomplete stitches. If at the end of a row you have more stitches than you started with, this is probably the cause. Turn to page 251 to see how to identify and fix an incomplete stitch.

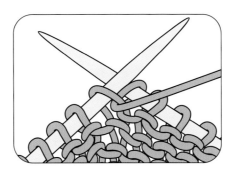

5 Pull the loop completely through the stitch, creating a new stitch on the right-hand needle.

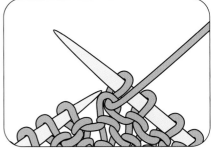

6 When it's safely through, slip the original stitch off the left-hand needle. The purl stitch is now complete.

Knit stitch (Continental)

If you are going to use the Continental techniques, this is how you work a knit stitch.

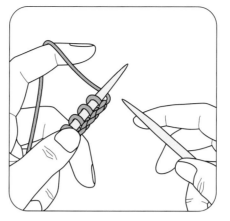

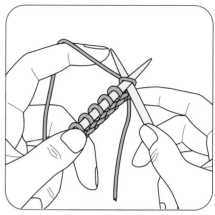

1 Hold the needles using the Continental method (page 37).

2 From front to back, put the tip of the right-hand needle into the first stitch on the left-hand needle.

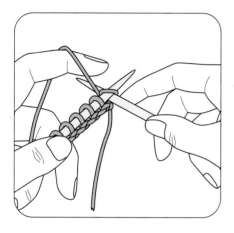

3 Lay the yarn that is held in your left hand over the right-hand needle, as shown.

4 With the tip of the right-hand needle, bring the strand through the cast on stitch. You will need to lower your left-hand index finger slightly to help this process.

5 Slip the original stitch off the left-hand needle. The knitted stitch is now complete.

Working back across a row

Even if you decide to use the English methods of knitting and purling (pages 38–39), it can be useful to be able to knit in the Continental style as well. This is because if you are knitting a very large project, such as an afghan, rather than having to turn the whole thing over at the end of each row, you can just change the way you knit and work back across the row without turning the project.

Purl stitch
(Continental)

This is how you work a purl stitch using the Continental technique.

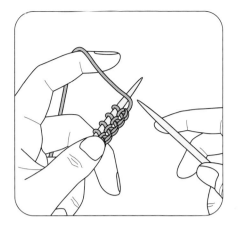

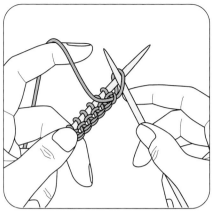

1 Bring the yarn to the front of the left-hand needle.

2 From back to front, put the tip of the right-hand needle into the first stitch on the left-hand needle.

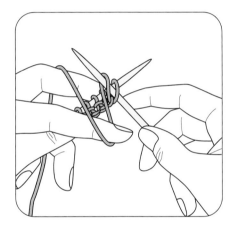

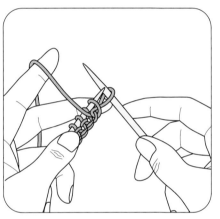

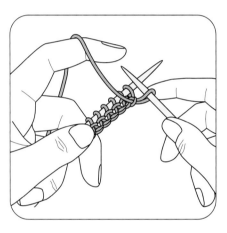

3 Lay the yarn over the tip of the right-hand needle and use the index finger of the left hand to keep the yarn taut.

4 Move the tip of the right-hand needle backwards through the stitch on the left-hand needle, making sure that this stitch remains on the needle.

5 When it's safely through, slip the original stitch off the left-hand needle. The purl stitch is now complete.

At the end of a row

You have learnt how to knit a stitch and then how to purl one, but how do you put these together?

The easiest thing to do is to cast on 20 or 30 stitches (pages 28–31) and then learn the knit stitch. When you have knitted every stitch from the left-hand needle to the right-hand needle you need to turn the work. Simply swap the needles in your hands so that the needle with the stitches on is now the left-hand needle and the empty needle is now the right-hand one. You are ready to start the next row.

If you are unsure as to which row – knit or purl – you should work next, look at the knitting in your left hand. If the purl side (page 24) is facing you, then you purl the next row. If the knit side is facing you, then you knit it.

If you have just finished purling a row, the yarn will be at the front of the work. Wrap it around to the other side of the work, which will tighten up the last stitch, and then swap the needles in your hands.

left-handed knitting

It is possible to knit left-handed, you just transfer the stitches from the right-hand needle onto the left-hand needle. The problem you will have is that if you want to work more complex textures in your knitting, you will find some designs are extremely difficult or even impossible to do. You will also have to make a number of alterations to some patterns for them to work out properly. Many left-handed knitters actually prefer to knit the right-handed way.

Left-handed knit stitch

Try this technique for knitting stitches and see if you find it easier than the right-handed method.

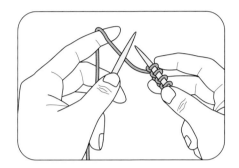

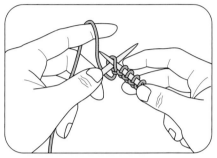

1 Hold the needle with the cast on stitches in your right hand and the yarn in your left hand.

2 From front to back, put the tip of the left-hand needle into the first stitch on the right-hand needle.

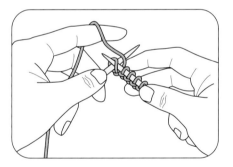

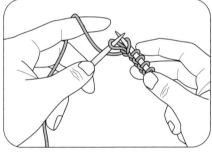

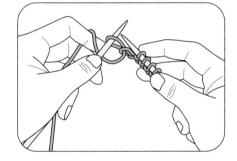

3 Wrap the yarn you are holding in your left hand under and then around the tip of the left-hand needle.

4 Bring the point of the left-hand needle, and the yarn wrapped around it, through the stitch on the right-hand needle.

5 When it is safely through, slip the original stitch off the right-hand needle. The knit stitch is now complete.

Casting on
Turn to page 31 to see how to cast on.

Holding the needles
Turn to page 37 to see how to hold the needles and yarn.

Left-handed purl stitch

This is the left-handed technique for purling stitches.

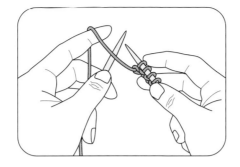

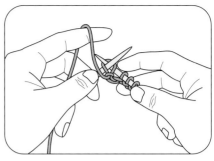

1 For purl stitch you need the yarn at the front of the work.

2 From back to front, put the tip of the left-hand needle into the first stitch on the right-hand needle.

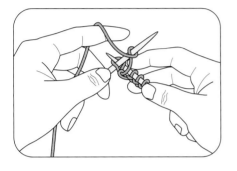

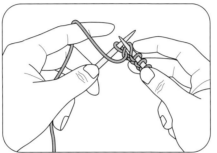

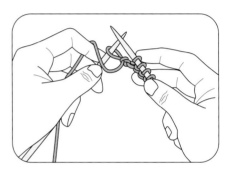

3 Wrap the yarn over and around the tip of the right-hand needle.

4 Bring the tip of the left-hand needle, and the yarn wrapped around it, backwards through the stitch on the right-hand needle, making sure that this stitch remains on the needle.

5 Pull the loop completely through the stitch, creating a new stitch on the left-hand needle. When it's safely through, slip the original stitch off the left-hand needle.

Using a mirror

If you are learning to knit left-handed and a technique illustrated for right-handed knitting in a book is defeating you, then hold the book up to a mirror and see if the reversed reflection makes it easier to understand. The best right-handed knitting technique for left-handers to try is the Continental method (pages 40–41).

simple knitted fabrics

Once you have learned the knit and purl stitches, a world of knitted fabrics is open to you.
Here are the most commonly used and simplest fabrics you can make.

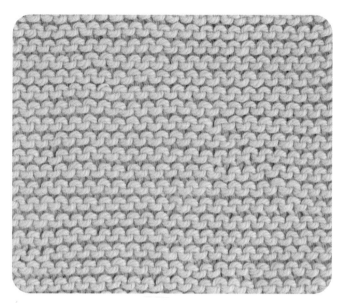

Garter stitch

If you knit every stitch and every row you will make a fabric
called garter stitch. This fabric is great for beginners and is
perfect for making a scarf as it is completely reversible.

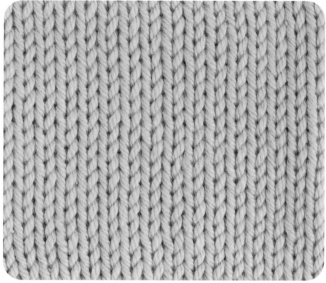

Stocking (stockinette) stitch

Stocking (stockinette) stitch is the most popular knitted
fabric and is used in all sorts of projects. This fabric is made
up of alternate rows of knit and purl stitches. It is a smooth
fabric that provides a good background for embellishments
(pages 176–197), as well as looking good in its own right.

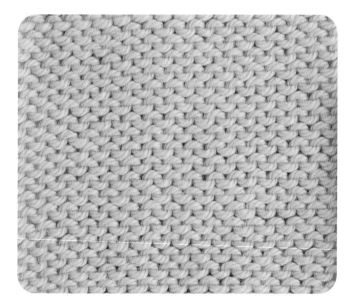

Reverse stocking (stockinette) stitch

This is quite simply the other side of stocking (stockinette)
stitch. This fabric is often used as a background for cables
and other textured stitches (pages 92–97).

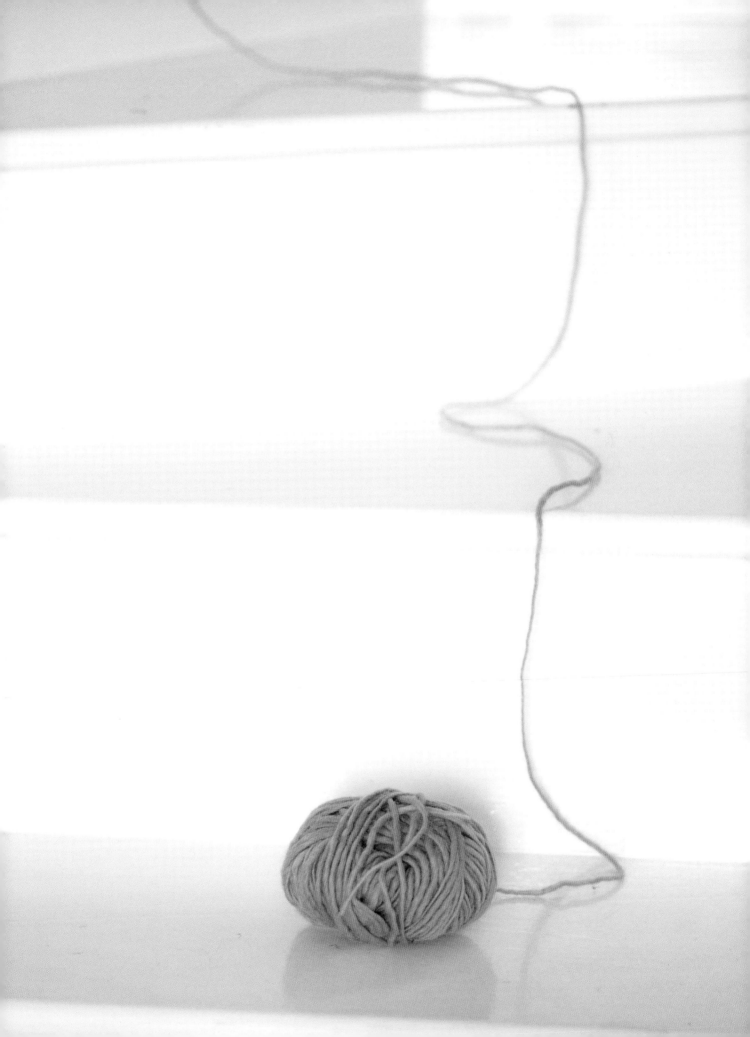

Rib

Rib is most commonly used on the lower edges, cuffs, neckbands and front bands of garments. If you were to cast on and work in stocking (stockinette) stitch straight away, the lower edge of your work would curl up. This is sometimes used as a feature, but to eliminate this curl you can use a rib for a neat edge with the knit and purl stitches forming distinctive columns. Rib is also very elastic, so it stretches to allow a hand or head to pass through and then closes up again for a snug fit.

Single rib (k1, p1 rib)

This is formed by alternately knitting one stitch and then purling one stitch.

Taking the yarn back

If you don't take the yarn to the front and back between stitches you will end up with loops lying across the needles. If you have more stitches than you should at the end of a row then this may have occurred. Baggy stitches, particularly on multiple stitch ribs, are a common problem (page 252).

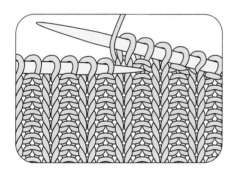

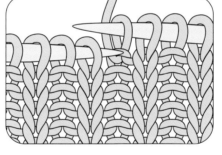

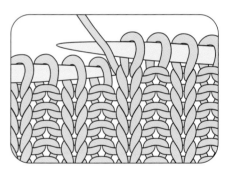

1 Knit one stitch with the yarn at the back of the work, then bring the yarn forward between the tips of the needles to the front in order to purl one stitch. When you have completed the purl stitch, take the yarn back between the needles ready for the next knit stitch.

2 Here the yarn is at the back of the work ready to knit the next stitch.

3 Here the yarn has come between the needles to be at the front ready for the purl stitch.

The stitches in single rib fabric run in columns.

Which stitch next in rib?

If you are a knitting novice it is easy to get lost as to which stitch in a rib pattern – knit or purl – you should work next. Here you can see how the knit and purl stitches differ: if the last stitch you worked has a bump across it, then it is a purl stitch and you knit the next stitch. Conversely, if the last stitch is a smooth V then it is a knit stitch and you purl the next stitch. The next stitch worked in the illustration (right) will be a knit stitch. As you knit more rows and the columns of knit and purl stitches grow, it becomes easier to see which stitch should come next.

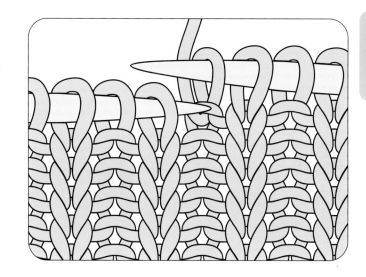

Rib patterns

Combining various numbers of knit and purl stitches will create different rib patterns. Working knit stitches through the back loop (page 51) twists them, giving the rib pattern a different look.

Double rib
Worked over a pattern repeat of
4 sts + 2 sts.
Row 1: [K2, p2] rep to last 2 sts, k2.
Row 2: P2, [k2, p2] rep to end.
Rep these 2 rows.

4x2 rib
Worked over a pattern repeat of
6 sts + 4 sts.
Row 1: [K4, p2] rep to last 4 sts, k4.
Row 2: P4, [k2, p4] rep to end.
Rep these 2 rows.

Twisted rib
Worked over an odd number of sts.
Row 1: [K1tbl, p1] rep to last st, k1tbl.
Row 2: P1, [k1tbl, p1] rep to end.
Rep these 2 rows.

Moss (seed) stitch

There is another commonly used fabric for areas such as edgings and collars and that is moss (seed) stitch. Like rib (pages 46–47), this is formed by knitting one stitch and purling the next, but the difference is that on the second row you work the opposite stitch to the one in the previous row. Rather than lining up in columns, the stitches produce a bumpy, textured fabric.

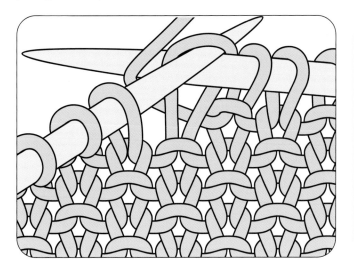

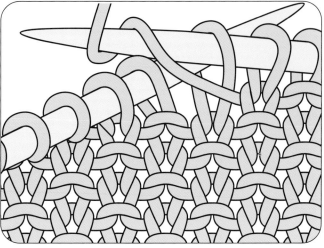

1 Knit one stitch with the yarn at the back of the work, then bring the yarn forward between the tips of the needles to the front in order to purl one stitch. When you have completed the purl stitch, take the yarn back between the needles ready for the next knit stitch.

2 On the second row, when you are faced with a knit stitch you purl it and when faced with a purl stitch, you knit it. Here, a stitch that was purled on the previous row will be knitted on this row.

The textural fabric produced by moss (seed) stitch.

Using moss (seed) stitch

Moss (seed) stitch is perfect for accessories such as scarves and bags as it is both stable and reversible. You can also use it as a background for Aran stitches (pages 92–97) as an alternative to the traditional reverse stocking (stockinette) stitch.

Next stitch in moss (seed)?

Look carefully at this illustration so that you are able to recognise which stitch you need to work next when working moss (seed) stitch.

If the next stitch has a bump across the bottom of it, then it is a purl stitch and you must knit into it. Conversely, if the next stitch is smooth then it is a knit stitch and you must purl into it. The next stitch worked in the illustration (right) will be a knit stitch.

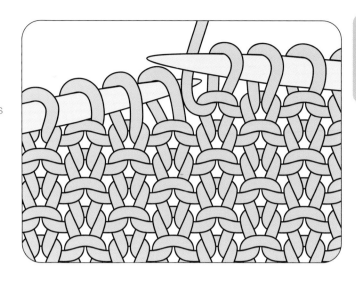

Moss (seed) patterns

As with rib (page 47), different combinations of knit and purl stitches will create different moss (seed) patterns.

Double moss (seed) stitch 1
Worked over a multiple of 4 sts.
Row 1: [K2, p2] rep to end.
Row 2: [K2, p2] rep to end.
Row 3: [P2, k2] rep to end.
Row 4: [P2, k2] rep to end.
Rep these 4 rows.

Double moss (seed) stitch 2
Worked over a multiple of 4 sts.
Row 1: [K2, p2] rep to end.
Row 2: [P2, k2] rep to end.
Rep these 2 rows.

Elongated moss (seed) stitch
Work over an even number of sts.
Row 1: [K1, p1] rep to end.
Row 2: [K1, p1] rep to end.
Row 3: [P1, k1] rep to end.
Row 4: [P1, k1] rep to end.
Rep these 4 rows.

slipping stitches

When you need to move a stitch from the left-hand needle to the right-hand needle without actually knitting or purling it, then you must slip it. This technique is used in different ways in knitting and is something you need to learn.

Slipping a stitch knitwise

You would usually slip a stitch this way on a knit row, though some effects involve slipping a stitch the opposite way to the stitches that are actually being worked.

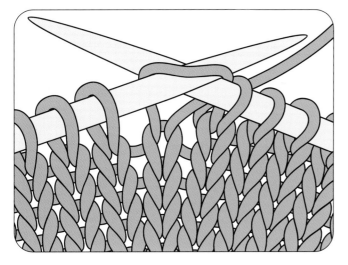

From front to back, put the tip of the right-hand needle into the next stitch on the left-hand needle and slip it over onto the right-hand needle.

Slipping a stitch purlwise

This is the method you use to slip a stitch purlwise, on a purl or a knit row.

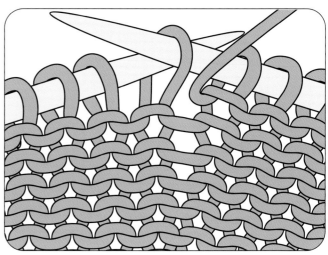

From back to front, put the tip of the right-hand needle into the next stitch on the left-hand needle and slip it over onto the right-hand needle.

Stretching stitches

When you are slipping a stitch be very careful not to pull on it and stretch it as there is nothing going through it to tighten it up again. Put the very tip of the needle into the stitch and allow it to find its own shape on the right-hand needle. A stretched slipped stitch will show in the finished knitting.

through the back loop of a stitch (tbl)

This is another technique that is worth knowing, as it can appear in several locations throughout a pattern. It actually twists the stitch, giving it a different appearance, so is mainly used for decorative detail. If you need to slip a stitch tbl, then slip it (opposite) by putting the needle through the back loop, as instructed below.

Knitting through the back loop

Here you are knitting through the back of the stitch, rather than through the front as is usual.

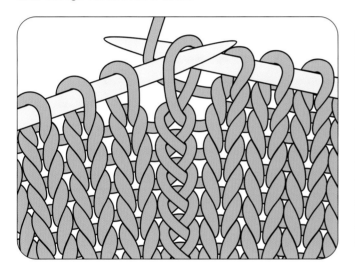

From front to back, put the tip of the right-hand needle into the back loop of the next stitch on the left-hand needle. Wrap the yarn around the tip of the needle and pull the new stitch through in the usual way.

Purling tbl

Purling tbl is slightly tricky and a good tip is to put the right-hand needle into the front of the stitch first and give it a slight stretch. Then hold the stitch in place with your left index finger on the left-hand needle while putting the right-hand needle into the stitch from the back.

Purling through the back loop

Though this looks complicated, you are simply purling through the back loop of the stitch.

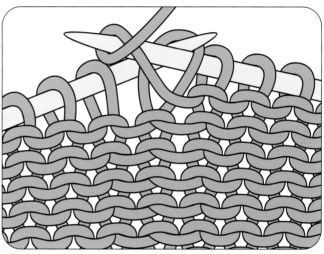

This is exactly the same technique, but worked in the purl direction. From back to front, put the tip of the right-hand needle into the back loop of the next stitch. Wrap the yarn around the tip of the needle and pull the new stitch through in the usual way. In both these illustrations, the column of stitches below the one being worked have all been worked through the back loop.

edge stitches

When working a piece of knitting it can become uneven at the edges. There are a few techniques that can neaten up the work, but some of them can cause you problems later if the edge has to be joined to another piece of knitting (pages 205–215), or you have to pick up stitches along it (pages 221–222). If either of these are the case, look at Troubleshooting (page 253) to improve your edge without using an edge stitch.

However, if the edges are not being sewn up (for example, on a scarf), then working an edge stitch – or selvedge as it is also called – can be a good option.

Slip stitch edge

A slipped stitch edge neatens your work but can cause you problems if later on you need to pick up any stitches from that edge.

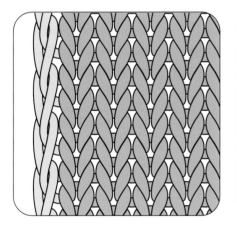

Simply slip the first stitch on every row. When you are slipping on the purl row, it is better to slip the stitch knitwise (page 50), then bring the yarn to the front for the purl stitches.

Double edge

Here the first two edge stitches are in garter stitch. This is an ideal selvedge for an edge that is not going to sewn to another piece.

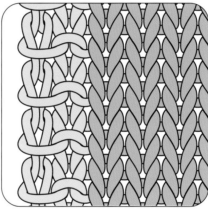

Slip the first stitch knitwise (page 50) through the back loop (page 51), knit the second stitch, work to last two stitches of the row then knit these two stitches. Repeat on every row.

Garter stitch edge

This creates a bumpy edge that is neat, but it can cause rough side seams, especially if you are using mattress stitch (pages 208–211) to sew up.

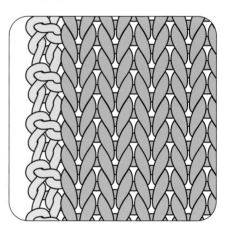

Simply knit the first stitch on every row.

Adding edge stitches

If you are adding an edge to an existing pattern, add the number of stitches required to work it to the existing stitch count. Work any increases or decreases inside the edge stitches.

joining in a new ball of yarn

Unless your project is very small, you will at some point finish a ball of yarn and need to join in a new one. If you run out of yarn half way across the row it's easy to think, 'Oh well, I'll join here, it will never show'. However, when you put on your finished sweater and stand in front of the mirror, the join will be horribly obvious. So, always join in new yarn at the edge, but how do you know if you will get to the other end of a row?

Calculating yarn for stocking (stockinette) stitch

If you are working in stocking (stockinette) stitch, spread the knitting out flat across the needle. If it is too wide to lie flat on one needle, measure the width and then measure the length of the yarn remaining instead of looping it across the needle.

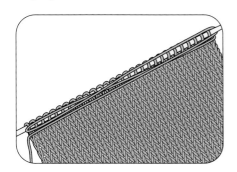

Loop the yarn back and forth across the knitting. If the yarn measures three times the width of your knitting then you have enough to do one more row. If it measures less, then start a new ball. Cut the long end, leaving 15cm (6in) to sew in (page 200). Keep the leftover pieces in a safe place in case you need to repair the project later on (page 257).

Calculating yarn for stitch patterns

You cannot measure the yarn in the same way if you are working a stitch pattern, as different patterns require different quantities of yarn.

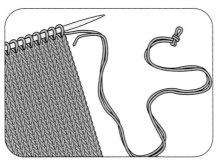

1 When you are getting near the end of the ball, fold the yarn remaining in half and place a slip knot at the fold.

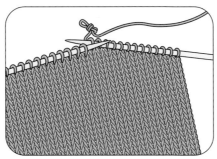

2 If you come to the slip knot on the next row, you know you won't have enough for another row as you have gone past the halfway marker. Simply undo the slip knot, continue and then join in the new ball before starting the next row.

Joining in a new ball

Whether you are joining in a new ball of the same colour yarn to complete a project or joining in a different colour to knit colour work (pages 146–175), the technique is the same.

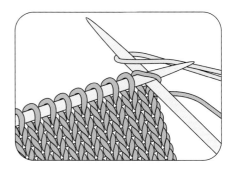

1 At the beginning of the row, slip the tip of the right-hand needle into the first stitch on left-hand needle in the usual way. Loop the new yarn around the tip of the right-hand needle.

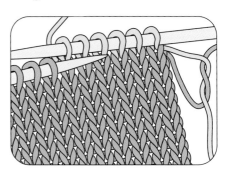

2 Work the next few stitches, then tie the two ends together using a single knot. When you have finished the knitting, you will sew the ends in (page 200).

casting (binding) off

Once you have completed your piece of work you need to finish the stitches so you can take out the needles without the knitting unravelling. This is called casting (binding) off. When casting (binding) off you use the same yarn and needles as for the work and either a knit stitch or a purl stitch, depending on whether the row would have been knitted or purled if the work was continued.

Casting (binding) off knitwise

This is the first, and most straightforward, way of casting (binding) off that you need to learn.

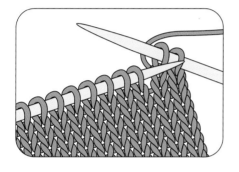

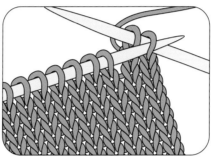

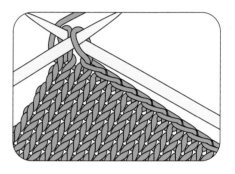

1 Knit the first two stitches in the usual way (page 38).

2 Slip the tip of the left-hand needle into the first stitch you knitted onto the right-hand needle. Lift it over the second stitch you knitted and drop it off the needle. You now have only one stitch on the right-hand needle.

3 Knit another stitch from the left-hand needle and then pass the previous stitch you knitted over it. Continue in this way until you have one stitch remaining on right-hand needle.

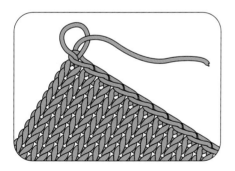

4 Cut the yarn leaving a 15cm (6in) tail to sew in later (page 200). Put the cut end through the remaining stitch and pull it tight.

A knitwise cast (bound) off edge lies flat on the stocking (stockinette) stitch side of the work.

Casting (binding) off purlwise

This is essentially the same as casting (binding) off knitwise,
but you are working with purl stitches.

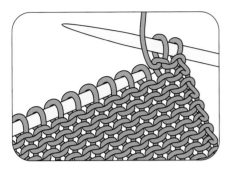

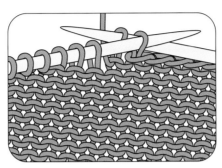

1 Purl the first two stitches in the usual way (page 39).

2 Take the yarn to the back. Slip the tip of the left-hand needle into the first stitch you purled onto the right-hand needle. Lift it over the second stitch you purled and drop it off the needle. You now have only one stitch on the right-hand needle. Continue in this way until you have one stitch remaining. Cut the yarn, leaving a 15cm (6in) tail to sew in later (page 200). Put the cut end through the remaining stitch and pull it tight.

Baggy last stitch

You will often find that the last stitch on the cast (bound) off row forms an ugly, baggy point. Knitters have different favourite methods for fixing this and here is mine. When casting (binding) off knitwise, work to the last stitch to be cast (bound) off: you will have one stitch on the right-hand needle and one stitch on left-hand needle. When you come to knit the last stitch, put the tip of the needle through the same stitch on the row below. Wrap the yarn around the tip of the right-hand needle and pull the loop through the stitch, slipping the original off the needle in the usual way. Cast (bind) off the last stitch and cut the yarn and put it through the loop in the usual way. As you pull it tight, give a little wiggle and you will see that you are not left with that unsightly point. The same principle applies when casting (binding) off purlwise.

A purlwise cast (bound) off edge lies across the top of the work.

Casting (binding) off in pattern

Casting (binding) off in pattern creates an edge that fits in with the rest of the fabric. The technique is shown here on rib stitch, but the principles apply to all stitch patterns.

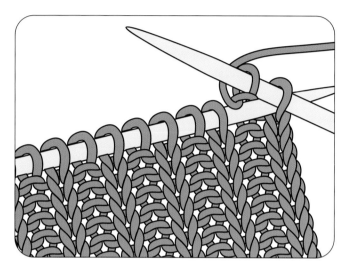

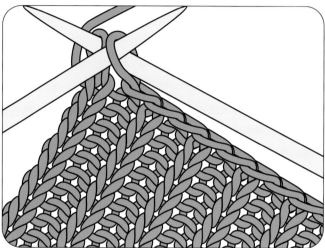

 1 Knit one stitch, then purl one stitch. Once you have two stitches on the right-hand needle, pass the first stitch worked over the second one. After working a purl stitch, make sure the yarn is at the back before lifting the previous stitch over it.

2 Continue across all stitches until one stitch remains, knitting the knit stitches and purling the purl ones. Cut the yarn, leaving a 15cm (6in) tail to sew in later (page 200). Put the end through the remaining stitch and pull it tight.

An edge cast (bound) off in rib pattern.

Using a larger needle

If you find that your cast (bound) off edge is much tighter than your knitted fabric, try casting (binding) off using a needle that is one size larger to give the edge more elasticity.

Casting (binding) off two edges together

This is a great technique for making the smooth seams, especially for shoulders. For a really professional shoulder, look at short row shaping (pages 132–134) to see how you can get perfectly sloped edges, and then cast (bind) off the edges together. You need three knitting needles the same size to work this technique.

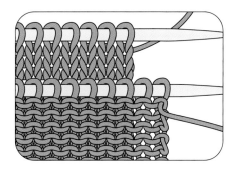

1 With the right sides of the work together, hold both needles, facing the same direction, in your left hand.

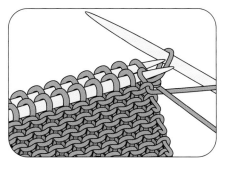

3 Squeezing the two needles in the left hand together, knit the two stitches together in a similar way to k2tog (page 78). Repeat Steps 2–3 again so that you have two stitches on the right-hand needle.

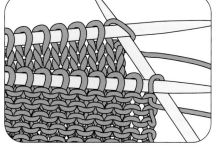

2 Hold a third needle in your right hand. Put the point of the right-hand needle into back of the first stitch on the front left-hand needle and then into the front of the first stitch on the back left-hand needle.

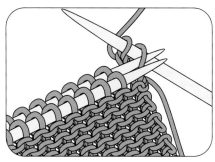

4 Using the tip of one of the left-hand needles, pass the first stitch on the right-hand needle over the second stitch and drop the stitch off the needle as if you were casting (binding) off in the usual way. Repeat the process until you have just one stitch on the right-hand needle. Cut the yarn, leaving a 15cm (6in) tail to sew in later (page 200). Put the end through the remaining stitch and pull it tight.

Two edges joined by casting (binding) them off together.

Picot edge cast (bind) off

This is a decorative cast (bind) off that creates a pretty edging that looks lovely on delicate designs such as baby clothes and evening wear.

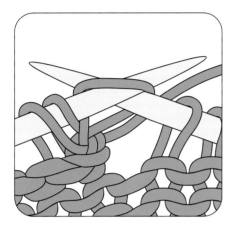 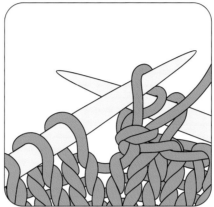 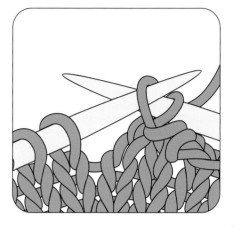

1 Cast (bind) off two knit stitches knitwise (page 54). *Turn the work and, using the cable cast on (page 28), cast on two additional stitches.

2 Turn the work again and cast (bind) off two of the three stitches on the right-hand needle by passing the second stitch over the first one and then the third stitch over the first one. One stitch remains on the right-hand needle.

3 Cast (bind) off two more stitches and then repeat from * until you have cast (bound) off all the stitches. Cut the yarn, leaving a 15cm (6in) tail to sew in later (page 200). Put the end through the remaining stitch and pull it tight.

A picot cast (bound) off edge creates a row of tiny points.

Choosing a cast (bind) off

Always consider the cast (bind) off as part of the overall design of a project and don't just settle for a straightforward one. Casting (binding) off in a different colour yarn can be a very effective way of adding a colour accent to a plain project.

Invisible cast (bind) off

For a very elastic edge, use this technique. It works extremely well on ribbing as it does not compromise the stretchiness of the rib.

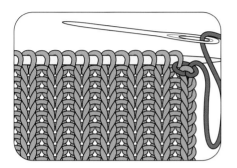

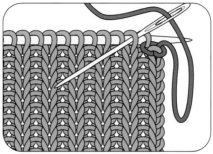

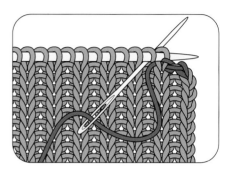

1 Cut the yarn, leaving a tail four times the width of the knitting. Thread a tapestry needle or knitter's sewing needle with the tail of yarn. Insert the needle purlwise through the first stitch, then knitwise through the second stitch. Insert the tapestry needle knitwise through the first stitch and slip this stitch off the knitting needle.

2 Insert the needle through the third stitch purlwise and then purlwise through the second stitch and slip the second stitch off the knitting needle.

3 Take the needle behind the third stitch and to the front, coming between the third and fourth stitches. Insert it knitwise through the fourth stitch.

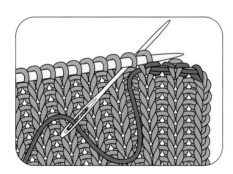

4 Repeat Steps 2–3, working into the third, fifth, fourth and sixth stitches. Continue in this way to the end of the row. Sew the yarn into the back of the work (page 200) and cut it.

An invisible cast (bound) off edge does not have the characteristic line of flat stitches across it.

Slip stitch crochet cast (bind) off

Crochet cast (bind) offs are good for yarns that have little elasticity, such as cotton, chenille and silk.

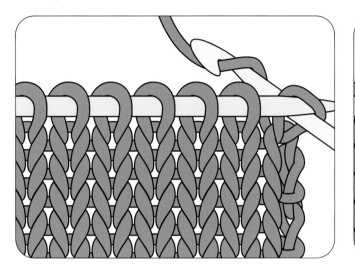

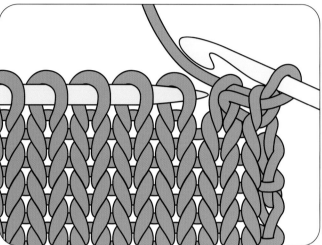

1 Holding the yarn in your left hand, put the crochet hook into the first stitch knitwise. Bring the yarn through and let the stitch drop off the left-hand needle.

2 *Repeat the process into the next stitch on the left-hand needle, but pull the loop through both the stitch on the left-hand needle and also the stitch on the hook. You now have one stitch on the crochet hook. Repeat from * until all the stitches are cast (bound) off. Cut the yarn, leaving a 15cm (6in) tail to sew in later (page 200). Put the end through the remaining stitch and pull it tight.

An edge cast (bound) off with slip stitch looks like a conventional cast (bound) off edge.

Using a crochet technique

If your cast (bound) off edges are often too tight, try using one of these crochet techniques instead to avoid the cast (bound) off edge pulling in. Use a crochet hook that is the same size as the knitting needles you have used.

Double (single) crochet cast (bind) off

This is a variation of the slip stitch crochet cast (bind) off that gives a slightly stiffer edge.

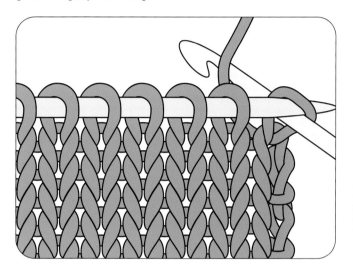

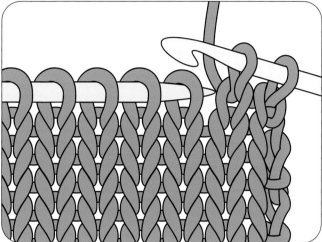

1 Use a crochet hook that is of a similar size to the knitting needles being used. Holding the yarn in your left hand, put the hook into the first stitch knitwise. Bring the yarn through and let the stitch drop off the left-hand needle.

2 *Work the next stitch in the same way. You should now have two stitches on the crochet hook.

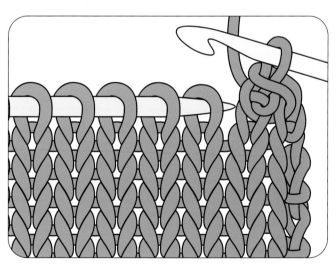

3 Wrap the yarn around the hook and pull the loop through both stitches on the hook. Repeat from * until all the stitches have been cast (bound) off. Cut the yarn, leaving a 15cm (6in) tail to sew in later (page 200). Put the end through the remaining stitch and pull it tight.

A double (single) crochet cast (bind) off can be a decorative edging.

structure and shaping

Now that you can knit it's time to learn more about how knitting projects are constructed. You also need to understand the secrets of shaping – a vital ingredient if you are to progress beyond knitting scarves.

how a garment is formed

Most knitted pieces are started from the lower edge and worked upwards. When working from a pattern you are always instructed to make the back of a sweater first, then the front and finally the sleeves. This is an unwritten rule, but the back is usually the largest piece and so is best got out of the way first.

Sweater body

Shown here is an outline of a simple sweater body. The coloured area shows the front of the garment and the dotted line indicates the neck shaping on the back of it.

You would start at the lower edge, where you cast on, and then usually work in a rib of some sort to form the welt (pages 46–47). After the welt you are usually asked to change to a larger needle and sometimes to increase some stitches as well. This is because the designer wants the welt to fit snugly and to stop the garment stretching out of shape over time.

Once the body is the length asked for in the pattern, you will be instructed to shape the armholes by casting (binding) off (pages 54–55) a few stitches and decreasing (pages 78–83) at the beginning and end of rows. This decreasing produces a shape like that shown, which helps the sleeve fit in place neatly.

You will then knit until the armholes are the length required; you are now up to the shoulders and neck shaping. This can always be a bit scary, but just follow the instructions carefully and all should be well. The worst thing you can do is to read a pattern right through before you start knitting. If you do this you may be too intimidated to ever start!

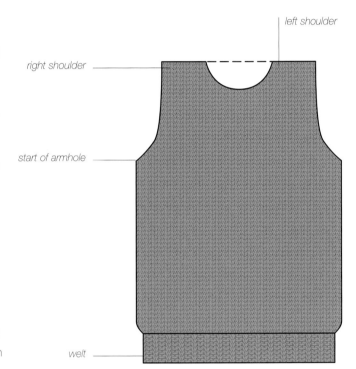

left shoulder

right shoulder

start of armhole

welt

Cardigan front

This illustration shows a front of a cardigan or jacket.

Again, you start at the lower edge and work up, shaping the armhole as for a sweater. When a pattern refers to the left front and left shoulder it is the left-hand side as if you were wearing the garment and not as if you were looking at it. The important point when working a cardigan front piece is to understand which edge is the front edge and which one is the side seam edge.

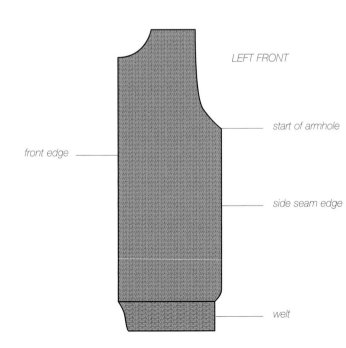

LEFT FRONT

start of armhole

front edge

side seam edge

welt

Sleeve

Knitting a sleeve will usually involve both increasing and decreasing.

You start with the cuff, usually in rib, and then change to a larger needle and possibly increase some stitches. On the main part of the sleeve there will certainly be increasing. You have to increase at both ends of rows to give you this shape. The pattern will tell you when and how to work the increases (pages 78–83).

Once you have all the stitches required to give you the sleeve width, the pattern will ask you to continue to a specified length and then you will have to shape the sleeve top, sometimes called the sleeve head or sleeve cap. This is similar to armhole shaping on a body and is a series of cast (bound) off stitches (pages 54–55) and decreases. The sleeve top will fit neatly into the armhole.

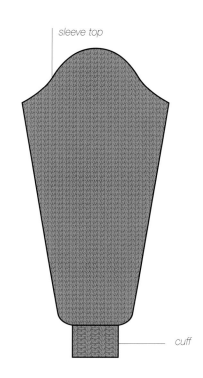

sleeve top

cuff

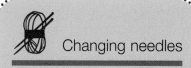

Changing needles

When you change needle size, you don't have to slip all the stitches off and put them on the new needle. You just knit the next row with the new size in your right hand and the old size in your left, then use both the new size needles.

Shaped garments

When knitting your first ever garment it is always best to choose a design that is quite simple, with no shaping at the side edges until you reach the armholes. You can usually tell when a pattern has side shaping as it will be accompanied by a diagram similar to those shown below. There will usually be sizes shown that, as long as your tension (gauge) is correct (page 18), the garment will knit up to.

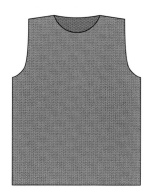

▲ Here is a simple design that doesn't have any side shaping until you get to the armholes.

▲ This illustration shows you what the shape of the sleeve is like. This one is quite basic with some shaping at the top.

▲ This garment diagram shows you that there is shaping on the side seams and it also has pockets. You can tell that it is a cardigan because there is a line running down the centre front.

understanding patterns

Designers and yarn companies all have their own way of writing a pattern. Though they look different, the same information should always be there. It is important to understand what means what before you decide on a pattern and buy your yarn.

The sample pattern opposite has the following sections:

Size When a designer chooses to work with small, medium, large etc., they will usually give the actual measurements. In which case, you will need to measure yourself (page 70) before deciding which size to knit.

If the pattern states, 'To suit bust…' or, 'To fit bust…', then the measurements given are not actual measurements. The designer has taken into account the shape of the garment and how they want it to fit, so you should make the size that is equivalent to that which you would usually buy in a shop, even if the finished measurements are larger than your actual measurements.

Materials The type of yarn the designer has used and the number of balls of that yarn needed to make each size. Also listed will be any buttons, ribbons, etc. that are needed.

Needles These are the knitting needles required to make this garment. There are three systems of measurement for knitting needles (page 294).

Tension (gauge) This tells you how many stitches and rows you must have to a certain measurement. Your tension (gauge) (page 18) must be correct to obtain the garment measurements given in the pattern.

Pattern The pattern then works through all the necessary parts of the garment, giving all the instructions needed.

Making up This tells you how to sew up your garment and if any borders or other elements are to be made.

You need to understand the use of round brackets to make the right size. If the sizes are extra-small, small, medium, large and extra-large and you choose to knit the medium size, then this will be the third size in the pattern instructions. The instructions will say something like:

Using 4mm (US 6) needles, cast on 80(84:88:92:96) sts
To knit the medium size you will need to cast on 88 stitches, the third number listed. The first size is always shown outside the brackets and the remaining sizes within them.

In some patterns you may encounter the following:
Knit 3(-:-:2:4) rows.
This would mean you wouldn't knit any rows as your size, the third size, has a '–', meaning a blank.

Continue until work measures
20(21:22:22:23)cm/8(8¼:8¾:8¾:9)in.
Brackets are used in the same way for specific measurements as well as for numbers of stitches and rows.

Be aware that many knitting patterns also use square brackets or parentheses [ ]. These are to do with repeating instructions (page 69) and have nothing to do with sizing.

Photocopying a pattern

Photocopy your pattern and work from the copy, crossing off rows as you do them. This way you will always know where you are.

This is the sizing information. The measurements given are to fit specific bust sizes and are not the actual measurements of the garment. The diagrams give the actual measurements. In this example the third size has been chosen and will be used throughout.

The pattern tells you what yarn to buy and the quantity needed for each size.

Here the pattern tells you the knitting needles you will need. In this pattern only one size is listed, though sometimes two or even three pairs could be needed for different areas of the garment. If multiple sizes are listed, the pattern will tell you when to change needles.

These are the important tension (gauge) details (page 18). Make sure you match the tension (gauge) or your garment may not knit up to the correct size.

This is the start of the knitting instructions and for a sweater you usually start with the back. The pattern will tell you which size needles to use and how many stitches to cast on. Here, 105 stitches will be cast on as the third size is being made (97 stitches for the first size, 101 for the second, 105 for the third and so on). If you are a beginner, it is advisable to mark all the numbers for your size before you start knitting.

For the front of the garment you have to work as for the back until ** (the end of the third line after **Shape armholes**). *After this point you continue with the instructions given for the front.*

These are the instructions for knitting the sleeves. You will make two identical pieces.

Here the pattern refers you to special instructions in another part of the book.

SIZE
8 10 12 14 16 18 20 22
To fit bust
82 87 92 97 102 107 112 117 cm
32 34 36 38 40 42 44 46 in

YARN
Details of yarn
Number of balls x 50gm

NEEDLES
1 pair 3¾ mm (no 9) (US 5) needles

TENSION
22 sts and 30 rows to 10 cm measured over stocking stitch using 3¾ mm (US 5) needles.

BACK
Using 3¾ mm (US 5) needles cast on 97 [101: 105: 111: 119: 125: 131: 139] sts.
Beg with a K row, work in st st, shaping side seams by dec 1 st at each end of 13th and every foll 6th row until 85 [89: 93: 99: 107: 113: 119: 127] sts rem.
Work 7 rows, ending with RS facing for next row.
Inc 1 st at each end of next and every foll 6th row until there are 93 [97: 101: 107: 115: 121: 127: 135] sts.
Cont straight until back meas 32 [32: 31: 34: 33: 35: 34: 36] cm, ending with RS facing for next row.
Shape armholes
Cast off 4 [5: 5: 6: 6: 7: 7: 8] sts at beg of next 2 rows.
85 [87: 91: 95: 103: 107: 113: 119] sts.★★
Dec 1 st at each end of next 3 [3: 5: 5: 7: 7: 9: 9] rows, then on foll 3 [3: 2: 2: 3: 3: 2: 4] alt rows.
73 [75: 77: 81: 83: 87: 91: 93] sts.
Cont straight until armhole meas 18 [18: 19: 19: 20: 20: 21: 21] cm, ending with RS facing for next row.
Shape back neck
Next row (RS): K21 [22: 23: 25: 25: 27: 29: 30] and turn, leaving rem sts on a holder.
Work each side of neck separately.
Dec 1 st at neck edge of next 4 rows.
17 [18: 19: 21: 21: 23: 25: 26] sts.
Work 1 row, ending with RS facing for next row.
Shape shoulder
Cast off.
With RS facing, rejoin yarn to rem sts, cast off centre 31 [31: 31: 31: 33: 33: 33: 33] sts, K to end.
Complete to match first side, reversing shapings.

FRONT
Work as given for back to ★★.
Divide for neck
Next row (RS): K2tog, K40 [41: 43: 45:

49: 51: 54: 57] and turn, leaving rem sts on a holder.
Work each side of neck separately.
Dec 1 st at armhole edge of next 2 [2: 4: 4: 6: 6: 8: 8] rows, then on foll 3 [3: 2: 2: 3: 3: 2: 4] alt rows **and at same time** dec 1 st at neck edge of 2nd and every foll alt row.
32 [33: 34: 36: 35: 37: 39: 38] sts.
Dec 1 st at neck edge **only** of 2nd and foll 9 [9: 7: 7: 6: 6: 4: 2] alt rows, then on every foll 4th row until 17 [18: 19: 21: 21: 23: 25: 26] sts rem.
Cont straight until front matches back to shoulder cast-off, ending with RS facing for next row.
Shape shoulder
Cast off.
With RS facing, rejoin yarn to rem sts, K2tog, K to last 2 sts, K2tog.
Complete to match first side, reversing shapings.

SLEEVES
Using 3¾ mm (US 5) needles cast on 53 [53: 55: 55: 57: 57: 59: 59] sts.
Beg with a K row, work in st st, shaping sides by inc 1 st at each end of 7th [7th: 7th: 7th: 7th: 7th: 5th: 5th] and every foll 8th [8th: 8th: 8th: 8th: 8th: 8th: 6th] row to 59 [69: 67: 77: 77: 87: 89: 69] sts, then on every foll 10th [10th: 10th: 10th: -: -: -: 8th] row until there are 77 [79: 81: 83: 85: -: -: 91] sts.
Cont straight until sleeve meas 43 [43: 44: 44: 45: 45: 44: 44] cm, ending with RS facing for next row.
Shape top
Cast off 4 [5: 5: 6: 6: 7: 7: 8] sts at beg of next 2 rows.
69 [69: 71: 71: 73: 73: 75: 75] sts.
Dec 1 st at each end of next 5 rows, then on every foll alt row to 29 sts, then on foll 3 rows, ending with RS facing for next row.
23 sts.
Cast off 4 sts at beg of next 2 rows.
Cast off rem 15 sts.

MAKING UP
Press as described on the information page.
Join both shoulder seams using back stitch, or mattress stitch if preferred.
Lace trim
Using 3¾ mm (US 5) needles cast on 20 sts.
Row 1 (RS): sl 1, K3, (yfwd, K2tog) 7 times, yfwd, K2.
21 sts.
Row 2: Knit.
Row 3: sl 1, K6, (yfwd, K2tog) 6 times, yfwd, K2.
22 sts.
Row 4: Knit.
Row 5: sl 1, K9, (yfwd, K2tog) 5 times, yfwd, K2.
23 sts.

Row 6: Knit.
Row 7: sl 1, K12, (yfwd, K2tog) 4 times, yfwd, K2.
24 sts.
Row 8: Knit.
Row 9: sl 1, K23.
Row 10: cast off 4 sts, K to end.
20 sts.
These 10 rows form patt.
Cont in patt until trim, when slightly gathered, is long enough to fit up centre front, from cast-on edge to base of V neck, and around entire neck edge, ending after patt row 10 and with RS facing for next row.
Cast off.
Using photograph as a guide, sew lace trim in place.
See information page for finishing instructions, setting in sleeves using the set-in method.

52 [52: 52: 55: 55: 57: 57: 59] cm
(20½ [20½: 20½: 21½: 21½: 22½: 22½: 24] in)

42.5 [44: 46: 48.5: 52.5: 55: 57.5: 61.5] cm
(16½ [17½: 18: 19: 20½: 21½: 22½: 24] in)

43 [43: 44: 44: 45: 45: 44: 44] cm
(17 [17: 17½: 17½: 17½: 17½: 17½: 17½] in)

This part of the pattern tells you how to complete the sweater. It is always advisable to read all the making up instructions before starting them so that you understand which bits you need to do first.

These are the instructions for a trim that goes around the neck.

These are the diagrams showing you the measurements of the finished garment. They also show you that the body is slightly shaped.

abbreviations

Knitting has a language of its own and what makes it more complicated are the abbreviations. These are used to save space because if patterns were written out in full they would go on for pages and pages.

Here is a list of the most commonly used abbreviations, but you should always look at the abbreviations listed in the book or pattern you are working from as they do sometimes differ. For example, 'k1b' can mean 'knit in back of stitch' or 'knit 1 in the row below'. There are also no hard and fast rules as to how capital letters are used.

alt	alternate; alternatively	k1b	knit stitch in row below	RT	right twist
approx	approximately	k2tog	knit two stitches (or number	sk	skip next stitch
BC	back cross		stated) together	sk2	skip next two stitches
beg	begin(s)(ning)	kfb	knit into the front and back of	skp(o)	slip one stitch, knit one stitch,
bet	between		a stitch		pass slipped stitch over
BO	bind (cast) off	ktbl	knit through back of loop	sl	slip
C4B	cable four stitches (or number	kwise	knitwise	ssk	slip one stitch, slip one stitch,
	stated) back	LH	left hand		knit slipped stitches together
C4F	cable four stitches (or number	LT	left twist	st st	stocking (stockinette) stitch
	stated) front	m	metres	st(s)	stitch(es)
CC	contract colour	M1	make one stitch	tbl	through back of loop
cm	centimetre(s)	MB	make bobble	tog	together
CN	cable needle	MC	main colour	WS	wrong side
CO	cast on	mm	millimetres	wyb	with yarn at the back
col	colour	oz	ounce(es)	wyf	with yarn at the front
cont	continue	p	purl	yb	yarn back
cr(oss) 2L	cross two stitches (or number	p2tog	purl two stitches (or number	yf	yarn front
	stated) to the left		stated) together	yfrn	yarn forward and round
cr(oss) 2R	cross two stitches (or number	patt(s)	pattern(s)		needle
	stated) to the right	pfb	purl into the front and back of	yfwd	yarn forward
dbl	double		a stitch	yo	yarn over needle
dec(s)	decrease(s)(ing)	pnso	pass next stitch over	yo2	yarn over twice
DK	double knit	psso	pass the slipped stitch over	yon	yarn over needle
dpn	double-pointed needle	ptbl	purl through back of loop	yrn	yarn round needle
FC	front cross	pwise	purlwise		
foll(s)	follow(s)(ing)	rem	remain(ing)		
g(r)	gram	rep	repeat		
g st	garter stitch	rev st st	reverse stocking (stockinette)		
in(s)	inch; inches		stitch		
inc	increase(s)(ing)	RH	right hand		
incl	include	rnds	rounds		
k	knit	RS	right side		

terminology

Various standard phrases used in knitting may mystify novices, so here are explanations of some of the most common ones.

Above markers Knitting worked above a row where markers have been placed.

After 16 rows have been worked Continue as instructed after the stated number of rows has been worked.

Alt rows this is used when you have to work something (usually shaping) on every alternate row.

At front edge The edge that meets in the centre; sometimes the edge that has a buttonhole band or button band.

At side edge The edge you will sew to another piece of knitting; usually referred to when knitting a cardigan or jacket.

At the same time Usually used when you are shaping a garment and you need to do different shapings on different edges. For example, you may be decreasing for the armhole and at the same time decreasing for the neck.

Cont in patt A stitch pattern will have been established in the instructions and now you need to continue working in that pattern until the pattern tells you to do otherwise.

Ending on a right side (RS) row The last row you knit must be on the right side.

Ending on a wrong side (WS) row The last row you knit must be on the wrong side.

From beg Usually used when you have to work a specified length from the beginning (cast on) edge of the piece. For example, 'Work until back measures 40cm (16in) from beg'.

Knitwise This means that you must follow the instruction putting the needle into the stitch as if you were going to knit it.

On foll 6 alt rows This tells you to work something (usually shaping) on the next six alternate rows.

On 5th and on every foll 4th row Usually used for shaping; work four rows then work the decrease or increase (whichever is specified) on the fifth row. Then work three more rows then decrease or increase as specified on the fourth row. You then continue to work three rows and increase or decrease on the fourth row until you have completed the required number of increases or decreases.

Pick up and knit 16 sts down left neck Pick up stated number of stitches along the edge specified.

Place markers at each end of last row Put a stitch marker into the first and last stitch of the specified row.

Purlwise This means that you must follow the instruction putting the needle into the stitch as if you were going to purl it.

Rep from * Repeat the instructions given after the *.

Reverse shaping This usually appears when you are working on a cardigan where you will only be given the instructions for the left front and then when you need to do the right front, you have to do everything in reverse. Depending on how complicated the shaping is, this can be tricky. If you are unsure of what to do, write the reverse shaping pattern out, carefully checking each row against the pattern.

Selvedge edge An edge that has been worked in a garter stitch or with a slip stitch edging to make a selvedge (page 52).

With right (wrong) sides together (facing) Place the right (wrong) sides of each piece of the work together.

With right side facing The right side of the work must be facing you to do the next stitch or row.

With wrong side facing The wrong side of the work must be facing you to do the next stitch or row.

Work across st holder If stitches have been placed on a stitch holder at some point in the pattern and now need to be knitted again, you simply use the stitch holder as your left-hand needle.

Work to last 2 sts Work across the row until you have two stitches (or the number stated) on the left-hand needle.

K2, [k2tog, k1] rep to end Knit two stitches then repeat the instructions in the square brackets to the end of the row.

which size do you knit?

Getting the right fit is important and you need to take time with this before you start knitting. Most patterns give you either a diagram or a full chart indicating the finished measurements. Don't assume that you are the medium or the large size because that is what you usually buy in a shop. The easiest way to get the correct measurements is by measuring an existing garment on yourself, or on the person you wish to knit for.

Measuring a garment

The garment you are going to measure doesn't have to be knitted, but it must be something that is comfortable. It should bear some resemblance to the shape of the diagram (page 65) in the knitting pattern and also fit you in the way you would like your finished knitwear to.

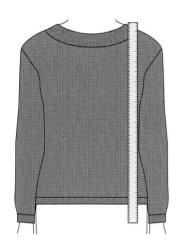

▲ Put the garment on and check that you are happy with everything about it. Do you need the sleeves to be shorter or longer? Do you want the body to be a different length?

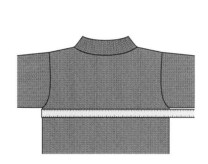

▲ Measure the width from one side seam to the other.

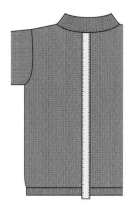

▲ Measure the length from the shoulder seam to the hem.

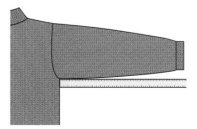

▲ Measure the sleeve length from the lowest point of the shoulder seam along to the cuff. Keep the ruler straight, not at an angle along the underarm seam.

Write down all these measurements and then compare them to the ones in the pattern. You can then see if they correspond to one of the sizes. It may be the case that you knit the medium body but the small sleeve to get the length correct. This gives you the opportunity to custom-fit your knitwear to your measurements. You can also alter measurements in a pattern (pages 270–273).

Measuring your work

If you have to knit to a length specified in the pattern, it is important to know how to measure your work correctly when it is on the needles.

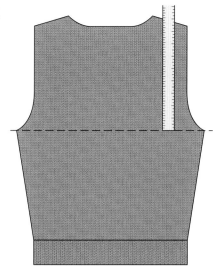

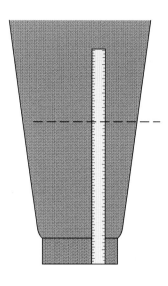

▲ To measure a shaped edge such as an armhole, you have to draw an imaginary line to know where to start your measurement from. You can put in a pin to mark the spot to measure from.

▲ Here a sleeve is being measured. You must measure straight up from the lower edge and not follow the shaped edge. The same principles apply to measuring all areas of your work.

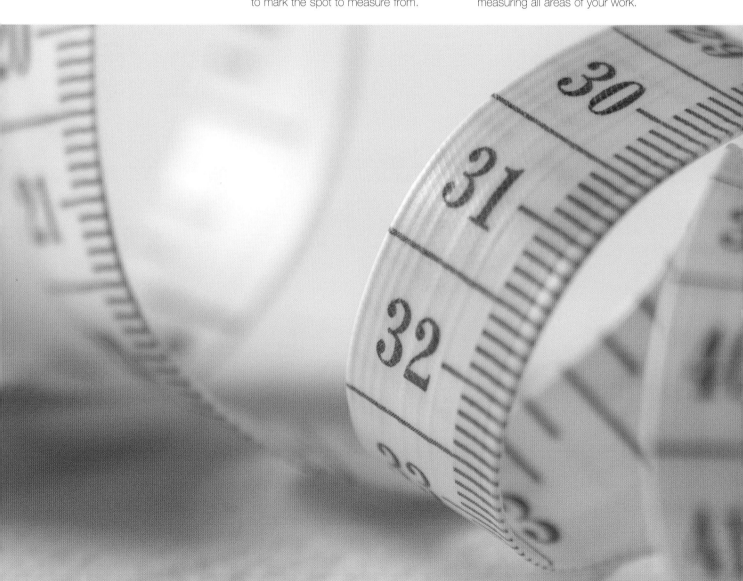

shaping

To be able to knit a project that is more complicated than a square or rectangle, you need to learn shaping techniques. There are two elements to shaping – increasing of stitches and decreasing of stitches – but different ways of doing both of them.

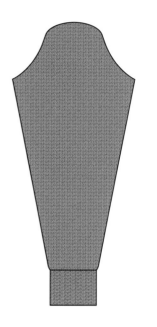

◀ On this sleeve the stitches have been increased to make it wider after the cuff. At the top the stitches have been decreased to create the rounder shoulder sleeve top.

◀ Here increasing and decreasing have been used to achieve the shaped edges at the side seams, the armholes and neck.

increasing

To increase stitches is to create more of them on your needle, thus making the knitting wider. Different increases slope in different directions in the knitting, as noted here with each one. This is important if you are going to work fully fashioned items (page 88) or if you want to mirror your increases at each end of a row for neatness.

Make one (M1)

(Slopes to the left on stocking [stockinette] stitch)

When you are asked to make a stitch in this way it is usually in the middle of a row. The increase is not obvious in the finished knitting.

Make one to the right

If you want to make a stitch and have it slope to the right instead, then pick up the strand from the back and knit into the front of it. The principle is the same on a purl row, but you are picking up and working in a purl direction.

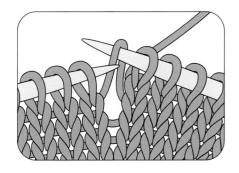

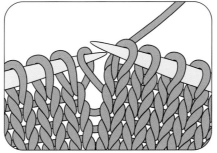

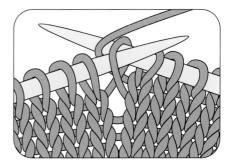

1 Work to the position of the increase. If you pull the tips of the needles apart slightly, you will see that there is a horizontal strand of yarn lying between the last stitch on the right-hand needle and the first on the left-hand needle. From the front, slip the tip of the right-hand needle under this strand.

2 Lift the strand and, from the front, slip the tip of the left-hand needle under it. Remove the right-hand needle, leaving the strand on the left-hand needle.

3 Knit into the back of the loop on the left-hand needle. You have made a completely new stitch and so increased by one stitch.

Stitches made in the middle of knit rows.

Increasing one knitwise (inc)

(Slopes to the left on stocking [stockinette] stitch)

This is the most commonly used type of increase. It is best used on an edge as the increased stitch has a small but visible bar across it: this will disappear into the seam when the project is sewn up. Used at the beginning of a row, as shown, the increased edge slopes to the right, but the stitch itself slopes to the left.

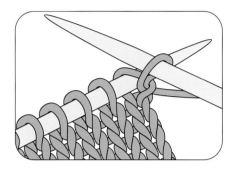

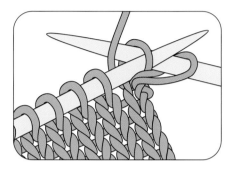

1 Work to the position of the increase. Knit into the front of the next stitch (page 38), but do not slip the original stitch off the left-hand needle.

2 Put the tip of the right-hand needle into the back of the same stitch on the left-hand needle.

3 Wrap the yarn around the right-hand needle in the same way you usually would to knit a stitch.

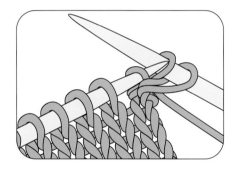

4 Bring the needle, and the yarn wrapped around it, through the stitch and now slip the original stitch off the left-hand needle. You have made two stitches out of one and so increased by one stitch.

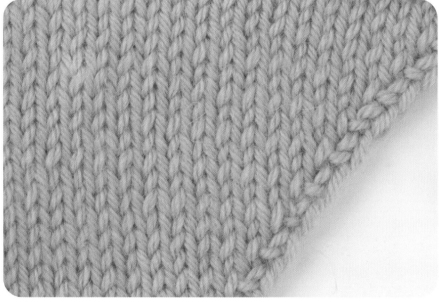

An edge increased knitwise on every knit row.

Increasing purlwise (inc)

(Slopes to the right on stocking [stockinette] stitch)

The way the yarn has to twist around makes this look trickier than it actually is. Again, this is an increase usually used on an edge that will disappear into a seam. Used at the beginning of a row, as shown, the increased edge slopes to the left, but the stitch itself slopes to the right.

Abbreviations

This style of increase is usually abbreviated as inc, whether it is on a knit or a purl row. Simply use the knit technique on a knit row and the purl technique on a purl row.

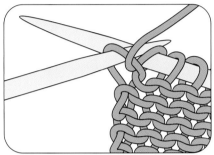

1 Work to the position of the increase. Purl into the front of the next stitch (page 39), but do not slip the original stitch off the left-hand needle.

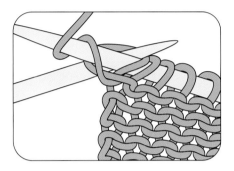

2 Put the tip of the right-hand needle into the back of the same stitch on the left-hand needle. Wrap the yarn around the right-hand needle in the same way you usually would to purl a stitch.

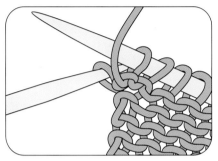

3 Bring the needle, and the yarn wrapped around it, through the stitch and now slip the original stitch off the left-hand needle. You have made two stitches out of one and so increased by one stitch.

An edge increased purlwise on every purl row.

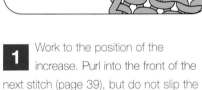

Increasing twice knitwise (inc2)

(Slopes to the left on stocking [stockinette] stitch)

You will sometimes need to increase by more than one stitch at a time. This technique uses the same principle as inc (page 74) to increase by two stitches on a knit row.

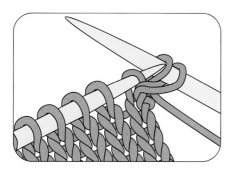

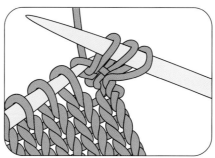

1 Work to the position of the increase. Knit into the front and then the back of the next stitch, but do not slip the original stitch off the left-hand needle yet.

2 Knit into the front of the same stitch again. You have made three stitches out of one and so increased by two stitches.

An edge increased twice on every knit row.

Increasing twice purlwise

(Slopes to the right on stocking [stockinette] stitch)

This technique allows you to increase by two stitches on a purl row.

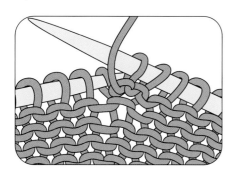

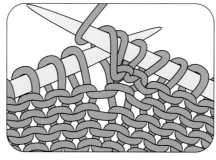

1 Work to the position of the increase. Purl into the front and then the back of the next stitch, but do not slip the original stitch off the left-hand needle yet.

2 Purl into the front of the same stitch again. You have made three stitches out of one and so increased by two stitches.

An edge increased twice on every purl row.

Increasing multiple stitches

Sometimes you will need to increase by multiple stitches at the beginning of a row. To do this you add the stitches at the end of the previous row so that the new row starts with the increased stitches.

1 Place the needle with the work on in your right hand and wrap the yarn from back to front around your left thumb.

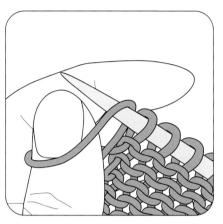

2 Put the tip of the right-hand needle into the loop around your thumb.

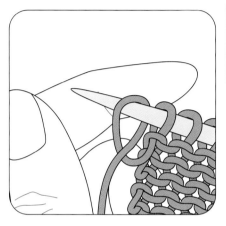

3 Slip your thumb out of the loop, using your index finger to make sure that the loop stays on the needle.

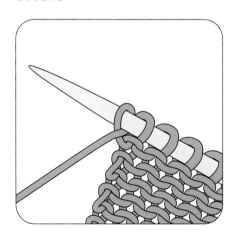

4 Pull the yarn tight to make a new stitch. Continue in this way until you have increased by the required number of stitches.

An edge increased by five stitches on every alternate knit row.

decreasing

As with increasing, decreasing is something you must master in order to make the simplest of garments. Decreasing is easy, it just sometimes reads as if it is difficult. As with increases, different decreases slope in different directions in the knitting, as noted here with each one, and this is important in fully fashioning (page 88) and in mirroring decreases for neatness.

Knit two stitches together (k2tog)

(Slopes to the right on stocking [stockinette] stitch)

This is the most basic of the decreases and the most commonly used. You would usually use it at the beginning or end of a row if the edge is to be seamed. Used at the beginning of a row, as shown, the decreased edge slopes to the left, but the stitch itself slopes to the right.

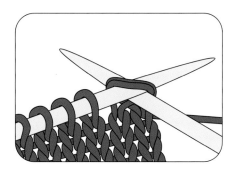

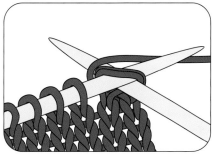

1 From front to back, put the tip of the right-hand needle into the next two stitches on the left-hand needle.

2 Knit the two stitches together in the usual way (page 38) as if they were one. You have made two stitches into one and so decreased by one stitch.

An edge decreased on every knit row.

Purl two stitches together (p2tog)

(Slopes to the right on stocking [stockinette] stitch)

This version of the basic decrease is used when working a purl row.

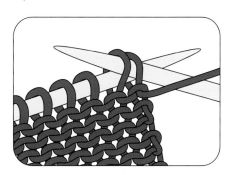

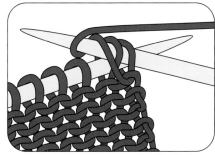

1 Put the tip of the right-hand needle into the next two stitches on the left-hand needle purlwise.

2 Purl the two stitches together as one. You have made two stitches into one and so decreased by one stitch.

An edge decreased on every purl row.

Slip one, knit one, pass the slipped stitch over (skpo)

(Slopes to the left on stocking [stockinette] stitch)

This stitch would often be used in fully fashioning (page 88), where it would be worked two or three stitches in from the edge. This technique is also often used when working lace stitches (pages 100–105).

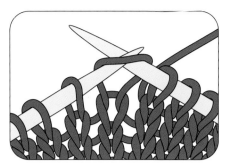

1 Put the tip of the right-hand needle into the next stitch and slip it knitwise (page 50) onto the right-hand needle.

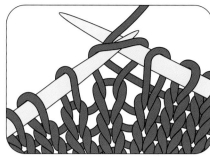

2 Knit the next stitch in the usual way (page 38).

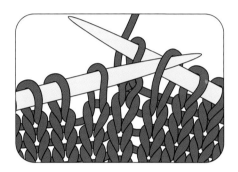

3 Put the tip of the left-hand needle into the front of the slipped stitch on the right-hand needle and lift it over the stitch just knitted. You have made two stitches into one and so decreased by one stitch.

Skpo used to decrease on every knit row.

Slip, slip, knit (ssk)

(Slopes to the left on stocking [stockinette] stitch)

This technique is also often used in fully fashioning (page 88). It produces a decrease that is slightly flatter than skpo.

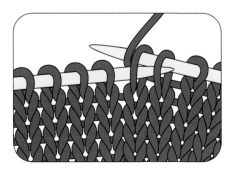

One at a time, slip the first and second stitches knitwise (page 50) onto the right-hand needle. From the left, put the left-hand needle into the fronts of these stitches and then knit them together.

Ssk used to decrease on every knit row.

Knit two stitches together through the backs of the loops (k2tog tbl)

(Slopes to the left on stocking [stockinette] stitch)

This is similar to k2tog (page 78) but you are knitting through the backs of the loops (page 51), which causes the decrease to slope in the opposite direction. Again, this is often used in fully fashioning (page 88).

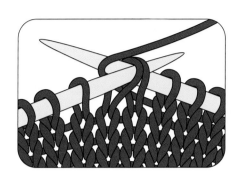

Put the tip of the right-hand needle into the backs of the first two stitches on the left-hand needle and knit these two stitches together as one. You have made two stitches into one and so decreased by one stitch.

An edge decreased on every knit row.

Purl two stitches together through the backs of the loops (p2tog tbl)

(Slopes to the left on stocking [stockinette] stitch)

When purling two stitches together you need to go through the backs of loops to make the decrease slant to the left. Another stitch used in fully fashioning (page 88); note that when it is used at the beginning of a row, as shown below, the decreased edge slopes to the right, but the stitch itself slopes to the left.

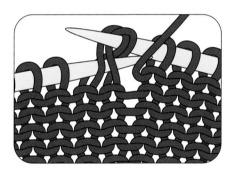

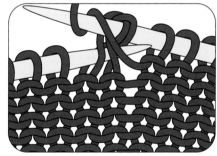

1 From back to the front, put the tip of the right-hand needle into the next two stitches on the left-hand needle.

2 Purl the two stitches together as one. You have made two stitches into one and so decreased by one stitch.

An edge decreased on every purl row.

Stretching the stitches

If you find it difficult to put the needle through the backs of the stitches, then put the needle into the front of the stitches first and stretch them slightly.

Slip one, knit two together, pass the slipped stitch over (sl1, k2tog, psso)

(Slopes to the left on stocking [stockinette] stitch)

This technique enables you to decrease by two stitches at the same time and would usually be used in the middle of a row.

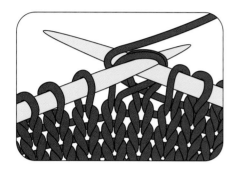

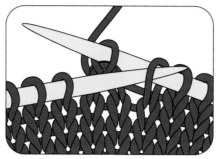

1 Slip the next stitch knitwise onto the right-hand needle then knit the following two stitches together (page 78).

2 Pass the slipped stitch over the two stitches knitted together. You have made three stitches into one and so decreased by two stitches.

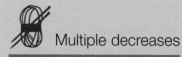

Multiple decreases

Two stitches at a time is the maximum number you can decrease by using these techniques. If you tried to decrease by more – for example, k4tog – the result would look ugly on the finished knitting. Larger decreases will be given as a special multiple decrease in a pattern.

There are two stitches between each decrease across the row.

Knit three together (k3tog)

(Slopes to the right on stocking [stockinette] stitch)

This is similar to k2tog (page 78), but you are decreasing by two stitches rather than by one. Again, this stitch will often be used in the middle of a row.

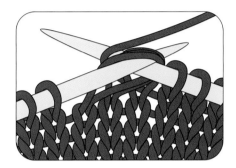

Put the tip of the right-hand needle knitwise into the next three stitches and knit them together as one. You have made three stitches into one and so decreased by two stitches.

K3tog is worked after every two stitches across the row.

Knit three together through the backs of the loops (k3togtbl)

(Slopes to the left on stocking [stockinette] stitch)

This is similar to k3tog (above), but you are knitting into the backs of the loops (page 50), which makes the decrease slant in the opposite direction.

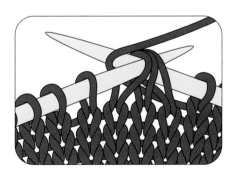

Put the right-hand needle into the backs of the next three stitches and knit them together as one. You have made three stitches into one and so decreased by two stitches.

There are two stitches between every k3togtbl decrease.

structure and shaping | 83

Working five stitches together (work 5 tog)

(The stitches slope towards the centre stitch on stocking [stockinette] stitch)

Use this technique to decrease by four stitches at the same time. This is sometimes used at the top of a bobble (pages 108–110) and for other decorative details.

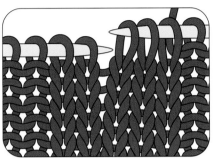

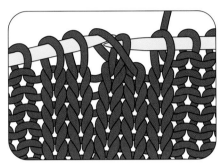

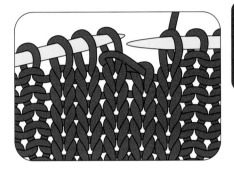

1 Keeping the yarn at the back of the work, slip the first three stitches onto the right-hand needle.

2 Pass the second stitch on the right-hand needle over the third one, (which is the centre stitch of the five).

3 Slip the centre stitch back onto the left-hand needle.

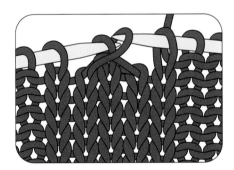

4 Pass the second stitch on the left-hand needle over the centre stitch.

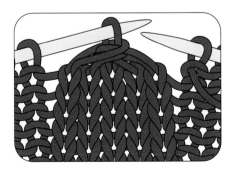

5 Slip the centre stitch back onto right-hand needle and repeat Steps 2, 3 and 4 once more. You have made five stitches into one and so decreased by four stitches.

The single stitch left after the decrease has been continued in st st on the rev st st background.

decorative increases and decreases

These increases and decreases can be used in textured patterns (pages 92–99) or lace patterns (pages 100–107) as part of the effect.

Working twice into the yarnover

With this increasing technique you are making two stitches from a yarnover (pages 100–105) that was made in the previous row.

Work to the yarnover. Knit into the back of the loop, drop the remaining part of the yarnover off the left-hand needle. Pick it back up with the tip of the left-hand needle, as shown, so that it turns the other way around, and knit into the front of it. The two stitches made will make a smooth V shape.

This increase produces an eyelet hole.

Double lifted stitch increase

This increase is useful when increasing in ribbed patterns (page 47). It increases by two stitches and can be varied by either knitting or purling into the back of the lifted stitch.

Work to the position of the increase. Lift the stitch from the row below onto the left-hand needle and knit it. Knit the following stitch on the left-hand needle then lift the stitch previously knitted onto the left-hand needle and knit it once again, as shown.

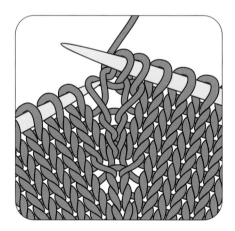

Increase worked in the middle of every knit row.

Balanced double decrease

Here is a technique that enables you to decrease symmetrically by two stitches at a time. You decrease each side of the centre stitch, which enables you to keep an even fabric.

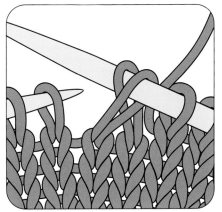

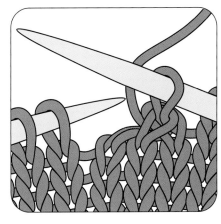

1 Put the tip of the right-hand needle knitwise into the second and then the first stitch on the left-hand needle and slip them together onto the right-hand needle.

2 Knit the next stitch then lift the two slipped stitches over the knitted stitch. The centre stitch of the decrease will lie on top.

Decrease worked in the middle of every knit row.

Working flares

These increases and decreases work very well in knitted skirts or peplums for jackets as they produce a pretty, flared effect. Look also at the techniques for creating flares, ruches and gathers (pages 142–143) to see other techniques that can be used in similar ways.

fully fashioning

Fully fashioning is when the designer wishes to make the increasing and decreasing an integral part of the design. It is a simple way of changing a plain garment into a more interesting one.

To work this technique you need to know which way the increases and decreases you use will slope, so refer back to the note given with each one. You can see here how the band of increases and then decreases along the edge of the knitting mirrors the shape of the fabric.

Stitch sampler

This sampler uses different increases and decreases, so follow the pattern to practise some of the techniques you have learned in this chapter.

Worked two or three stitches in from the edge of the knitting, the increases and decreases will be visible when the knitting is sewn up.

Cast on 15 sts.
Work 2 rows in st st.
Row 3: K3, m1, knit to last 3 sts, m1, k3.
Row 4: Purl.
Rep rows 3–4 until you have 33 sts.
Work 4 rows straight st st.
Next row: K2togtbl, knit to last 4 sts, k2tog, k2.
Next row: Purl.
Rep last 2 rows until you have 11 sts.
Work 4 rows straight st st.
Next row: Inc in every st.
Work 4 rows straight st st.
Cast (bind) off.

texture
with stitches

Swapping groups of stitches on the needle gives you cables, crosses and twists, while increasing and decreasing creates bobbles. Cable and bobble stitches are sometimes referred to as Aran stitches, named for the islands off the coast of Scotland where the techniques are thought to have originated. Aran patterns are traditionally knitted in cream yarn, but can look wonderful in vibrant colours.

cables

Many knitters avoid cabling as it looks complex, but just try it and you will see that it is deceptive and is really quite a simple technique to master. Cables are stitches that have been lifted with a third needle and crossed to another place in the work, and it's the third needle that puts people off. The actual cables are usually worked in stocking (stockinette) stitch on a background of reverse stocking (stockinette) stitch or sometimes moss (seed) stitch.

All cables use the techniques shown, but they can involve different numbers of stitches. For example, 'C6B' means 'cable six back'. You would slip three stitches onto the cable needle and hold it at the back, then knit three from the left-hand needle and finally the three from the cable needle. The pattern you are working from will tell you how many stitches to put on the cable needle and how many to knit.

Cable 4 back (C4B)

Holding the cable needle at the back of the work makes the cable twist across to the right.

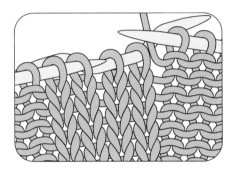

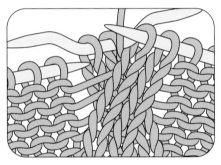

1 Work to the position of the cable. Slip the first two stitches from the left-hand needle onto the cable needle and leave it at the back of the work.

2 Coming in front of the cable needle that is holding the two stitches, knit the next two stitches from the left-hand needle.

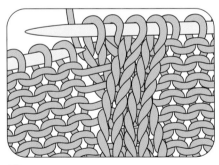

3 Now knit the two stitches from the cable needle to complete the cable four back. If you find that the first stitch purled after the cable needle is baggy, try purling into the back of it (page 51) to tighten it.

This cable twist is worked on every sixth row.

Cable four front (C4F)

Holding the cable needle at the front of the work makes the cable twist across to the left.

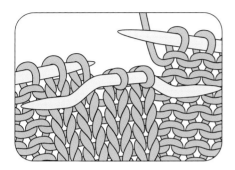

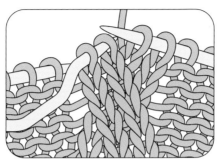

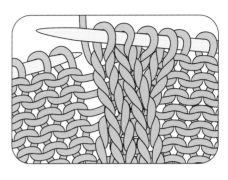

1 Work to the position of the cable. Slip the first two stitches from the left-hand needle onto the cable needle and leave it at the front of the work.

2 Going behind the cable needle that is holding the stitches, knit the next two stitches from the left-hand needle.

3 Then knit the two stitches that are on the cable needle to complete the cable.

Cable needles

Using a cranked cable needle like the one shown (see also page 11), makes it almost impossible for the stitches to slip off while you are working the next stitches on the left-hand needle. Once you are confident with cabling, try using a straight cable needle, which makes the process a bit quicker.

A band of cable four front.

twisted stitches

This technique is similar to cabling (pages 92–93) but is used to move stitches worked in stocking (stockinette) stitch across a background worked in reverse stocking (stockinette) stitch. Twisted stitch patterns can vary, but these are the ones most commonly used. As with cables, this technique can be used with different numbers of stitches.

Twist 3 back (T3B)

A back twist enables your stitches to move to the right. Here, two knit stitches are being moved.

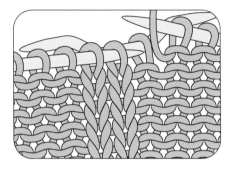 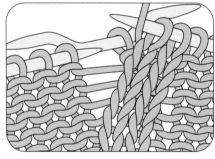 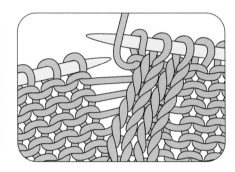

1 Work to one stitch before the stitches you wish to move. Slip this next stitch onto the cable needle, slipping it to match the background stitches – purlwise if the background is reverse stocking (stockinette) stitch – and leave it at the back of the work.

2 Knit the next two stitches from the left-hand needle.

3 Now work the stitch from the cable needle in the stitch required – purl if the background is reverse stocking (stockinette) stitch.

The stitches are moved on every eighth row.

Stretched stitches

The illustrations for some of these techniques will show the stitches stretched out a little. This is done so that you can see exactly what is happening. In the actual knitting the stitches should sit neatly next to one another.

Twist 3 front (T3F)

A front twist enables your stitches to move to the left.

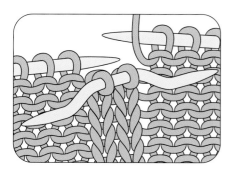 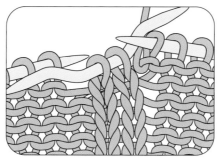 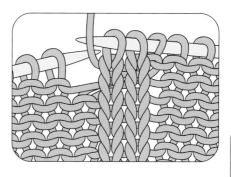

1 Work to the stitches that you wish to move and slip these two stitches onto the cable needle, leaving it at the front of the work.

2 Work the next stitch on the left-hand needle in the stitch required – purl if the background is reverse stocking (stockinette) stitch.

3 Now knit the two stitches on the cable needle.

A band of two stitches twisted to the left.

crossed stitches

If you are only moving one stitch, a cable needle is not required. Stitches are referred to as crossed when you are moving one stitch across a background worked in the same stitch, usually stocking (stockinette) stitch.

Cross 2 back (C2B)

A back cross moves a single stitch to the right.

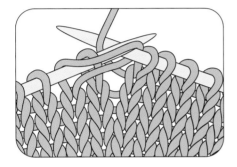

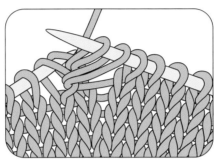

C2B worked on every knit row.

1 Work to the position of the cross. Put the tip of the right-hand needle knitwise into the second stitch on the left-hand needle and knit it, without dropping the original stitch off the left-hand needle.

2 Put the tip of the right-hand needle knitwise into the first stitch on the left-hand needle. Knit this stitch and then drop both original stitches off the left-hand needle together.

Cross 2 front (C2F)

A front cross moves a single stitch to the left.

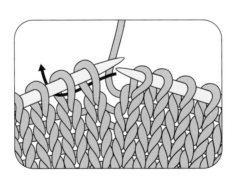

Worked in the same position every time, the crossed stitches form a vertical column.

1 Work to the position of the cross. Put the tip of the right-hand needle knitwise into the back of the second stitch on the left-hand needle and knit it, without dropping the original stitch off the left-hand needle. Knit into the front of the first stitch on the left-hand needle and drop both original stitches off the left-hand needle together.

twist stitches

These techniques use the same principles as cross stitches to move a single stitch knitted in one stitch pattern across a background knitted in a different stitch pattern. Here, a single knit stitch is being moved across a background of reverse stocking (stockinette) stitch.

Twist 2 back (T2B)

A back twist moves a single stitch to the right.

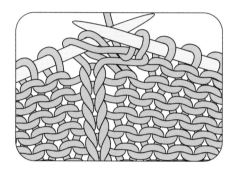

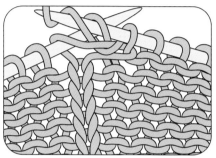

1 Work to the position of the twist. Put the tip of the right-hand needle knitwise into the second stitch on the left-hand needle and knit it, without dropping the original stitch off the left-hand needle.

2 Bring the yarn to the front of the work and purl the first stitch on the left-hand needle. Drop both original stitches off the left-hand needle together.

T2B worked on every right-side row.

Twist 2 front (T2F)

A front twist moves a single stitch to the left.

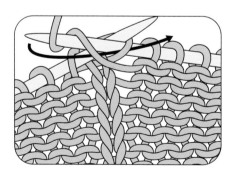

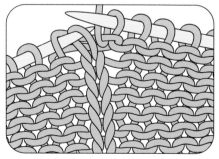

1 Work to the position of the twist. Purl the second stitch on the left-hand needle by going through the back of the loop, without dropping the original stitch off the left-hand needle.

2 Bring the right-hand needle to the front and take the yarn to the back and knit the first stitch on the left-hand needle. Drop both original stitches off the left-hand needle together.

Twist stitches create a raised line.

working from a chart

Older patterns have written instructions for cable, cross and twist stitches, but with the aid of computers most pattern writers use charts to show texture as well as colour. Texture charts can look really complicated, but in fact they can become easier to use than a written pattern. They have an advantage in that you can see what you are producing, whereas with written instructions you are often not sure what the finished result should look like until you have completed a piece of the work. If you look at this chart you can see that the groups of cable and twist stitches move apart by one stitch on every right-side row until just one stitch of reverse stocking (stockinette) stitch remains between them. Understanding how a pattern moves helps you get into the rhythm of it and you may not need to check every row on the chart as the knitted fabric grows.

When working from a chart you work from right to left on the right-side rows and from left to right on the wrong-side rows unless you are working in the round (page 120), in which case you will work from right to left on every row as you would with colour knitting (page 152).

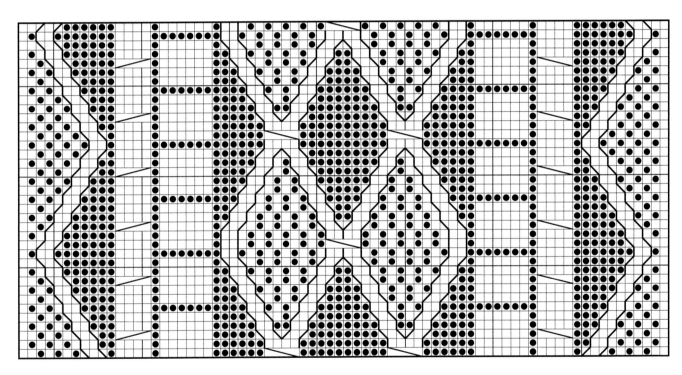

●	P on RS, k on WS
□	K on RS, p on WS
	T3B
	T3F
	C4B
	C4F

Chart symbols

Symbols used in texture charts are not universal so always check the key that comes with the chart before starting the pattern.

This swatch was knitted following the chart opposite.

lace knitting

Lace knitting is a series of loops and decreases that make open-work patterns. If you are tackling lace knitting for the first time it is advisable to find a pattern where every alternate row is plain knit or purl. This will make it easier if you need to unravel (page 249) to fix a mistake.

Bringing the yarn over the needle to make a hole is known as a yarnover and it can be described in several ways. Some designers use the term 'yo' for all types of yarnover and others will use different terms, depending on where the yarn has been left after the previous stitch has been worked. Here are all the different stitch combinations with specific instructions as to how to work yarnovers between them.

Yarn forward (yfwd)

This yarnover is used when you have just worked a knit stitch and need to do another knit stitch after the yarnover.

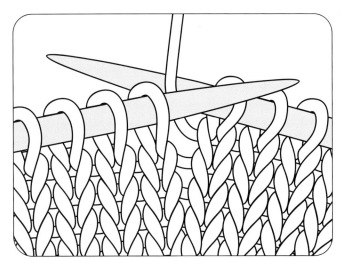

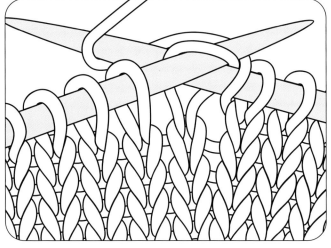

1 Work to the position of the yarnover. Bring the yarn forward between the tips of the needles.

2 Take the yarn backwards over the right-hand needle and knit the next stitch.

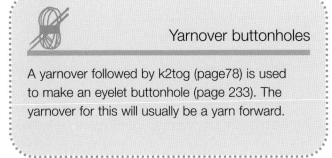

Yarnover buttonholes

A yarnover followed by k2tog (page78) is used to make an eyelet buttonhole (page 233). The yarnover for this will usually be a yarn forward.

Yarn over needle (yon)

This yarnover is used when you have just worked a purl stitch and the following stitch will be a knit stitch.

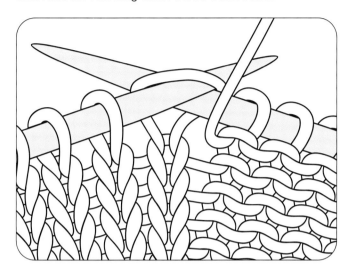

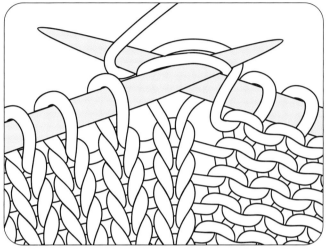

1 Work to the position of the yarnover. After having purled the last stitch, put the tip of the right-hand needle knitwise into the next stitch.

2 As the yarn is already at the front it will automatically go over the needle as you knit the next stitch.

Multiple yarnovers

For a larger hole, wrap the yarn around the needle more than once. When you work back across the row, work into one of the yarnover loops and drop the other one off the needle.

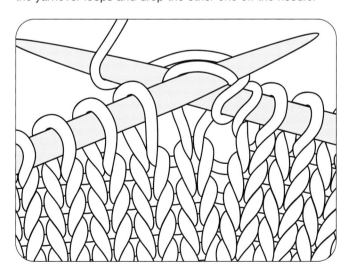

The yarn is wrapped twice around the needle for a multiple yarn forward. The same principle applies for all yarnovers: follow the instructions for wrapping the yarn once, but do it twice instead.

Yarn forward round needle (yfrn)

This yarnover is used when you have just worked a knit
stitch and the following stitch will be a purl stitch.

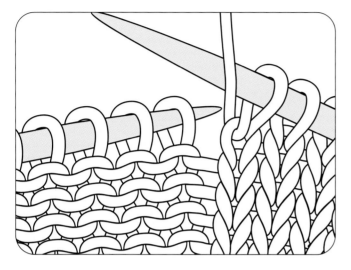

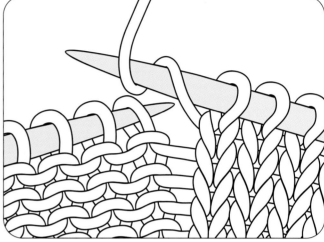

1 Work to the position of the yarnover. After having knitted
the last stitch, bring the yarn forward between the two
needles as if to purl.

2 Wrap the yarn once over and around the needle until it is
back in the right position to purl the next stitch.

Yarn round needle (yrn)

This yarnover is used when you have just worked a purl
stitch and wish to do another purl stitch after the yarnover.

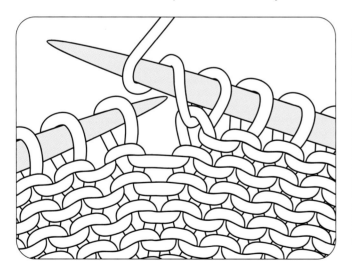

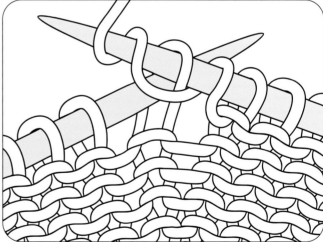

1 Work to the position of the yarnover. Take the yarn over
the right-hand needle to the back of the work and then
through between the tips of the needles and to the front of the
work again.

2 Purl the next stitch.

Slip one, knit one, pass the slipped stitch over (skpo)

This technique is used in decreasing (page 79) as well as in working lace stitches.

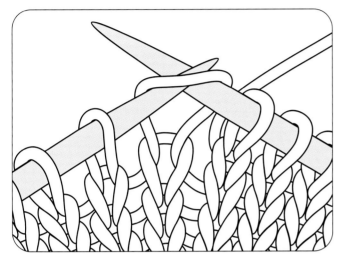

1 Put the tip of the right-hand needle into the next stitch and slip it onto the right-hand needle.

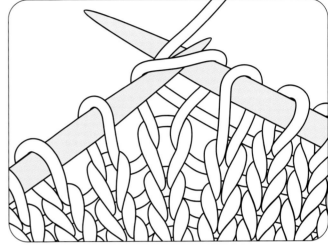

2 Knit the next stitch in the usual way.

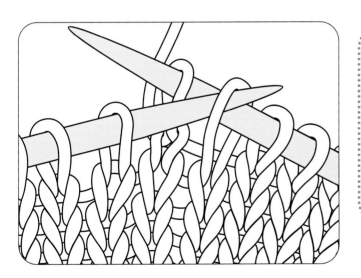

3 Put the tip of the left-hand needle into the front of the slipped stitch on the right-hand needle and lift it over the stitch just knitted.

Stretching the stitch

When working skpo be careful not to pull on the slipped stitch or it will stretch and as you are not knitting into it, it is not possible to tighten up it again. A stretched stitch will show as a baggy loop at an angle on the finished knitting.

Yarnover at the beginning of a knit row

In some lace patterns it is necessary to have a yarnover at the beginning of the row. On a knit row, work it as follows.

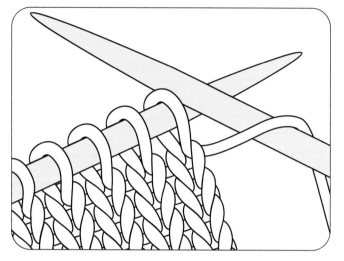 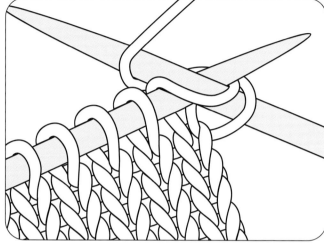

1 Hold the yarn in front of the work, as if you were going to purl the first stitch, and drape it over the right-hand needle.

2 Put the tip of the right-hand needle knitwise into the first stitch on the left-hand needle. Bring the yarn around to the back and knit the stitch.

Yarnover at the beginning of a purl row

At the beginning of a purl row work the yarn over in this way.

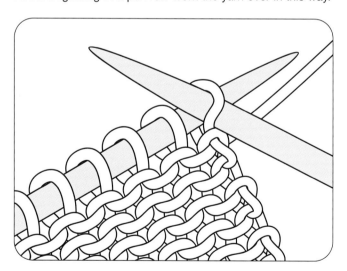 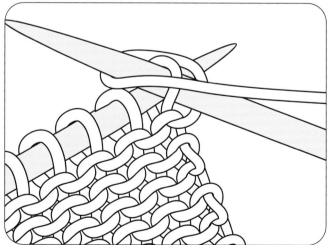

1 Put the tip of the right-hand needle purlwise into the first stitch on the left-hand needle. Make sure the yarn is at the back and below the right-hand needle.

2 Bring the yarn over the tip of the left-hand needle and under the right-hand needle. Purl the stitch, pulling the yarn through the stitch only – not through the extra loop as well.

working from a chart

As with cable patterns (page 98), lace patterns are often now shown as charts rather than as written instructions, though sometimes the pattern will have both.

Always ensure that you understand the key and know how to work all the techniques needed before you start the project. If necessary, practise any unfamiliar techniques with scrap yarn. When working from a chart you work from right to left on the right-side rows and from left to right on the wrong-side rows.

Photocopy and enlarge the chart so that you can mark off the completed rows as you work. This will help you keep track of where you are in the pattern.

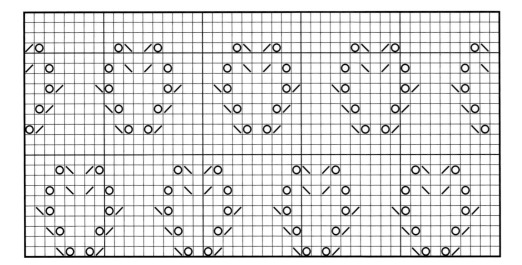

□	K on RS, p on WS
◙	yon
⊘	k2tog
⊠	k2togtbl

This swatch was knitted following the chart above.

How to work a pattern repeat

Rather than displaying a whole charted design, sometimes a pattern will give a smaller chart showing a section that needs to be repeated to make up the complete design: this is called a pattern repeat. Shown below is a charted pattern repeat for a lace pattern. The lace you knit will have the same arrangement of holes as that charted in full opposite, but the chart is presented differently.

There are two edge stitches on either side and then a 12-stitch pattern repeat. You would work the two edge stitches, then work the pattern repeat as many times as instructed in the pattern and then finally work the last two edge stitches.

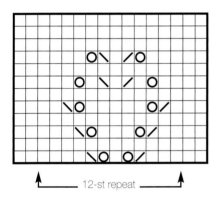

← |____ 12-st repeat ____| →

This lace pattern has a 12-stitch horizontal repeat.

Keeping patterns correct in lace

Obviously it is important to keep the pattern of the lace correct. It is best to count the number of stitches you have after each row until you get into the rhythm of the pattern. It can be hard to see if the pattern looks right until you have worked at least 20cm (8in) of it.

Some lace patterns have a different number of stitches at the end of some rows due to yarnovers, but no decreases, being made on those rows. Most patterns will give you a stitch count on these rows, so check that you have the correct number of stitches against the stitch count, not against the original number of stitches cast on.

Working increases and decreases into lace knitting and keeping the pattern correct can be difficult. It is best to place a round marker (page 12) one stitch in from the beginning and end of a row before starting the increases. Work the increases before the marker at the beginning of a row and after it at the end and then you can easily see how many stitches have been increased. When you increase a stitch, work in stocking (stockinette) stitch until you have increased by enough stitches to do a complete pattern repeat.

However, if the pattern repeat is large the increase section can create an unsightly stocking (stockinette) stitch triangle. In this case you can look at the pattern repeat and see if half of it can be worked once enough stitches have been increased.

At the top of the swatch a half-pattern repeat has been worked into the increased section.

bobbles

Another traditional stitch that is seen in both lace and Aran design is the bobble. These can differ in size and in how they are made and a pattern will give instructions for how to work the particular bobble in the project you are knitting. Bobbles are usually made in stocking (stockinette) stitch.

Here are two different sizes of bobble to practise your techniques on, plus a neat large bobble that doesn't involve turning the work: particularly useful if you are knitting a large project such as an afghan.

Small bobble

These tiny bobbles are worked on one row and are sometimes called popcorn bobbles.

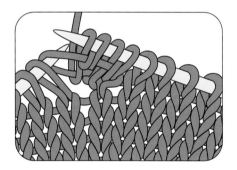 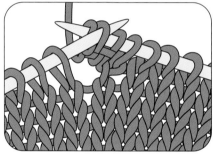 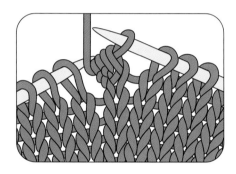

1 Work to the position of the bobble. In the same way as for increasing knitwise (page 74), knit into the front, then the back, the front again and then the back again of the next stitch and then slip the original stitch off the left-hand needle. You have made four stitches out of one.

2 With the tip of the left-hand needle, lift the second stitch on the right-hand needle over the first one.

3 Lift the third and fourth stitches in turn over the first one. One stitch remains and the bobble is complete.

Baggy stitches

If the first stitch knitted after a bobble is a little baggy, you can knit into the back of it (page 51) to tighten it. The twisted stitch will be partly hidden by the bobble and should not show too much.

A scattering of little bobbles.

Bobble without turning

These bobbles can be made with different numbers of stitches and rows to achieve the size you need.

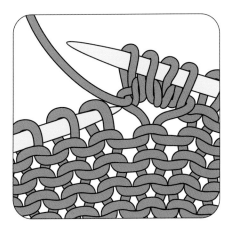

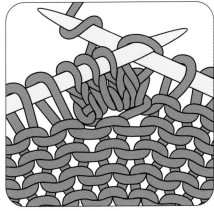

1 In the same way as for increasing knitwise (page 74), knit into the front, then the back, the front again and then the back again of the next stitch and then slip the original stitch off the left-hand needle. You have made four stitches out of one.

2 *Slip the four stitches knitwise (page 50) back onto the left-hand needle. Bring the yarn across the back of the four stitches and, pulling it gently taut, knit the four stitches again. Repeat from * three times more. You have worked four rows over the four bobble stitches.

3 Using the tip of the left-hand needle, pass the second stitch over the first one. Then pass the third and fourth stitches in turn over the first one.

4 One stitch remains and the bobble is complete. Work the rest of the row as instructed in the pattern.

This technique produces tight, round bobbles.

Large bobble

This bobble involves turning the work to make a big bobble that will be prominent.

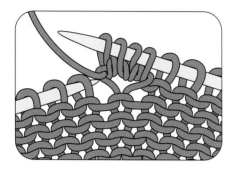

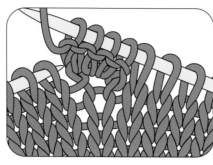

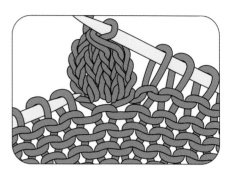

1 Work to the position of the bobble. Knit, then purl, then knit, then purl into the next stitch and then slip the original stitch off the left-hand needle. You have made four stitches out of one.

2 Turn the work so that the wrong side is facing you and purl the four stitches you have just made. Turn the work again and knit the four stitches. Turn the work once more and purl the four stitches. You have now worked three rows over the four bobble stitches.

3 Turn the work again so that the right side is facing you. Slip the first two stitches knitwise (page 50) from the left-hand needle to the right-hand needle. Knit the next two stitches together (page 78), then pass the two slipped stitches over it.

4 One stitch remains and the bobble is complete. Work the rest of the row as instructed in the pattern.

Chunky bobbles on a reverse stocking (stockinette) stitch background.

loop knitting

Loop knitting can be used to lend a fur effect to knitted fabric. It can be used all over or just as an edging. Bear in mind that these techniques use a lot of yarn, approximately 5cm (2in) for each loop, so if you decide to add loops to a project you will need to buy more yarn than the original pattern specifies.

Single loop

This is worked on the right side of the fabric. The part of the loop where you wind the yarn around your left thumb might sound awkward, but it just takes a bit of practice. You need to hold the right-hand needle against your right palm with your second, third and little fingers and use your right index finger and thumb to wrap the yarn around your left thumb. Here, the loop is shown in a different colour for clarity.

Wrapping the yarn

If you find wrapping the yarn around your thumb a bit tricky, you can cut a strip of cardboard the desired depth of the loop and wrap the yarn around that instead.

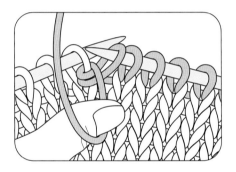

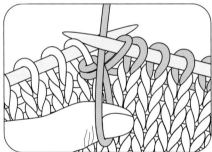

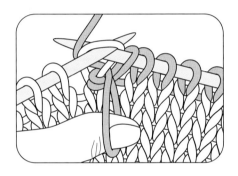

1 Work to the position of the loop. With the right side of the work facing you, knit the next stitch but do not allow the original stitch to drop off the left-hand needle. Bring the yarn forward between the tips of the needles to the front. Stretch out your left thumb so that it is in front of the knitting and wrap the yarn under and around it.

2 Take the yarn back between the tips of the needles to the back.

3 Knit into the same stitch again and then drop the original stitch off the left-hand needle. At the same time, take your left thumb out of the loop.

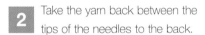

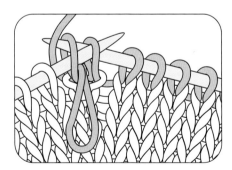

4 In a similar way to ssk (page 79), put the tip of the left-hand needle through the front of the two stitches just made and knit them together. When you have finished the loop row and the next row, give all the loops a gentle tug to even them out and tighten the stitches.

Loops worked on alternate stitches on knit rows.

Clustered loops

If you want denser groups of loops, then this technique is the answer. Again, the loop row and loops are shown in a different colour for clarity.

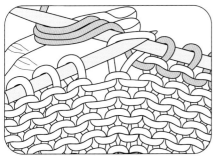  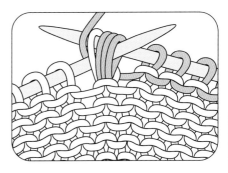

1 To make a cluster of loops you need to work with the wrong side of the work facing you. Work to the position of the loops, then take the yarn between the tips of the needles to the back of the work. Put the right-hand needle knitwise (page 69) into the next stitch. Put one or two fingers (depending how long you would like the loops to be) of your left hand behind the right-hand needle and wind the yarn in a clockwise direction around the fingers and right-hand needle three times.

2 Using the right-hand needle, draw the ends of the loops up through the stitch, without dropping the original stitch off the left-hand needle.

3 Remove your fingers from loops. Slip the ends of the loops onto the left-hand needle and knit them together with the original stitch through the back loops (page 51). If necessary, keep the loops taut at the back of the work with your left hand. Pull the loops firmly on the right side of the work to tighten the stitches.

Embellished loops

You can use a different yarn to knit the loop stitch sections of a project: mohair yarn makes fluffy fur cuffs on a jacket knitted in smooth yarn. You can also add beads to loops. Thread beads onto the yarn (page 178) and push one down onto each loop as you wrap the yarn around your fingers.

Cluster loops worked on alternate stitches on purl rows.

grouping stitches

There are various ways of grouping or bunching stitches together to create different effects. Traditionally these techniques are used to create knitted smocking, but they can also be used to great effect in more contemporary designs.

Clustered stitches

This example shows you how to cluster six stitches together, but the same technique can be used with different numbers of stitches. Here, the knitted fabric is a knit two, purl two rib (page 47) and the clustering is worked over two knit, two purl and two knit stitches.

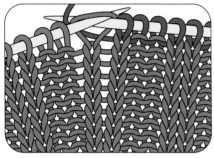

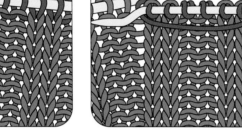

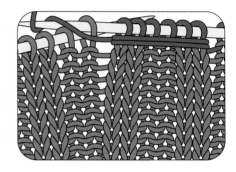

1 Work to the position of the cluster. Knit two, purl two, knit two from the left-hand needle.

2 Slip these last six stitches onto a cable needle. From front to back, wrap the yarn twice around the stitches on the cable needle.

3 Slip the stitches back onto the right-hand needle. Pull the yarn to bunch the stitches together. Continue in the rib pattern until you get to the next group of stitches to be clustered.

Using colour

You can wrap the stitches with a different colour yarn to emphasise the effect. It is best to use a yarn that is the same weight as the project yarn and to strand it across the back of the work between the clustered stitches using a Fair Isle stranding technique (pages 170–173).

A group of six stitches clustered together.

Smocking

If you want to introduce classic smocking into a design, it is important to establish a fabric stitch pattern that will work with the clustered stitches to create the smocking pattern you want. Here, the background is a knit one, purl three rib, with one purl stitch at the beginning and end.

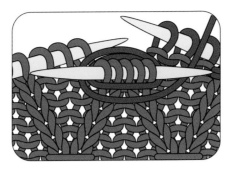

On a right-side row, purl one, then cluster together one knit, three purl and one knit stitches. Purl to the next knit stitch, and then repeat the cluster and continue to the end of the row. On the following sixth row, purl one, knit one, purl three, then work the cluster with the next five stitches. Purl three, repeat the cluster and continue to the end of the row. This will create a diamond smocking pattern.

A traditional diamond smocking pattern.

Bound stitches

For a more subtle effect you can bind a smaller number of stitches together without using a cable needle. This example is worked on stocking (stockinette) stitch.

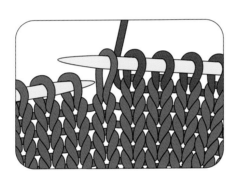

1 Work to the first of the stitches to be bound together. Slip the first stitch purlwise onto the right-hand needle, keeping the yarn at the back of the work.

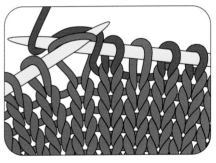

2 Knit the following stitch on the left-hand needle and then bring yarn forward and knit the next stitch (page 100).

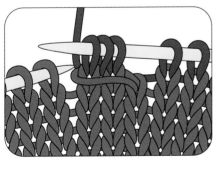

3 Put the tip of the left-hand needle into the slipped stitch and lift it over the first knitted stitch, the yarnover and the second knitted stitch, so binding these stitches together.

Bound stitches worked on every eighth row.

stitch samplers

Here are samplers of different textured stitch patterns for you to practise your techniques with. Follow the pattern instructions carefully and refer back to the specific techniques if you need to.

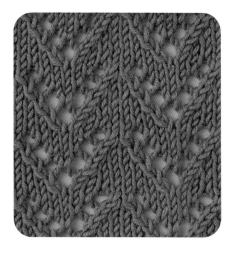

Chevron lace

Worked over a multiple of 9 sts.

Row 1 (RS): *K4, yfwd, skpo, k3, rep from * to end.

Row 2 and all WS rows: Purl.

Row 3: *K2, k2tog, yfwd, k1, yfwd, skpo, k2, rep from * to end.

Row 5: *K1, k2tog, yfwd, k3, yfwd, skpo, k1, rep from * to end.

Row 7: *K2tog, yfwd, k5, yfwd, skpo, rep from * to end.

Row 8: Purl.

Rep these 8 rows.

Trefoil lace

Worked over a multiple of 8 sts.

Row 1 (RS): Knit.

Row 2 and all WS rows: Purl.

Row 3: K3, *yfwd, ssk, k6, rep from * to last 3 sts, k3.

Row 5: K1, *k2tog, yfwd, k1, ywfd, ssk, k3, rep from * to last 2 sts, k2.

Row 7: As row 3.

Row 9: Knit.

Row 11: K7, *yfwd, ssk, k6, rep from * to last st, k1.

Row 13: K5, *k2tog, yfwd, k1, yfwd, ssk, k3, rep from * to last 3 sts, k3.

Row 15: As row 11.

Row 16: Purl.

Rep these 16 rows.

Diamond lace

Worked over a multiple of 12 sts + 1 st.

Row 1 (RS): *P1, k2tog, k3, yfwd, k1, yfwd, k3, skpo, p1, rep from * to last st, p1.

Row 2 and all WS rows: Purl.

Row 3: *P1, k2tog, k2, yfwd, k3, yfwd, k2, skpo, p1, rep from * to last st, p1.

Row 5: *P1, k2tog, k1, yfwd, k5, yfwd, k1, skpo, p1, rep from * to last st, p1.

Row 7: *P1, k2tog, yfwd, k7, yfwd, skpo, p1, rep from * to last st, p1.

Row 9: *K1, yfwd, k3, skpo, p1, k2tog, k3, yfwd, rep from * to last st, k1.

Row 11: *K2, yfwd, k2, skpo, p1, k2tog, k2, yfwd, k1, rep from * to last st, k1.

Row 13: *K3, yfwd, k1, skpo, p1, k2tog, k1, yfwd, k2, rep from * to last st, k1.

Row 15: *K4, yfwd, skpo, p1, k2tog, yfwd, k3, rep from * to last st, k1.

Row 16: Purl.

Rep these 16 rows.

Cable

Panel of 32 sts.

Rows 1 and 3 (RS): P2, k12, p4, k12, p2.

Rows 2 and all WS rows: Knit the knit sts and purl the purl sts.

Rows 5: P2, C6B, p4, C6F, p2.

Rows 7: As row 1.

Rows 8: As row 2.

Rep these 8 rows.

Twisted stitches

Worked over a multiple of 13 sts + 7 sts.

Row 1: * P2, k3, p2, k6, rep from * to last 7 sts, p2, k2, p2.

Row 2: Work sts as set.

Row 3: P2, twist 2 sts right, k1, p2, [twist 2 sts right] 3 times, rep from * to last 7 sts, p2, twist 2 right, k1, p2.

Row 4: As row 2.

Row 5: P2, k1, twist 2 sts left, p2, k1, [twist 2 sts left] twice, k1, rep from * to last 7 sts, p2, k1, twist 2 sts left, p2.

Rep rows 2–5.

Cable and bobble

Panel of 11 sts with rev st st background. For bobble, see page 110.

Row 1: P2, k3, p1, k3, p2.

Row 2: Knit the knit sts and purl the purl sts.

Row 3: P2, sl 4 sts onto CN and hold at back, k3, sl last st from CN back onto LH needle and knit this st, k3 from CN, p2.

Row 4: Knit the knit sts and purl the purl sts.

Row 5: Sl 2 sts onto CN and hold at back, k3, then p2 from CN, p1, sl 3 sts onto CN and hold at front, p2, then p3 from CN.

Row 6: Knit the knit sts and purl the purl sts.

Row 7: K3, p2, MB, p2, k3.

Row 8: Knit the knit sts and purl the purl sts.

Row 9: P7, sl 1st onto CN and hold at back, k3, then p1 from CN.

Row 10: Knit the knit sts and purl the purl sts.

Row 11: P6, (sl 1st onto CN and hold at back, k3, then p1 from CN, p1.

Row 12: Knit the knit sts and purl the purl sts.

Row 13: P5, (sl 1st onto CN and hold at back, k3, then p1 from CN, p2.

Row 14: Knit the knit sts and purl the purl sts.

Row 15: P4, sl 1st onto CN and hold at back, k3, then p1 from CN, p3.

Row 16: Knit the knit sts and purl the purl sts.

Row 17: P3, sl 1st onto CN and hold at back, k3, then p1 from CN, p4.

Row 18: Knit the knit sts and purl the purl sts.

Row 19: P2, sl 1st onto CN and hold at back, k3, then p1 from CN, p5.

Row 20: Knit the knit sts and purl the purl sts.

Row 21: P1, sl 1st onto CN and hold at back, k3, then p1 from CN, p6.

Row 22: P3, k4, p3, k1.

Row 23: Sl 1st onto CN and hold at back of work, k3, then p1 from CN, p4, k3.

Row 24: Knit the knit sts and purl the purl sts.

Row 25: K3, p2, MB, p2, k3.

Row 26: P3, k5, p3.

Row 27: Sl 3 sts onto CN and hold at front, p2, then p3 from CN, p1, sl 2 sts onto CN and hold at back, k3, then p2 from CN.

Rep rows 2–27.

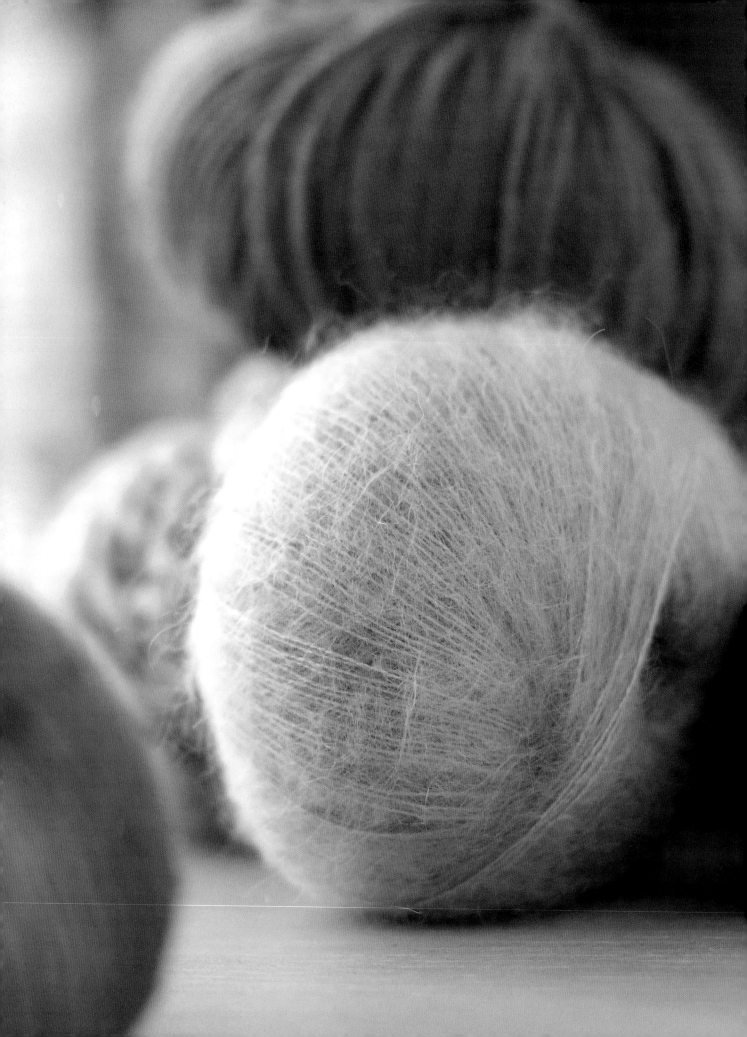

types of knitting

Usually we think of knitting as a flat fabric made using two needles and some yarn, but it doesn't have to be that way. You can knit various shapes, such as tubes, pleats and corners. This chapter looks at different knitting techniques and includes pockets, as they are elements you need to think about while knitting a project, rather than a piece that is added on afterwards.

circular knitting

The easiest way to knit in the round is to use a circular needle. It has two pointed ends joined with a cord, usually made from plastic or nylon. A circular needle enables you to knit a tube with no side seams to sew up. You can knit a sweater this way up to the armholes, then you have to divide the front and back. This is particularly useful when knitting in a complicated Fair Isle pattern (pages 164–173), as it makes it easier to match the pattern at the side seams. Another place where circular knitting is useful is on a neckband, especially a polo neck, as working in the round eliminates any seams. Some knitters also find it an advantage that you only work in the stitch making the right side of the fabric, usually knit stitch.

Starting circular knitting

Circular needles come in different lengths and a pattern should tell you which length to use. Using the two pointed tips of the circular needle, cast on in the usual way (pages 28–31). If the needle is the right length, the cast on stitches should fill it without having to stretch them out (which can make the knitting hard work or impossible).

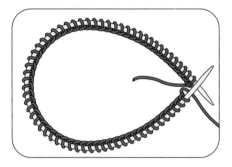

1 Once you have cast on the correct number of stitches, check carefully that the cast on row is not twisted around the needle. If it is, you will end up knitting a Mobius strip, which can be fun for a scarf but is useless for a sweater.

2 Place a round marker (page 12) on right-hand point of the needle after you have cast on the correct number of stitches. When knitting the first stitch that was cast on, make sure you pull it tight to prevent a hole forming.

Knitting with circular needles

Circular needles can also be used for knitting conventionally (backwards and forwards), by swapping the points in your hands at the end of each row. With heavy projects, such as afghans, you can cast on a lot of stitches easily and stretch them out to see how the pattern is growing. As the work progresses, you can hold the weight of the knitted fabric in your lap and not on the needles, thus sparing you aches and pains in your wrists and arms. It is very easy to travel with circular needles as they pack away neatly and if you are knitting on a train or plane (if the airline allows it), you won't nudge your travelling neighbour as you would with the ends of straight needles.

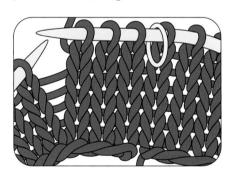

3 Knit until you come to the marker; you have completed one round. Slip the marker onto the right-hand point of the needle and knit the next round.

Circular for a yoke

A circular needle is also used for joining work together to work a yoke or large neck. The body and sleeves are completed to the underarm and then they are joined. The stitches for the underarm are placed on holders and are later grafted together. You must finish knitting the body at the left underarm on the back of the sweater.

Keeping track

Make sure you mark the front and back of the body so that you don't loose track of where you are.

1 On the body, if you need ten stitches for the underarm, place the five stitches either side of the seam marker on a thread or stitch holder.

2 Do the same on the sleeves: place the five stitches either side of the seam marker on a thread or stitch holder.

3 Beginning at the front left underarm, work across the front body stitches to the right underarm. Now work across all the right sleeve stitches, except those on the thread. Work across the stitches for the back and then finally across the stitches for the left sleeve, except those on the thread. You now have all the stitches for the yoke on one needle. Leave the stitches on the threads until the yoke is complete and then graft (page 205) them together.

A tube of knitting on a circular needle.

Working on double-pointed needles

Double-pointed needles can also be used to work in the round and create a tube of knitting. Novice knitters are often put off knitting in this way because of the extra needles, but they are nothing to be afraid of. You are still only knitting on two needles at any one time and after a bit of practice you will find that you can just ignore the needles you are not actually using.

You can choose to work on four or five needles; usually you would work on four needles on a small project, like a sock, and for larger projects you would use five needles. The example shown here uses four needles. You need to divide the number of stitches between three of the needles and the fourth will be the needle you knit with.

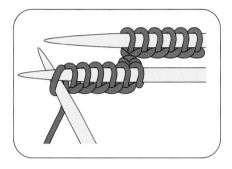

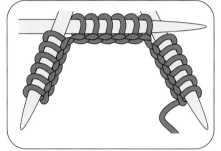

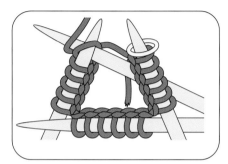

1 Cast on the required number of stitches onto the first needle, plus one extra stitch. Slip the extra stitch onto the second needle then repeat the process until the required number of stitches is cast on to all the needles.

2 Lay out the needles with the tips overlapping as shown here. Make sure that the cast on edge faces into the middle of the triangle all the way around and is not twisted at any point.

3 Place a round marker (page 12) on the needle after the last stitch has been cast on. Using the free needle, knit the stitches off the first needle. When all the stitches are knitted, the first needle becomes the free one, ready to knit the stitches off the second needle with. Continue knitting off each needle in turn until you come to the marker and then slip the marker from the left-hand needle to the right-hand needle and knit the next round.

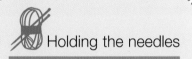
Holding the needles

The four needles will feel awkward in your hands at first, so before you start a project, cast on some stitches using spare yarn and knit a few rounds. On each round, the lower tip of the left-hand needle should lie in front of the tip of the needle making up the bottom of the triangle and the lower tip of the right-hand needle should lie behind the other tip of the bottom needle.

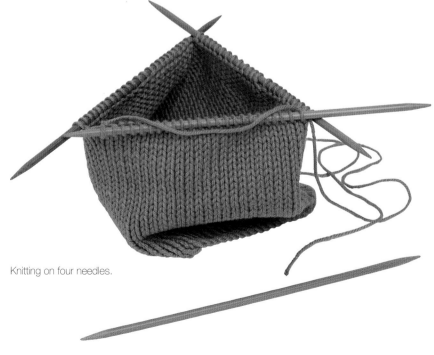

Knitting on four needles.

knitted socks

Knitting socks has become very popular and there are beautiful yarns on the market that are dyed in such a way that when you knit the yarn it produces a striped fabric. The best way to knit a sock is on four needles (opposite).

The anatomy of a sock

The greatest challenge when knitting a sock is to know where exactly you are on the sock at any given point in the pattern. This drawing should help you understand how a sock is made and so which bits of the pattern relate to which bits of the actual sock.

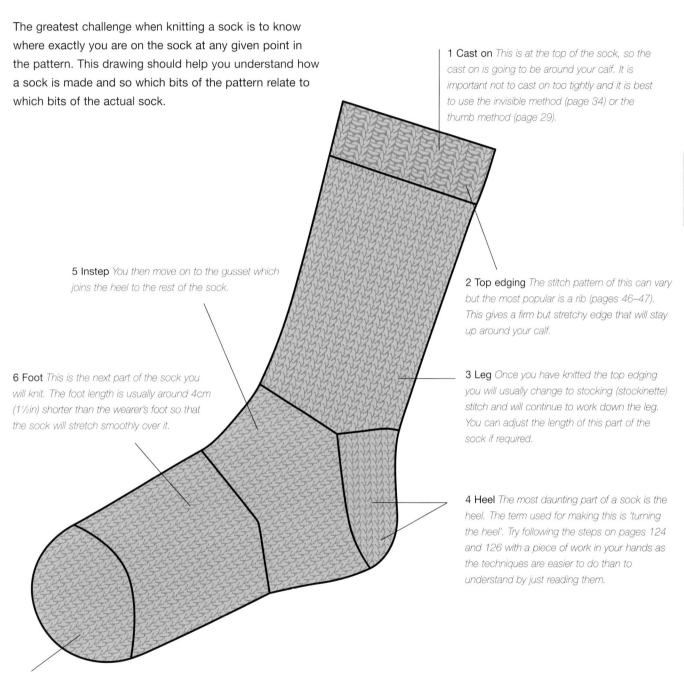

1 Cast on *This is at the top of the sock, so the cast on is going to be around your calf. It is important not to cast on too tightly and it is best to use the invisible method (page 34) or the thumb method (page 29).*

5 Instep *You then move on to the gusset which joins the heel to the rest of the sock.*

6 Foot *This is the next part of the sock you will knit. The foot length is usually around 4cm (1½in) shorter than the wearer's foot so that the sock will stretch smoothly over it.*

2 Top edging *The stitch pattern of this can vary but the most popular is a rib (pages 46–47). This gives a firm but stretchy edge that will stay up around your calf.*

3 Leg *Once you have knitted the top edging you will usually change to stocking (stockinette) stitch and will continue to work down the leg. You can adjust the length of this part of the sock if required.*

4 Heel *The most daunting part of a sock is the heel. The term used for making this is 'turning the heel'. Try following the steps on pages 124 and 126 with a piece of work in your hands as the techniques are easier to do than to understand by just reading them.*

7 Toe *The toe is then shaped and finally knitted (page 57), grafted (page 205) or sewn (page 208) up. Grafting gives the best finish.*

Knitting a sock

Here is a sample pattern for a child's sock, which is worth knitting to practise all the techniques. Choose a double-knit or Aran-weight yarn and four double-pointed needles the size recommended on the yarn ball band.

Cast on 42 stitches, casting 14 stitches on to each needle (page 122). Place a round marker after the last stitch cast on.

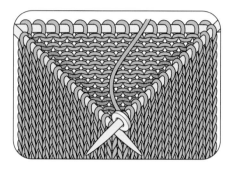

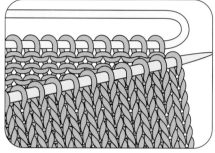

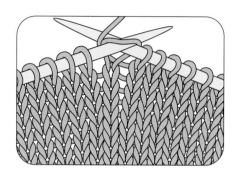

1 Work 6 rounds (page 122) of single rib (page 46). The top edging is complete. Change to stocking (stockinette) stitch (remembering that in the round this means knitting every row), and knit until the leg is the required length. (This is the measurement from the cast on to the top of the heel.) Cut the yarn, leaving a 15cm (6in) tail to sew in later (page 200). The leg is complete.

2 Slip the first 11 and the last 11 stitches of the last round onto one needle: these 22 stitches will be used for the heel. Slip the remaining 20 stitches onto a stitch holder (page 12) or spare needle: these will be picked up when working the instep.

3 With the right side of the work facing you, re-join the yarn (page 53) to the right-hand side of the heel stitches. Using a spare needle, knit across these stitches. Continue working back and forth on these 22 stitches in stocking (stockinette) stitch (remembering that when working back and forth you knit and purl alternate rows), for approximately 5cm (2in), ending with a wrong side (purl) row.

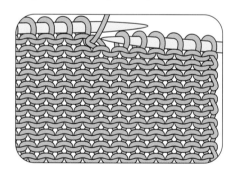

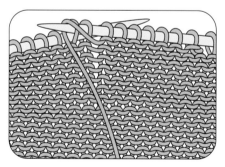

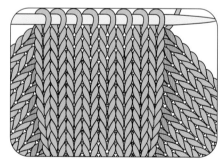

4 With the right side facing, knit 14 stitches then skpo (page 79) to decrease by 1 stitch. Leave the last 6 stitches not worked and turn the work by swapping the needles in your hands. The right-hand needle holds 6 stitches from the previous row and the left-hand needle holds 15 stitches.

5 Purl the next 7 stitches then p2tog (page 78) to decrease by 1 stitch. Leave the last 6 stitches not worked and turn the work.

6 On the next row, knit 7 stitches, skpo, turn. On the next row, purl 7 stitches, p2 tog, turn. Repeat these 2 rows until 8 stitches in total remain on the needle, ending with a wrong side row. Turn the work.

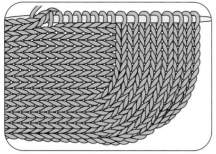

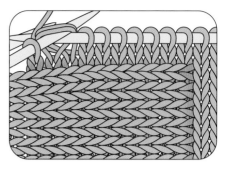

7 Now start working in rounds again. Knit across the 8 heel stitches then pick up and knit (page 127) 10 stitches along the side of the heel. Using a second needle, knit across the 20 instep stitches that are on the stitch holder.

8 Using a third needle, pick up and knit 10 stitches along the other side of the heel then knit across 4 of the stitches on the first needle. Place a marker after the last stitch knitted. There should be a total of 48 stitches on the three needles: 14 stitches on the first needle, 20 on the second needle and 14 on the third needle.

9 Knit 1 round. On the next round, knit to the third stitch from the end on the first needle, then k2tog (page 78). Knit the last stitch on the first needle.

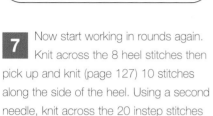

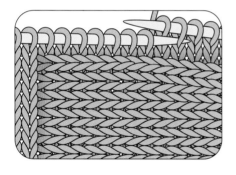

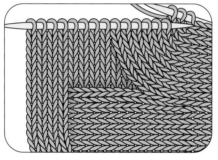

10 Knit across the 20 instep stitches. Knit 1 stitch from the third needle, then skpo. Knit to the end of the round.

11 Repeat this decrease round three more times so that 40 stitches remain on the needles. Turning the heel is now completed.
Continue in stocking (stockinette) stitch until the foot is the required length. (This is the measurement from base of the heel to the start of the toes.)
To shape the toe, on the next round decrease 1 stitch at the end of the first needle and the beginning of the third needle, as instructed in Steps 9 and 10.

Repeat this round four more times. There should be a total of 30 stitches on the three needles. Divide the stitches equally between the three needles and continue the shaping by working k2tog at the beginning and end of each needle on every round until 2 stitches remain on each needle. Rearrange the stitches so that there are 3 stitches on each of two needles. Cast (bind) off (page 57), graft (page 205) or sew (page 208) these stitches together.

picking up stitches

There will be times when you have to pick up a number of stitches from a finished piece of knitting in order to knit another part of the project. There are two ways of doing this, the difference between them being whether you are picking up stitches right across the finished piece or picking up a smaller number of stitches within the finished piece.

Picking up with a knitting needle

This technique is also known as 'pick up and knit' and is used if you need to pick up stitches right across a piece. For example, you would use this method to pick up stitches around a neck (page 221).

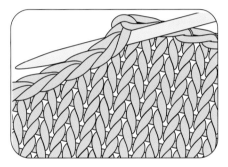

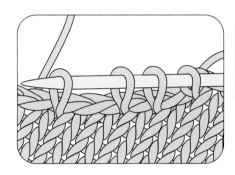

1 From the right side, put the tip of a needle into the space between the edge stitch and the next stitch.

2 Loop the yarn around the needle. Make sure that the loop is at least 15cm (6in) from the cut end, so leaving a tail to be sewn in later (page 200).

3 Bring the needle, and the yarn looped around it, through the space to the front of the work. Continue in this way, picking up stitches from the finished edge as required.

Picking up with a crochet hook

You would use this technique if you wanted to pick up a number of stitches within a finished piece. For example, picking up for a picked-up patch pocket (page 131).

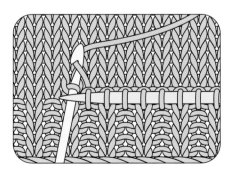

Thread a tapestry needle with the end of the yarn and take it through the finished piece to the wrong side, at the left-hand edge of where you want to start picking up stitches. (Remember, this is the left-hand edge as you wear the garment, not as you look at it.) Fasten the yarn to the back of the piece. Put the crochet hook into the first stitch to be picked up from and under the upper loop of that stitch. Catch the yarn with the hook, pull it through and slip it onto a knitting needle. Pull the yarn gently to make sure the stitch sits snugly around the needle. Continue in this way, picking up one stitch from the knitted fabric as required.

pockets

There are several types of pocket and the type you choose to knit will depend on how much of a feature of the garment you want the pockets to be. Inserted pockets, which are mainly used on cardigans and jackets, are neat, discreet and are less of a feature of the garment than a patch pocket. There are two types of inserted pockets: horizontal and vertical. There are also two ways of making patch pockets, though the results are visually similar so usually the method you use will be simply the one you prefer.

Horizontal inserted pocket

This is a pocket with a top opening. Knit the pocket lining before you start the piece of the garment in which the pocket is to be, usually the front. The pattern will tell you how many stitches to knit for the lining, which should be two stitches more than are cast off for the pocket. Finish the lining with a right side row (knit row on stocking [stockinette] stitch), and leave the stitches on a stitch holder until required. Here, the lining is shown in a different colour for clarity.

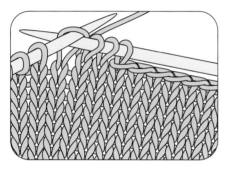 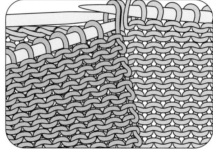 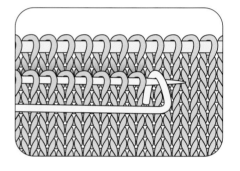

1 Work on the garment piece that requires the pocket to the row before the pocket, which should be a wrong side row. On the next row (right side), knit to the position of the pocket. Cast (bind) off the required number of stitches and knit to the end of the row.

2 On the next row (wrong side), purl to one stitch before the cast (bound) off stitches. Right side down, lay the lining on top of the work and purl together the last stitch before the cast (bind) off with the first stitch of the lining. Purl across the lining stitches until one stitch remains. Purl this stitch together with the first stitch on the left-hand needle after the cast (bind) off. Purl to the end of the row. Work the rest of the garment piece. When you are making up the garment, whipstitch (page 231) the lining to the back of the piece.

3 In Step 1, instead of casting (binding) off the stitches for the pocket opening you can leave them on a stitch holder. When you have finished the rest of the piece, go back to these stitches and work a decorative border for the pocket opening. Mattress stitch (page 208) the sides of this border to the front of the piece.

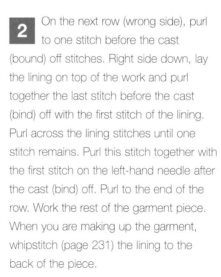

Horizontal pocket with ribbed border.

Vertical inserted pocket

Vertical pockets have the opening at the side and the lining is worked at the same time as the pocket. You will need two stitch holders and a spare knitting needle to work this pocket.

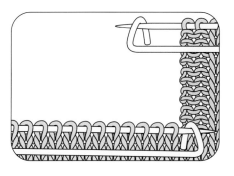

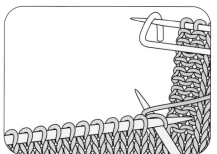

Using colour

You can add a flash of colour to a plain jacket by knitting the pocket lining in a contrast colour yarn.

1 Work the garment piece to the row before the pocket, which should be a wrong side row. On the next row (right side), knit to the position of the bottom edge of the pocket. Slip the remaining stitches on the left-hand needle onto a stitch holder. Turn the work and work the stitches on the needles (these make the the front of the pocket) until the pocket is the required depth, finishing with a wrong side row. It is best to work the edging of the pocket as you go: here, it is a 2-stitch garter stitch edge (page 52). Slip all the stitches onto the second stitch holder.

2 Slip the stitches on the first stitch holder onto a needle and hold it in your left hand. Using the cable method (page 28), cast on the number of stitches required for the lining. Work this section to same depth as the front pocket section, finishing with a wrong side row.

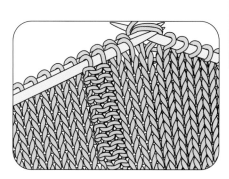

3 Slip the stitches on the second holder onto a needle. Using the spare needle, knit across the piece until you reach the position of the inner edge of the lining. Hold the needle with the lining stitches on behind the front of the pocket then knit together the stitches from the lining and the front of the work. Do this in the same way as for casting (binding) off two edges together (page 57), but do not actually cast (bind) the stitches off, just knit them all. Work the rest of the garment piece. When you are making up the garment, whipstitch the lining to the back of the piece (page 231).

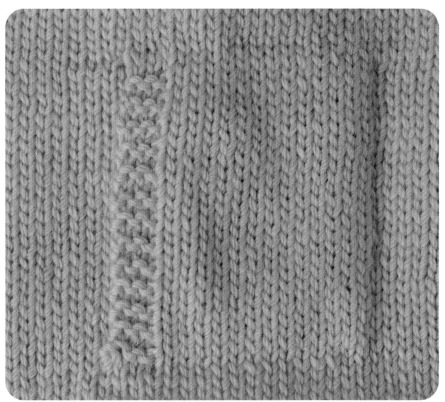

Vertical pocket with garter stitch border.

Patch pockets

Patch pockets are the simplest type to make. The trick to making them look good is placing them attractively and making sure that the sewing is not visible.

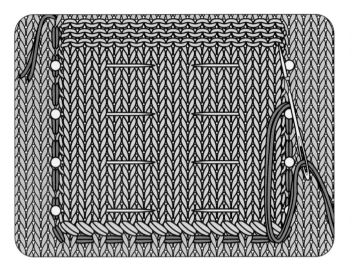

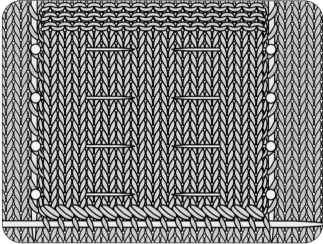

1 Before making up the garment, press the pocket piece (page 258) and the piece of the garment it is to be sewn to. Tack or pin the pocket in position. Using contrast colour yarn on the garment piece, work running stitch (page 185) around the side and lower edges of the pocket. Make sure the lines of running stitch are straight: use the stitches and rows to guide you. Then sew the pocket to the garment using either slip stitch or mattress stitch (page 208).

2 An alternative way marking out the pocket placing is to slip knitting needles vertically and horizontally through the stitches of the garment piece around the edges of the pocket.

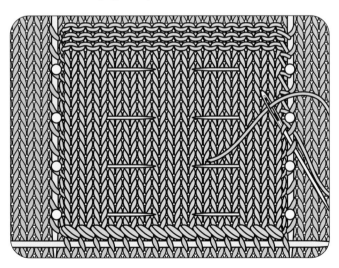

3 Slip stitch the pocket in place, sewing a stitch from the side of the pocket to one of the stitches on the knitting needles.

A patch pocket with a double rib border.

Pick up and knit patch pocket

This is another way of making a patch pocket. As you pick up the stitches from the garment piece, there is less sewing up to do afterwards. Here the stitches are being picked up at the top of the rib.

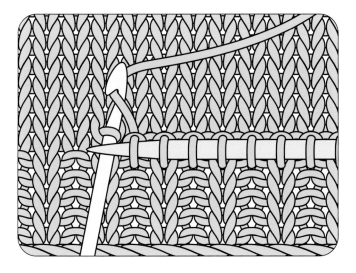

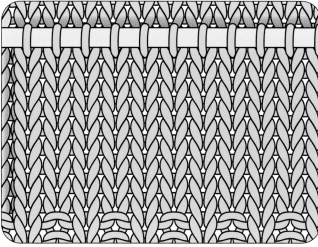

1 Take the tail end of the yarn to the back of the garment piece and fasten it at the position of the bottom left-hand corner of the pocket. (Remember, this is the left-hand side as you wear the garment, not as you look at it.) Using a crochet hook, pick up the required number of stitches (page 127) and place them on a knitting needle.

2 Beginning with a wrong side row, work in the stitch required to the depth required. Add rib or an edging if required and cast (bind) off. Follow Step 1 of Patch Pockets (opposite) to sew the sides of the pocket to the garment.

Adding pockets

With care, patch pockets can be added to a finished garment. This is perfect if you have knitted a cardigan and when you first wear it you are constantly running your hands down the front, wishing it had pockets.

short-row shaping

Short-row shaping is a technique that enables you to turn the knitting and work extra rows in a certain area of a project without cast (binding) off any stitches or creating holes. This technique is most useful in shoulder shaping. When you cast (bind) off shoulders in steps, it is nearly impossible to sew the pieces together and create a smooth seam. Short-row shaping can also be used to create a curved hem or to turn the heel on a sock. Wherever you use it, the technique is the same. You wrap the stitch before the turn on one row and then pick the wraps up on another row.

Wrapping a stitch on a knit row

Wrapping the stitch before you turn the work will prevent a
hole forming in the fabric. This is how you do it on a knit row.

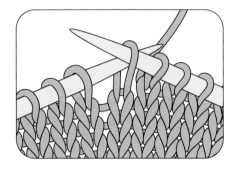

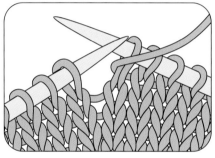

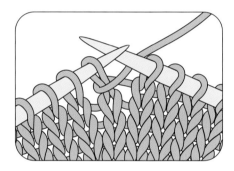

1 Work to the position of the turn. Slip the next stitch purlwise (page 50) off the left-hand needle and onto the right-hand needle.

2 Bring the yarn forward between the two needles.

3 Slip the stitch back onto the left-hand needle and take the yarn to the back. The wrap lies around the base of the slipped stitch. Turn the work and work the next row as instructed in the pattern.

Picking up wraps on a knit row

At a given point in a pattern you need to work across the row of wrapped stitches and pick up all the wraps so that they don't show on the finished project. This is how you do it on a knit row.

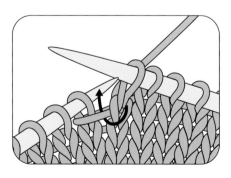

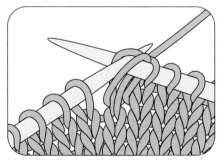

1 Knit to the first wrapped stitch. Put the tip of the right-hand needle up through the front of the wrap.

2 With the wrap on the needle, put the tip of this needle into the stitch it is wrapped around and knit the loop and stitch together. Continue across the row, picking up wrapped stitches as you go.

Wrapping a stitch on a purl row

This is how you wrap a stitch on a purl row.

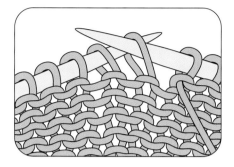

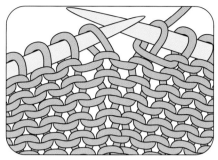

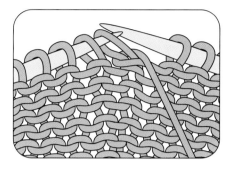

1 Work to the position of the turn. Slip the next stitch purlwise off the left-hand needle and onto the right-hand needle, keeping the yarn at the front of the work.

2 Take the yarn between the two needles to the back of the work.

3 Slip the stitch back onto the left-hand needle and bring the yarn between the two needles to the front of the work. Turn the work and work the next row as instructed in the pattern.

Picking up wraps on a purl row

This is how you pick up wraps on a purl row.

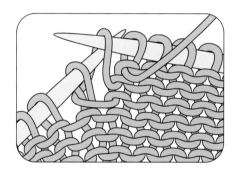

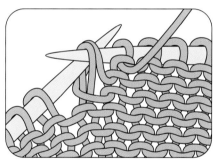

1 Purl to the first wrapped stitch. Using the tip of the right-hand needle, pick up the wrap from the back to the front.

2 Slip the loop onto the left-hand needle and purl it together with the stitch it was wrapped around. Continue in this way across the row, picking up all the wrapped stitches as you come to them.

Picking up stitches

If you pick up all of the wrapped stitches using these techniques, the wraps will almost completely disappear on the right side of the finished knitting.

Short-row shaping exercise

It can sometimes be difficult to understand how to put short-row shaping into practice when following shoulder shapings in a pattern. Here, are typical pattern instructions for shoulder shaping on the left front of a garment and instructions on how to adapt them to short-row shaping and so create a smoothly curved shoulder. To practise the technique, first cast on 30 stitches and work 10 rows in stocking (stockinette) stitch.

The existing pattern reads:
Cast (bind) off 10 sts at beg of next and foll alt row.
Work 1 row.
Cast (bind) off rem 10 sts.

On your practice piece, follow these instructions to work the same shaping using short-row shaping.

Next row: Knit across all stitches. (This is where you would be casting (binding) off the first 10 stitches if you were following the original pattern.)
Next row: Purl 20 sts, wrap stitch (slip next stitch purlwise, take yarn to back, slip stitch back onto left-hand needle, yarn forward, turn work).

Next row: Knit 20 sts.
Next row: Purl 10 sts, wrap stitch (as before).
Next row: Knit 10 sts.
Next row: Purl across all stitches, when you come to a wrapped stitch, pick up the loop, slip onto left-hand needle and purl together with stitch.
Leave all stitches on a stitch holder. When making up the garment, graft (page 205) these stitches to those on a holder for the left shoulder of the back of the garment.

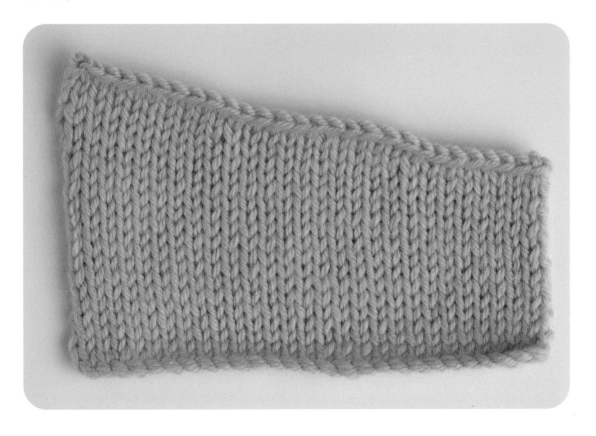

The smoothly sloping cast (bound) off edge you can achieve with short-row shaping.

panel knitting

This technique is ideal if you are making a throw and are not sure how big you want the finished item to be. It also allows you to work with fewer stitches on the needle at any one time. Panel knitting is great for Aran designs and for creating more unusual projects.

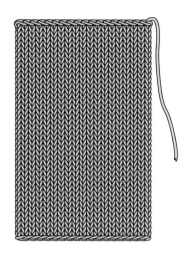

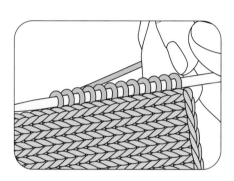

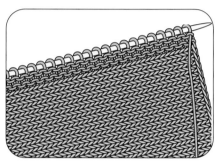

1 Knit one panel in the stitch of your choice. Either cast (bind) off or hold the stitches on a thread.

2 Using a circular needle, pick up and knit (page 127) along the right-hand side edge of the panel, picking up one stitch from each row end. You can use a contrasting yarn, as here, or the same yarn to do this.

3 You may choose to work a few rows at this stage: here three rows have been knitted.

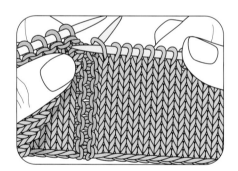

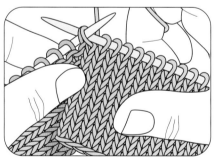

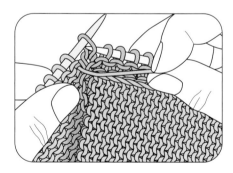

4 Using straight needles, cast on the next panel. You can work it in the same stitch as the first panel, or a different one. However, remember that stocking (stockinette) stitch and garter stitch do not knit up to the same length. On the first row, knit until one stitch remains on the left-hand needle. Put the tip of the right-hand needle into this stitch.

5 Slip this stitch onto the circular needle and knit it together through the backs of the loops (page 51) with the first stitch on the circular needle.

6 Turn the work. Slip one stitch from the circular needle onto the left-hand needle and, with the right-hand needle, work it together through the backs of the loops with the first stitch on the left-hand needle. Work to the end of the row.

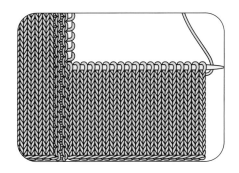

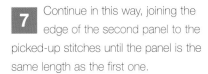

Shaping panels

On shaped panel knitting, using fully fashioned increases and decreases (pages 72–83) adds to the effect. Working them two stitches in from the edges makes it easy to pick up for the next panel.

7 Continue in this way, joining the edge of the second panel to the picked-up stitches until the panel is the same length as the first one.

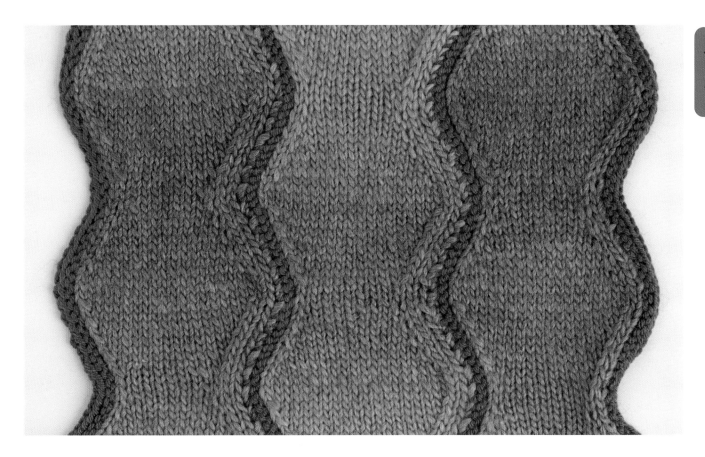

In the example shown here, the first panel is shaped by decreasing 1 stitch at each end of the row for 10 rows. Then work 10 rows straight, followed by 10 rows with an increase of 1 stitch at each end of the row.

On the second panel you have to do the opposite: increase first then decrease. Using variegated yarn gives a really unusual appearance and makes the knitting look complex, which in fact it isn't.

pleats and tucks

Pleats use purl and slipped stitches to create vertical folds. The knitted fabric is double thickness and is much bulkier than pleats made in cloth, which are heavily pressed. Tucks involve picking up stitches on a row below the working row to make horizontal folds across the fabric. They are rather like pintucks on cloth.

Pleat structure

To understand how knitted pleats work, study this diagram and the photographs of the pleat swatches on page 140. The face, fold-under and return sections of the pleat all have the same number of stitches. The face is divided from the fold-under and the fold-under from the return by slip stitches or purl stitches, depending on which way you want the pleats to fold. In the diagram below, the pleats fold to the left.

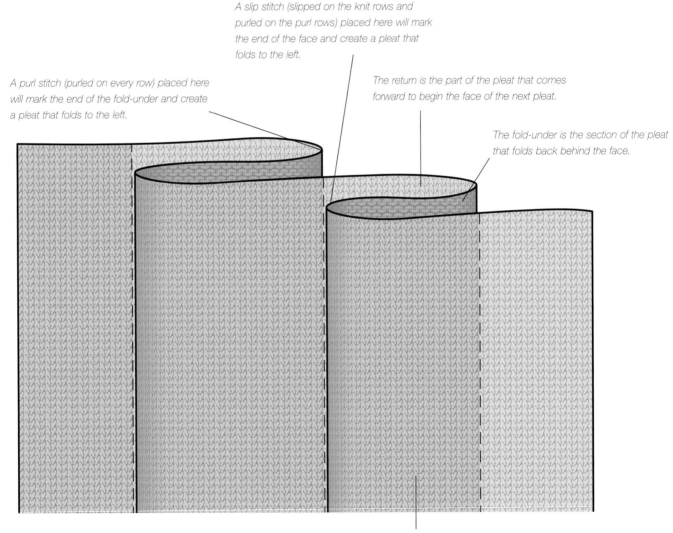

A slip stitch (slipped on the knit rows and purled on the purl rows) placed here will mark the end of the face and create a pleat that folds to the left.

A purl stitch (purled on every row) placed here will mark the end of the fold-under and create a pleat that folds to the left.

The return is the part of the pleat that comes forward to begin the face of the next pleat.

The fold-under is the section of the pleat that folds back behind the face.

The face of the pleat is the main area that will be visible in the finished knitting.

Knitting pleats

To knit a piece of pleated fabric, first decide how many pleats you want and how many stitches wide they will be. You need to multiply the number of stitches for the pleat width by three (the face, fold-under and return all need the same number of stitches), and then add one slipped stitch and one purl stitch for each pleat.

For example, if ten pleats were required, each 5 stitches wide, you would do the following calculation.
5 (width of pleat in stitches) x 3 = 15
15 (number of pleat stitches) + 2 (1 slip and 1 purl stitch) = 17 (total number of stitches in each pleat)
17 x 10 (number of pleats required) = 170 (number of stitches to cast on)

To work pleats that fold to the left, follow this pattern.

Cast on 170 sts.
Row 1: [Knit 5 sts, slip 1 st, knit 5 sts, purl 1 st, knit 5 sts] repeat to last st.
Row 2: Purl to end of row.

To work the pleat fabric for pleats that fold to the right, follow this pattern.
Cast on 140 sts.
Row 1: [Knit 5 sts, purl 1 st, knit 5 sts, slip 1 st, knit 5 sts] repeat to last st.
Row 2: Purl to end of row.

Casting (binding) off pleats

When casting (binding) off the stitches of a pleat it is important to do it properly so that the pleat lies flat. Handle the needles carefully to prevent stitches slipping off as you work. Here, the pleat fabric is knitted following the pattern above and the pleats will fold to the left.

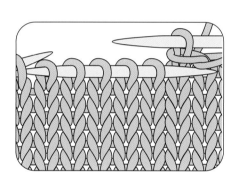

1 Cast (bind) off until you reach the first pleat. With one stitch on your right-hand needle (the first stitch of the face), slip the other four stitches for the face of the pleat and the slip stitch purlwise onto a double-pointed needle.

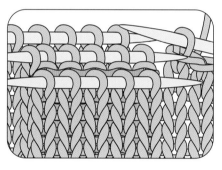

2 Slip the five stitches for the fold-under of the pleat and the purl stitch onto a second double-pointed needle. Turn these stitches so the wrong sides of the pleat are together.

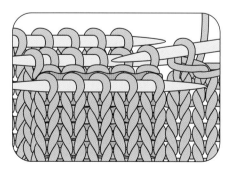

3 Slip one stitch from the fold-under stitches onto the right-hand needle. Knit the first stitch from the return (the first five stitches on the left-hand needle) and pass the two stitches over it one at a time.

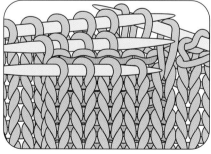

4 *Slip one stitch from face and one from fold-under onto right-hand needle. Knit next stitch from return, pass the three stitches over it one at a time. Repeat from * until all stitches are cast (bound) off.

Pleat samplers

Practice your pleat techniques by following the patterns for these three samplers. When the pleated fabric is the required length, cast (bind) the pleats off (page 139).

Multi-pleats

Cast on 70 sts.

Row 1: *K9, sl 1, k9, p1, rep from * to last 10 sts, k10.

Row 2: P10, *sl 1, p9, rep from * to end.

Rep rows 1–2.

Box pleat

Cast on 42 sts.

Row 1: K10, sl 1, k5, p1, k10, p1, k5, sl 1, k10.

Row 2: P16, sl 1, p10, sl 1, p16.

Rep rows 1–2.

Triangle box pleat

Cast on 42 sts.

Row 1: K10, sl 1, k5, p1, k10, p1, k5, sl 1, k10.

Row 2: P16, sl 1, p10, sl 1, p16.

Rep rows 1–2 twice more.

Row 7: K10, sl 1, k3, skpo, p1, k2tog, k6, skpo, p1, k2tog, k3, sl 1, k10.

Row 8: P15, sl 1, p8, sl 1, p15.

Cont to dec as set on every 4th row until 2 sts rem in centre fold.

Work across all sts.

Tucks

Tucks can be used to form ridges in the fabric and add texture to a project, or as an edging. A tuck can be worked in a different colour to the rest of the project, as here. If you are working it in the main colour, then mark the pick up row by weaving a thread through the stitches before picking up the tuck, as you would for unravelling to a thread (page 249), but along the back of the work. Pull out the thread as you knit the tuck.

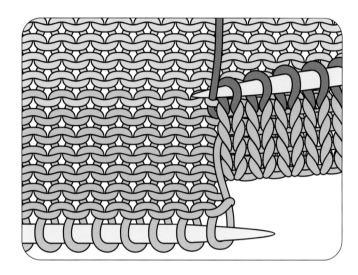

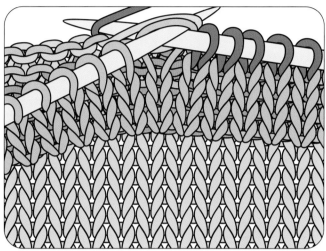

1 Work stocking (stockinette) stitch for twice the required depth of the tuck. Fold the tuck fabric in half, wrong sides facing. Put the tip of the left-hand needle into the lower loop of the first stitch of the last row in the main project colour.

2 Knit the loop together with the first stitch on the left-hand needle. Continue in this way across the row, knitting corresponding stitches and loops together.

Ruching

You can create ruched effects by working tucks across just part of a row. Work in the same way as for a full tuck, but just picking up the loops for the required number of stitches and knitting the rest of the row in the usual way.

Two tucks of different depths.

types of knitting

gathers and flares

Increasing or decreasing stitches across a row of knitting widens or narrows the knitted fabric and can be used to create decorative effects.

Gathers

In knitting it is best to work gathering using the stitches themselves, rather than running a thread through the fabric, as you would with cloth. There are several different techniques you can use, depending on the effect you want to achieve.

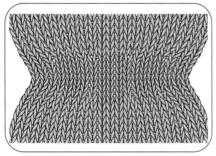

1 This gathered area has been achieved by decreasing (pages 78–83) then using smaller needles for a number of rows. Then the needles are changed again and increases (pages 73–77) are worked.

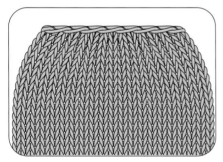

3 The gathering here would be ideal for puffed sleeves. To get this finish you need to work three stitches together (pages 82–83) at the time as casting (binding) off.

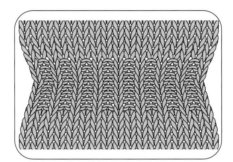

2 This gather has been achieved by using rib stitches (page 56) worked on smaller needles than those used for the main part of the project. Remember that with rib, the deeper the area, the more it will gather in.

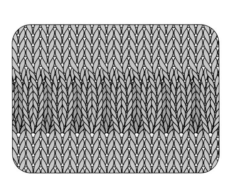

4 To create this gathered effect you need to double the number of stitches by increasing (pages 73–77) in every stitch, then work a few straight rows, and then decrease by working 2tog (page 78) across a row.

Flares

Flares are made by increasing or decreasing stitches in a pattern to widen or narrow the fabric. Flares can be used for lots of things, but the most common use would be for a skirt.

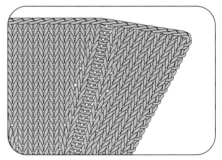

1 Combining different stitches can add to the lines of a flare. Here, the fabric is made by knitting four stitches, then purling two stitches. The increases (pages 73–77) are made every fourth row on either side of the purl stitches. Therefore, the purl stitches remain in straight lines, adding to the flared effect. This flare could also be made by casting on a large number of stitches and then decreasing in the same pattern.

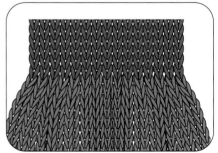

2 This flare is made by decreasing (pages 78–83) every third or fourth stitch and then working straight.

corners

Outer corners have obvious uses for borders on projects such as blankets and throws, while inner corners can be used to create V-necks (page 273).

Outer corner

You need to create enough extra fabric for a border to go around an outer corner and still lie flat.

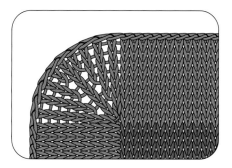

Work to the one stitch before the corner. Make one stitch (page 73) and then mark the following stitch with a stitch marker (page 12); this will be the centre stitch for the corner. Make one more stitch in the stitch following the centre stitch. Continue to increase in this way on either every row or every alternate row, depending on the angle you require. When it comes to casting (binding) off, you may need to increase in the stitches at the same time as casting (binding) off around the corner. Do this by casting (binding) off to the increase position, make one and pass the last stitch over the made stitch before knitting the next stitch.

Inner corner

For an inner corner you need to decrease the amount of fabric so that it turns the corner but still lies flat.

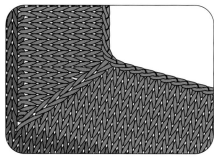

For an inner corner you need to decrease each side of a centre stitch. It is best to mark the centre stitch first, then work to two stitches before it. Work two stitches together using skpo (page 79). Knit the centre stitch and then work k2tog (page 78). Continue to decrease in this way on either every row or every alternate row, depending on the angle required. Working mirrored decreases in this way keeps the pattern around the corner symmetrical.

Tight inner corner

For a tighter inner corner try the following technique.

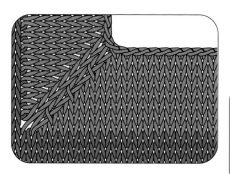

Work to one stitch before the centre stitch, slip two stitches knitwise (page 50) together, knit one stitch then pass the two slipped stitches over the knitted one. Then complete the row. Work in this way on every row or every alternate row, depending on the angle required. You will probably need to decrease as you cast (bind) off round the corner. To do this, simply work to the decrease position, skpo, then pass the last stitch over the skpo before knitting the next stitch.

Sewn corners

If these techniques don't appeal, then you can make a border by knitting straight strips and sewing them to the edges of the project. At the corners, butt the strips up and sew them together.

gores and gussets

Gores are used mainly for skirts and for peplums on cardigans and jackets and are achieved by increasing or decreasing either side of a centre stitch. Gussets are produced by either increasing or decreasing and then decreasing or increasing to create a diamond shape. They are usually used under the arms in traditional Guernsey designs to allow for free movement.

Increase gore

This gore is produced by increasing either side of a centre stitch.

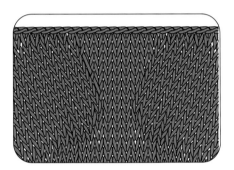

Place a round marker (page 12) either side of the centre stitch. Work to the first marker, slip it onto the right-hand needle, make one stitch (page 73). Knit the centre stitch, make another stitch, slip the second marker onto the right-hand needle and continue the row. You can increase in this way on every row, alternate row or even every third or fourth row, depending on how deep and how wide the gore needs to be.

Decrease gore

Here the gore is produced by decreasing: you would have cast on the number of stitches for the widest point of the gore.

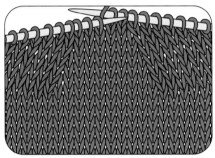

Place a round marker at each end of the gore. Work to the first marker and slip it onto the right-hand needle, then decrease two stitches using skpo (page 79). Knit to two stitches before the second marker and k2tog (page 78), slip the marker onto the right-hand needle and continue the row. As for the increase gore, work the decreases on every row, alternate row or even every third or fourth row, depending on the depth of gore. Make sure you look at fully fashioning (page 88) to understand how to use the correct decreases to achieve slopes in the right directions.

Gusset

Gussets are worked in the same way as gores but, use increasing and then decreasing (or vice versa).

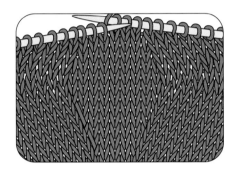

Work an increase gore (far left) until you have created a triangle of the desired width. Then work a decrease gore (left) until you have just one stitch remaining.

Shaping bags

Knitted bags are usually made by sewing various pieces together to create the three-dimensional shape. However, bags can be beautifully shaped by knitting gores instead of by sewing in a separate gusset strip.

bias and chevron knitting

These techniques alter the angle of the knitted fabric, sloping it in different directions. Bias pieces can slope to the right or left and chevrons can point up or down.

Bias knitting

You can achieve bias-shaped pieces by decreasing and increasing at the edges of a piece of knitting. Working different numbers of straight rows between the increase and decrease row will alter the angle of the slant. Working mirrored increases and decreases (page 88) will create neat edges.

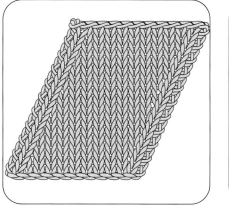

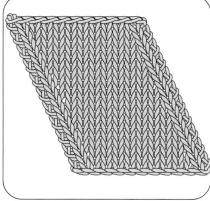

1 For a bias to the right, simply increase at the beginning and decrease at the end of every alternate row.

2 For a bias to the left, decrease at the beginning and increase at the end of every alternate row.

Chevron knitting

To make a chevron you need to mark a centre stitch on your work.

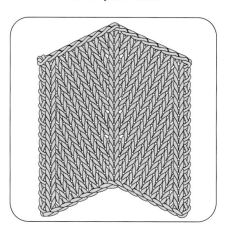

1 For the chevron to point upwards, decrease at each end of the row and increase by making one stitch (page 73) each side of the centre stitch.

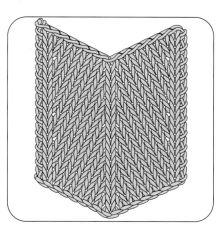

2 For a chevron to point downwards, increase at each end of the row and work a balanced double decrease (page 87) at the centre stitch.

Bias knitted fabric

Unlike woven cloth fabric, bias knitted fabric is not stretchier than straight knitted fabric. Knitting on the bias is used just to create an effect. Bias knitted colour stripes are interesting and can look very effective when the bias piece is sewn to a piece with straight stripes.

knitting
with colour

Working with colour takes your knitting to a new level and involves mastering several skills. Colour effects will look gorgeous but are sometimes frustrating as getting the finished appearance as neat as your usual stocking (stockinette) stitch can be a challenge.

knitting stripes

The easiest way to introduce colour work into your knitting is by working stripes. They are simple and fun and can be added to almost any existing pattern.

Joining in a new colour stripe

You can simply join in a new colour at the side seam (page 53), but to eliminate some of the ends at the side it is best to join in the new colour before the end of the last row of the old colour. This technique leaves you with fewer ends to sew in (page 200) when the knitting is complete.

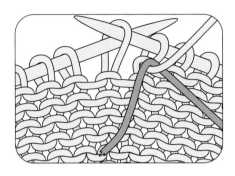

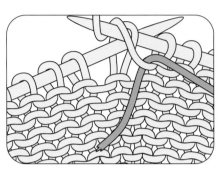

1 On the row before the new colour is needed, stop about ten stitches before the end of the row. Lay the new colour over the existing colour.

2 Hold the new colour down with your left thumb and work the next stitch in the existing colour, catching the new colour into the back of the stitch.

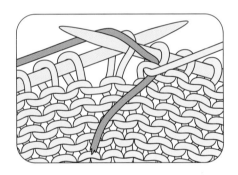

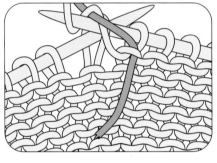

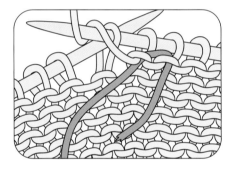

3 To weave the new colour in as you work, lay it over the tip of the right-hand needle.

4 Work the next stitch using the existing colour and keeping the new colour held high to stop it from going through the stitch.

5 Holding the new colour down, work the next stitch with the existing colour. Continue in this way, weaving the new colour in on every alternate stitch to the end of the row. Turn the work and the new colour is safely secured and ready to do the next row. If you no longer need the old colour, cut the end and weave it in on the following row on every alternate stitch using the same technique.

The new colour woven in on the previous row.

Carrying yarn up the side of the work

When you are working stripes, do not join in a new colour for every stripe. Instead, carry the colours not in use up the side of the work until you need them again. The colours must be caught into the knitting at the end of every alternate row to prevent big loops appearing.

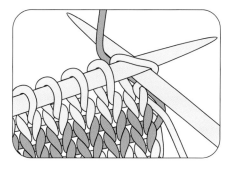

If you are working a two-row stripe, then just knit the first stitch of the third row with the new colour. For wider stripes, catch in any yarns being carried up the side at the start of the next row. Put the right-hand needle into the first stitch, lay the yarn to be carried over the working yarn and work the first stitch in the working yarn.

Working stripes

If the stripes are over an odd number of rows, the next time you need a specific colour it will be at the wrong side of the work. Rather than joining in the new colour (page 53), work back and forth on a circular needle and when the yarn is at the wrong end, simply slide your stitches to the other end of the needle and turn the work and the right colour will be there ready to knit with. If you are not working on a circular needle and the yarn you need is at the wrong end, slip the stitches back onto the left-hand needle, then start the next row. Remember to carry the yarn up both sides of the work.

different stripe effects

It's very easy to be really creative with stripes, you just need to use your imagination a little when it comes to choosing colours, stitches and stripe widths. Here are four different stripe samplers you can try to give you some ideas.

Different stripe effects

▲ Stripes

Using shades A and B and working in st st throughout.

Rows 1–5: A.

Rows 6–9: B.

Rows 10–13: A.

Rep rows 6–13.

▲ Texture stripes

Using shades A, B and C and working in st st unless otherwise stated.

Rows 1–4: A.

Row 5: B.

Row 6: C.

Rows 7–10: C in moss (seed) stitch.

Row 11: B.

Rows 12–15: D.

Row 16: B.

Row 17: C.

Rows 18–20: C in moss (seed) stitch.

Row 21: B.

Rep these 21 rows.

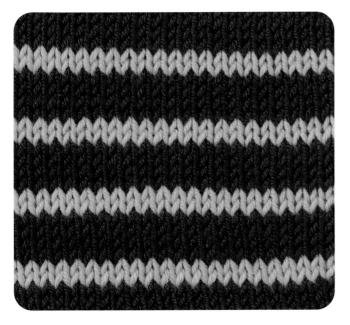

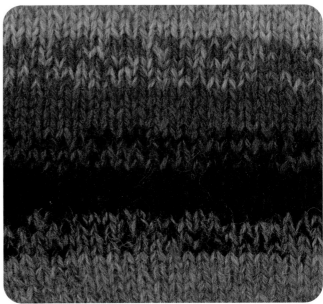

▲ Uneven stripes

Using shades A and B and working in st st throughout.

Rows 1–3: A.

Rows 4–5: B.

Rows 6–9: A.

Rep rows 4–9.

▲ Blurred stripes

Using shades A, B, C, D and E and working in st st throughout.

Rows 1–6: A and B (1 strand of each).

Rows 7–10: B and C (1 strand of each).

Rows 11–14: C (2 strands).

Rows 15–18: C and D (1 strand of each).

Rows 19–22: D (2 strands).

Rows 23–26: D and E (1 strand of each).

Rows 27–30: E (2 strands).

Rep these 30 rows.

Vertical stripes

Vertical stripes need to be worked using the intarsia technique (pages 158–159). However, do look carefully at the project you are making and see if it would be possible to knit it sideways, thus working the stripes horizontally. This can cut out a lot of the work of joining yarns and preparing and using bobbins.

Vertical stripes worked using the intarsia technique.

The shape of a stitch

Knitted stitches are not square; as you can see from the
illustration (right), they are in fact wider than they are tall.
Therefore, a shape plotted out on squared graph paper
in a pattern book may look odd, but when knitted up it
will be fine.

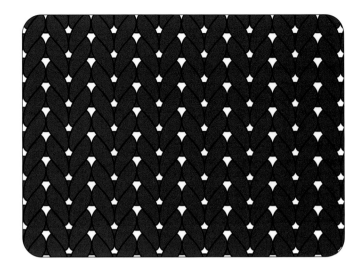

How graph and knitted fabric differ

Here you can see the difference between a graphed shape
and the completed knitted motif. On the graph the circle
looks a bit like an egg lying on its side, but knitted up it
is perfectly round.

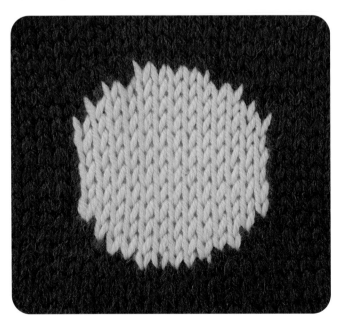

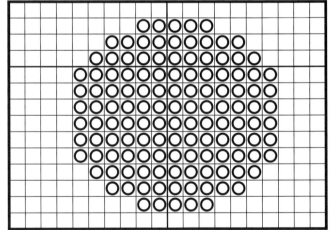

A circle motif knitted following the chart on the right.

Knitter's graph paper

It is possible to obtain special knitter's graph paper, which you can find on the Internet. As you can see (right), the boxes that represent the stitches are rectangular and so reflect the actual shape of a stitch. It is worth investing in this graph paper if you plan to design your own motifs.

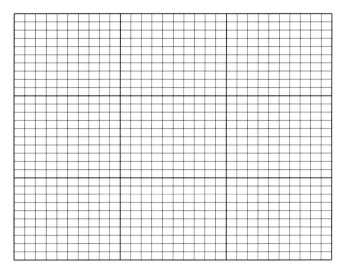

Square graph paper

If you have to work on squared graph paper you must make the design about one-third wider than it is tall to allow for the shape of a stitch. Imperial graph paper is best as the squares are quite large.

bobbins

Bobbins are a key to having an enjoyable time while knitting with colour; they keep the yarns organised when working with several colours. If you work with whole balls, the yarns will twist and tangle. There are two types of bobbin, purchased and hand-made. The purchased type are usually made of plastic and you wind the amount of yarn required around them. They are quite good, but they can catch on each other and if you are using quite a bulky yarn you can't get very much on them.

Making a bobbin

The best type of bobbin to use is a hand-made one, and they are very easy to make.

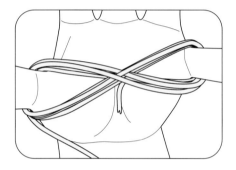

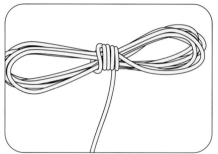

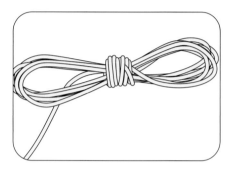

1 With the tail of the yarn in your palm, wrap the working end in a figure-of-eight pattern around your thumb and little finger.

2 When you have enough yarn wrapped (below), slip the bundle off your hand and wrap the tail end tightly around the centre to tie the bundle together. Make sure that the free end sticks out of the bundle.

3 When you use the bobbin, pull the free end gently to pull the yarn from the centre, making sure not to pull out too much at a time. The key to intarsia work is to keep the bobbins short at the back of the work to avoid tangling them.

A hand-made bobbin.

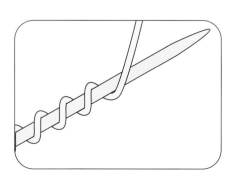

If you need to know how much yarn to make into a bobbin for a specific area of colour, work out how many stitches the area occupies and twist the yarn around a needle that number of times. Add a little extra for sewing in the ends (page 201).

A purchased bobbin wound with yarn.

intarsia

Intarsia is colour work where the fabric remains single-thickness throughout. You have to join the areas of colour that are next to each other as you work. Like all new techniques it takes practice, but it is one of the most enjoyable types of knitting. The intarsia technique is used to knit individual motifs where the background colour remains the same on either side.

A daisy knitted using the intarsia technique.

Joining in a new colour

When working in intarsia you will find yourself needing to join in a new colour in the middle of a row.

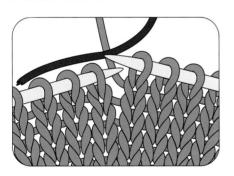

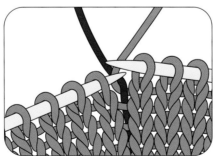

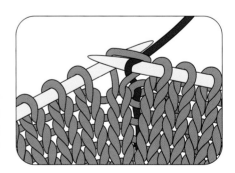

1 On a knit row, knit to the change in colour. Lay the new colour over the existing colour and between the two needles, with the tail to the left.

2 Bring the new colour under and then over the existing colour.

3 Knit the stitch with the new colour. Go back and pull gently on the tail to tighten up the first stitch in the new colour after you have knitted a couple more stitches.

Changing colours in a straight vertical line

Once you have joined in a new colour you may need to work for a number of rows changing these colours on both the knit rows and purl rows. This is often confusingly referred to as 'twisting' the yarns but it is a link rather than a twist. It is a common mistake to over-twist the yarns at this point and then the fabric will not lie flat.

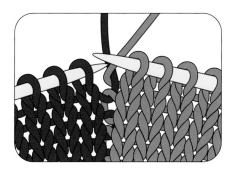

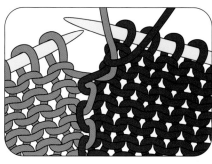

1 On a knit row, knit to the change in colour. Bring the new colour up from under the old colour and drop the old colour so that the new colour is ready to work with.

2 On a purl row, knit to the change in colour. Bring the new colour from the left under the old colour and up to the top. Drop the old colour and continue with the new colour.

A straight colour change on the right side.

A straight colour change on the wrong side.

Small areas of colour

When working a very small area of colour in intarsia it is better to work with a strand of the yarn rather than a bobbin to help prevent tangling.

Changing colours on the diagonal

The technique is the same as for changing colours in a straight line (opposite), but you will find that sometimes the yarn you want is in a different place and if you get the technique wrong you may end up over-twisting the yarns.

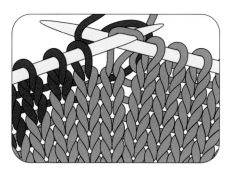

1 On a knit row with the diagonal going to the right, bring the new colour from underneath the old colour and knit with it.

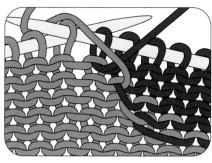

2 On a purl row with the diagonal going to the left, bring the new colour from underneath the old colour and purl with it.

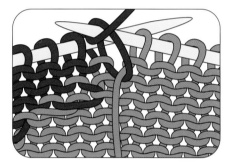

3 On a purl row with the diagonal going to the right, bring the new colour under the old colour and purl with it.

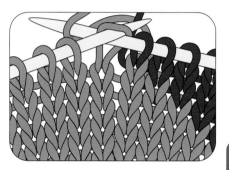

4 On a knit row with the diagonal going to the left, bring the new colour from underneath the old colour and knit with it.

A diagonal colour change on the right side.

A diagonal colour change on the wrong side.

Bringing a colour across the back

When working in intarsia you will sometimes need to carry a contrast yarn across the back for a few stitches, ready for the next row where it will be needed earlier than where it was left on the previous row. You can do this by weaving in the contrast yarn along the row (page 148), but if you have missed doing this, there is another technique.

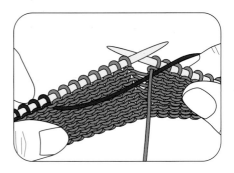

1 On a purl row, bring the contrast colour across the stitches to where it is needed, keeping the loop quite loose. Bring it under the original colour and purl a stitch with the contrast colour.

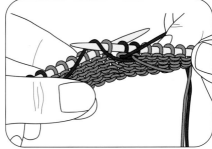

2 To anchor the contrast loop as you purl across the row, put the tip of the right-hand needle into the next stitch and then under the loop.

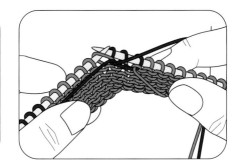

3 Purl the stitch, making sure that the loop doesn't go through the stitch. Repeat on every alternate stitch until the loop is anchored across the fabric.

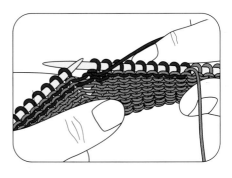

4 Here you can see the back of a knit row and the dark purple yarn that needs to come across the stitches.

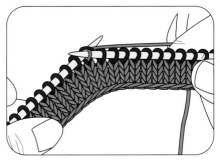

5 Bring the yarn across the back of the stitches to where it is needed, keeping the loop quite loose, and knit the stitch with it.

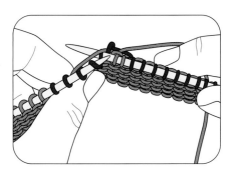

6 To anchor the loop as you knit across the row, put the tip of the right-hand needle into the next stitch and then under the back of the loop. Knit with the new colour, not allowing the loop to come through the stitch. Repeat on every alternate stitch until the loop is anchored across the fabric.

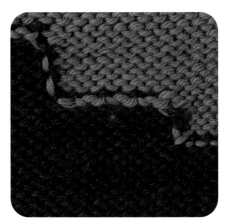

A loop anchored across the back of stitches.

Eliminating ends

If you are working a complex design it is always best to look for ways of eliminating ends so that you can cut down the number of hours that will be needed to sew them all in (page 201). Look for shapes that perhaps have an outline, as with this diamond motif.

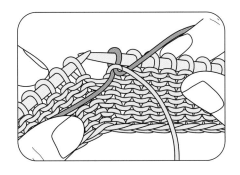

1 Take a length of the yarn required to work the whole motif and fold it in half. On the centre stitch of the motif, loop the fold over the right-hand needle.

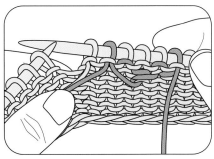

2 On the next row, take one end of the yarn to the right and the other to the left, linking the outline and background colours on each row (pages 158–159). If the motif is very small and the background colour remains the same, it is best to carry the background colour across the back of the motif, weaving it in if necessary (pages 170–173).

How to approach a complex design

Some intarsia designs become so complex that you might consider using Fair Isle techniques (pages 164–173) for parts of them. Before you start such a project, spend time looking at the chart and work out which techniques you are going to use to knit which parts of the design. Look at the notes below the chart (opposite), to see how this design was worked.

An intarsia panel made up into a small bag.

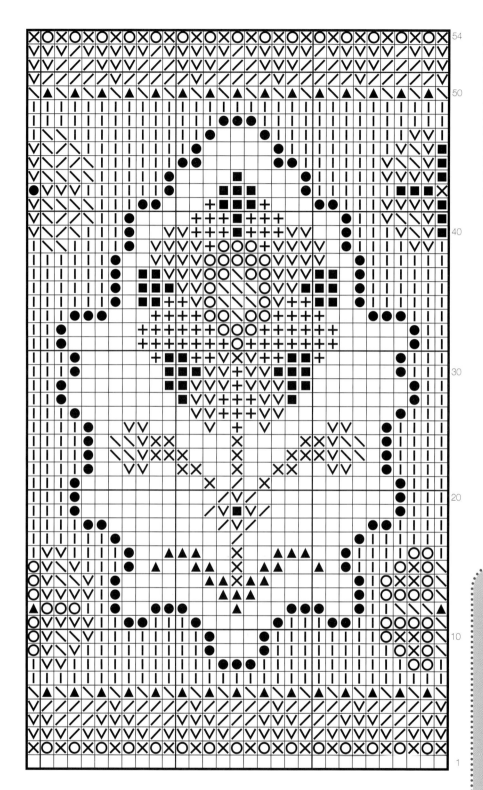

Colour key:

- □ cream
- ● black
- ☒ lime green
- ☑ pale blue
- ⊞ purple
- ⊡ damson
- ◎ pale pink
- ◺ lilac
- ■ mid-pink
- ☑ deep pink
- ▲ mid-blue

To work this chart the intarsia technique was used for the outer and inner background and the outline and lower leaves were worked using the eliminating ends technique (opposite). The stalk used a single strand of yarn. The border across the bottom and the flower itself were worked using Fair Isle techniques.

Using bobbins

Generally with intarsia designs if you are trying to decide if you need to make another bobbin or not it usually means that you should! Always work on the principle that the more bobbins you use the better the outcome will be. On an intarsia-only design the motif should be as visible on the back as it is on the front.

knitting with colour

fair isle knitting

With this type of colour knitting you are working with one or more colours in stocking (stockinette) stitch and the pattern is a repetitive design. Yarns that are not being used have to be carried (or stranded, as it is known), across the back of the work, thus making the fabric double thickness. The art of good Fair Isle is to keep the fabric elastic and supple and to achieve this you must be careful not to pull the yarns too tightly. When worked properly the yarns should not tangle.

Once you have joined in the yarns, there are three possible techniques to use when knitting in Fair Isle and they all take practice to master. The techniques differ in whether you hold the yarns only in your right hand or in both hands. Whichever technique you use, it is advisable to only strand the yarn across the back for a maximum of three stitches. If the design requires you to carry the yarn for more than three stitches then you need to catch the yarn into the back of the work. If you do not do this you will end up with large loops that you will catch your fingers in as you put the garment on. You will also tend to pull the strands too tight and this will cause the work to pucker on the front.

The front of a piece of Fair Isle knitting.

The back of a piece of Fair Isle knitting showing the stranded yarns.

Even fabric

To keep the fabric an even thickness, always carry both yarns (pages 170–173) right to the edge of the work, even if the last few stitches do not use one of the colours.

Joining in a new colour on a knit row

When working Fair Isle, it is better to join in a new colour at the beginning of a row, but if you have to join it in mid row, this is how to do it on a knit row.

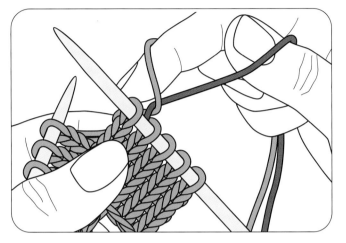

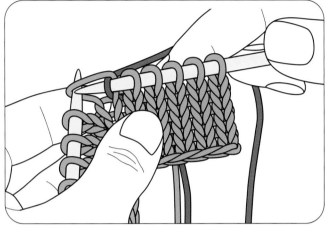

1 Lay the new colour (B) over the original colour (A). Twist the yarns over themselves and hold them in place.

2 Knit with the new colour (B). You can always go back and tighten the join after a couple of stitches.

Joining in a new colour on a purl row

This is how you join in a new colour mid-row on a purl row.

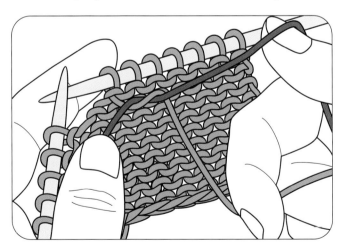

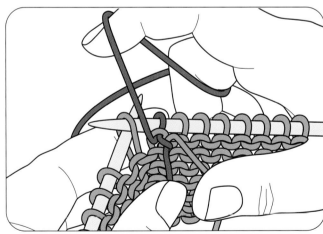

1 Lay the new colour (B) over the original colour (A). Twist the yarns over themselves and hold them in place.

2 Purl with the new colour (B).

Holding yarns one at a time on a knit row

With this technique you are holding just one of the different coloured yarns in your right hand at any one time. This is the simplest yet slowest of the Fair Isle techniques.

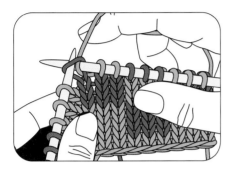  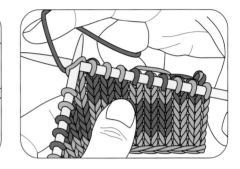

1 Knit the stitches as usual in yarn A (green yarn).

2 Drop yarn A and pick up yarn B (purple yarn), making sure yarn B comes under yarn A.

3 Knit with yarn B in the usual way, making sure not to pull the yarn too tight.

Holding yarns one at a time on a purl row

On a purl row the principle is the same. This links the yarns around one another, joining the different-coloured areas into one fabric.

Spreading stitches

Keep the stitches on the right-hand needle spread out; this will help stop you pulling the yarns too tightly as you carry them across the back.

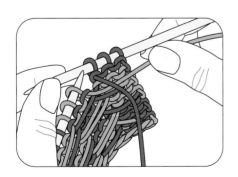 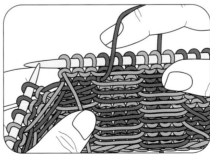 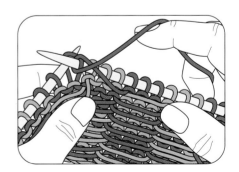

1 Purl stitches as usual in yarn B (purple). Drop B and pick up yarn A (green), making sure A comes under B.

2 To change colours back to yarn B (purple), drop A and bring B across over yarn A.

3 Purl with yarn B in the usual way.

Holding both yarns in your right hand on a knit row

Once mastered, this is a speedier technique than holding one yarn at a time (opposite).

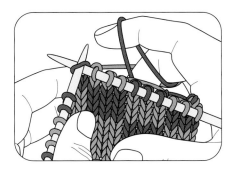 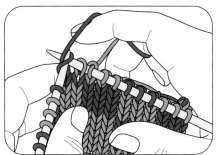 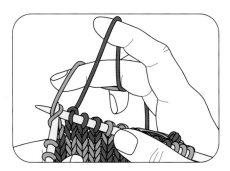

1 Put the tip of the right-hand needle into the stitch and place both yarns in your right hand. Place the yarn to be used first over your index finger and the other over your second finger.

2 Using your index finger, knit the number of stitches required in that colour yarn.

3 Using your second finger, knit the stitches in the other colour, making sure that the yarn comes up from under the first yarn knitted with.

Holding both yarns in your right hand on a purl row

Place the yarns in your right hand as you would for working a knit row.

Tension (gauge)

If your Fair Isle knitting is very tight, go up a needle size in order to obtain the right tension (gauge) (page 18).

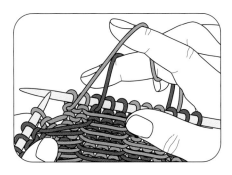 

1 Purl the required number of stitches using the yarn that is held over your index finger.

2 Alternate fingers as the different-coloured yarns are needed.

Holding yarns in both hands on a knit row

This is usually the technique that people find hardest to master, but once you can work it you can knit Fair Isle very quickly and evenly. So, if you do want to improve your colour knitting, this is the technique it is worth spending time perfecting. Start by practising knitting a simple check pattern, like the one shown here, so that you don't have to concentrate on the design, just on your hands.

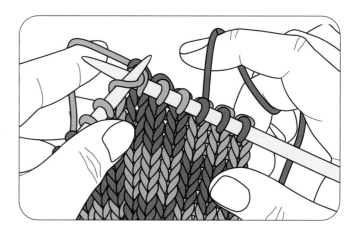

1 Place the yarn to be used first (A, purple) in your right hand and the other (B, green) over the index finger of your left hand. Turn to Continental knitting (pages 40–41) to see how best to hold the yarn and knit the stitches with your left hand.

2 Knit the required number of stitches with your right hand and yarn A.

3 When yarn B is needed, simply place the right-hand needle over yarn B.

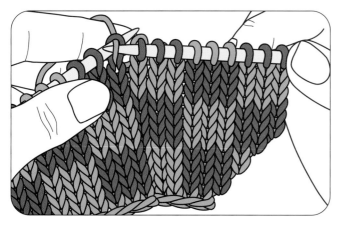

4 Bring the stitch through.

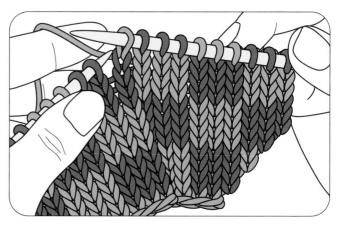

5 Complete the stitch, keeping yarn B on your left hand.

Holding yarns in both hands on a purl row

This is how to use the same two-handed technique on a purl row.

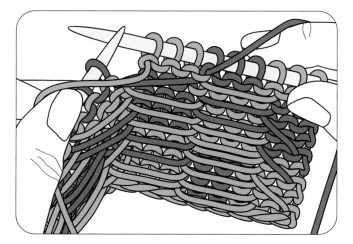

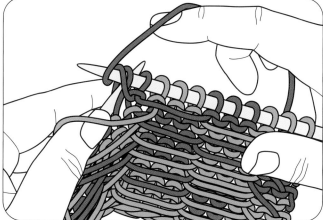

1 Hold yarn B in your left hand and yarn A in your right hand.

2 Purl in yarn A, keeping yarn B over your left thumb.

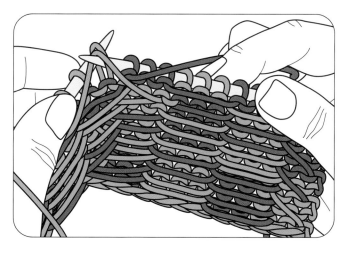

3 When yarn B is needed, place the right-hand needle under yarn B.

4 Push the stitch through. Complete the stitch, keeping yarn B on your left hand.

stranding yarns

When you have to catch the yarn into the back of the work because it needs to cross more than three stitches before being used again, you have to strand it across the fabric. There are two ways of doing this and the technique you choose will depend on how you work Fair Isle. If you work Fair Isle with your right hand (pages 166–167), then use the right-hand technique for stranding and similarly, use both hands if you use both to knit Fair Isle (pages 168–169).

Stranding yarns using the right-hand technique on a knit row

On this example there are five stitches between the colours, so you would strand the yarn on the third stitch of the five. Knit to the right stitch.

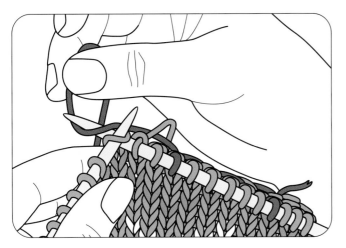

1 Drop yarn A (green) and pick up yarn B, making sure you pass it under A, and place B over the left-hand needle.

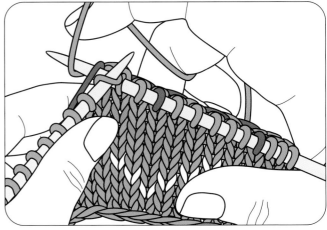

2 Knit using yarn A.

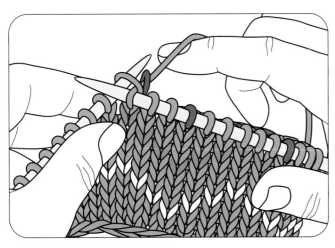

3 Make sure that you do not bring yarn B through the stitch as well as yarn A.

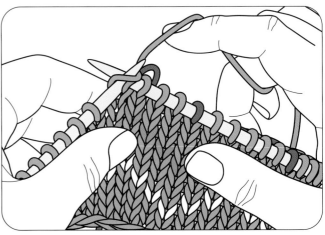

4 Knit the next stitch to lock the stranding into place.

Stranding yarns using the right-hand technique on a purl row

This is how the same technique is worked on a purl row.
Purl to the right stitch.

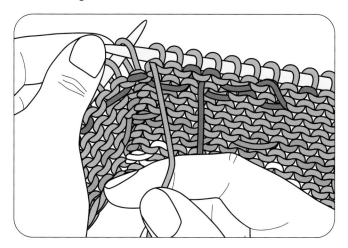

1 Hold yarn A (green) down at the back of the fabric.

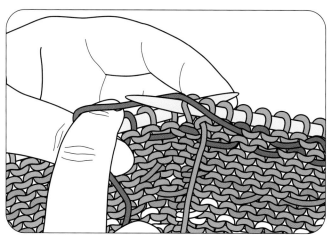

2 Bring yarn B across and lay it across the left-hand needle.

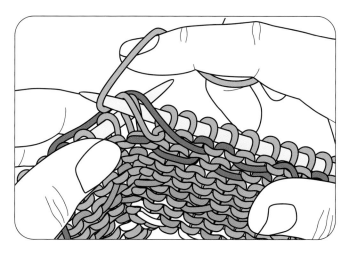

3 Purl using yarn A.

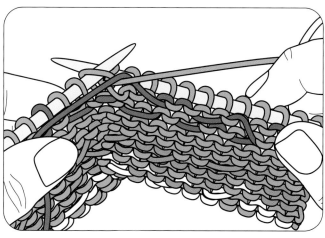

4 Make sure yarn B doesn't come through the stitch as well. Purl the next stitch to lock the stranding into place.

Knitting know-how

You can't strand on the last stitch of a row or the stitch before you need the colour. Stranded yarns need a following stitch to lock them in place.

Stranding yarns holding yarns in both hands on a knit row

Again, the yarn is being stranded into the third stitch of a group of five that it has to go across. Hold the yarns in both hands as for two-handed Fair Isle (pages 168–169), making sure the yarn to be stranded is in your left hand.

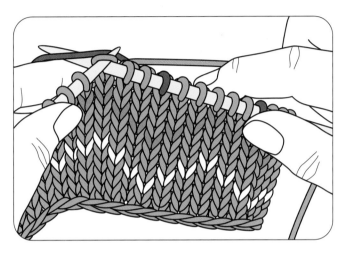

1 Knit to the right stitch then place the right-hand needle under yarn B (purple) on your left hand.

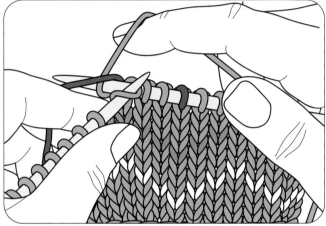

2 Knit the stitch with yarn A (green) in your right hand.

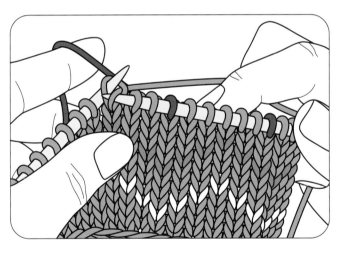

3 Make sure yarn B doesn't come through stitch as well.

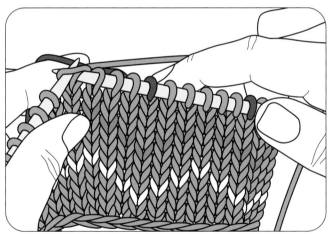

4 Knit the next stitch to lock the stranding into place.

Stranding yarns holding yarns in both hands on a purl row

Hold the yarns as for stranding with both hands on a knit row (opposite).

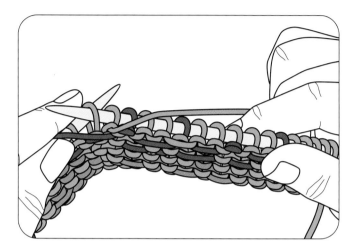

1 Purl to where you need to strand the yarn.

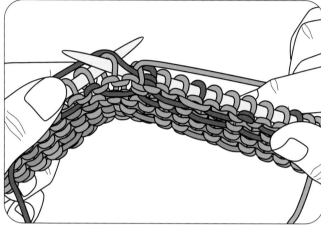

2 Place the right-hand needle under yarn B (purple) held in your left hand.

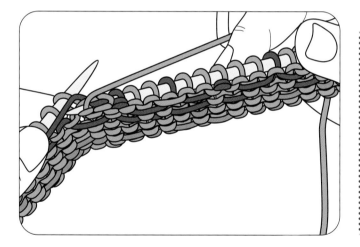

3 Purl with yarn A (green), making sure yarn B stays in front and doesn't go through the stitch. Purl the next stitch to lock the stranding into place.

Knitting know-how

When stranding yarn on a repetitive design it is easy to catch it in to the back of the same stitch on each row, but try not to do this as it will cause ridges on the front of the work. If you stranded into the third stitch of a group of five on one row, strand into the second stitch of the group on the next row.

colour knitting samplers

Here are some charts for you to practise your colour knitting techniques with. The first two use the Fair Isle technique while the second two should be worked using intarsia knitting.

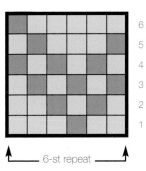

A simple Fair Isle border.

A three-colour Fair Isle pattern.

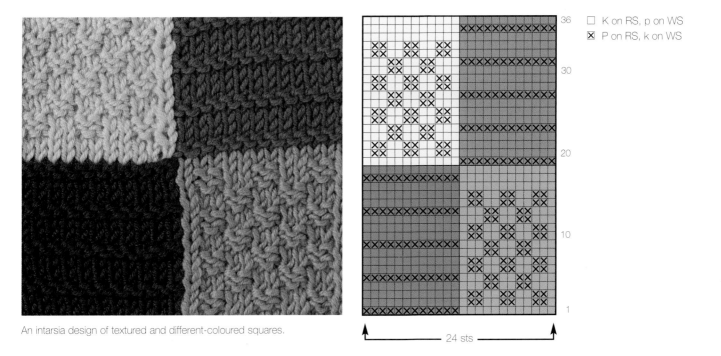

An intarsia design of textured and different-coloured squares.

□ K on RS, p on WS
☒ P on RS, k on WS

A daisy motif knitted in intarsia.

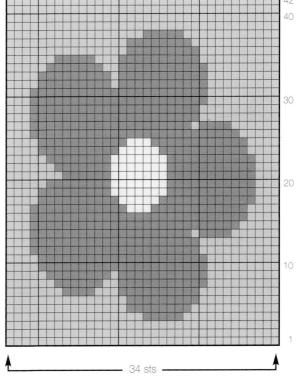

embellishments

The plainest knitted project can be made stylish and interesting by the addition of sparkling beads, colourful embroidery, perky pom-poms or an elegant fringe. Add various embellishments to your knitting and watch it transform from ordinary to extraordinary.

beading

Beading is one of my favourite embellishments. It is simple to do and a basic sweater design can be made glamorous by a row of beading around the cuff or edge of the collar. There are two most commonly used types of beading – slip stitch beading and knitted-in beading. Whichever you use, there are a couple of things to bear in mind when buying the beads. Firstly, the hole in the bead must be large enough for the yarn to pass through and secondly, the bead must not be too heavy for the yarn. Using a heavy bead on a fine yarn will cause the stitches, and possibly the whole garment, to stretch.

Threading beads onto yarn

Whichever beading technique you are going to use, the first step is to get the beads onto the yarn.

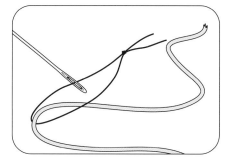

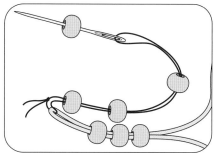

1   Thread a sewing needle with a short length of sewing cotton and knot the ends. Put the tail end of the yarn through the loop of cotton.

2   Pick up the beads with the needle, slide them down the thread and onto the yarn.

Slip stitch beading

This is the simplest and most often used beading technique, though beads can only be placed on every alternate stitch and row. Generally slip stitch beading will not affect your tension (gauge), so you can add beads to an existing plain pattern. It is usually worked on stocking (stockinette) stitch.

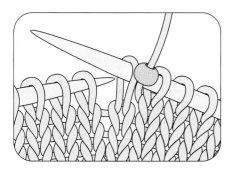

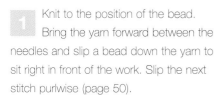 **1** Knit to the position of the bead. Bring the yarn forward between the needles and slip a bead down the yarn to sit right in front of the work. Slip the next stitch purlwise (page 50).

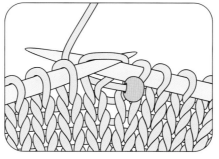 **2** Take the yarn between the needles to the back of the work, making sure the bead stays in front of the slipped stitch. Knit the next stitch quite tightly.

Purling beads

Beads can be placed on a purl row by taking the yarn to the back, sliding the bead down, slipping the next stitch knitwise, then taking the yarn to the front again.

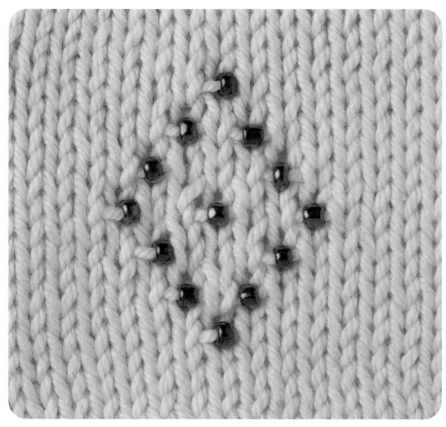

Slip-stitch beaded motif.

Knitted-in beading on a knit row

This technique allows you to place a bead in every stitch on every row. However, if you bead an item heavily you may affect your tension (gauge) and will certainly affect the drape of the finished project. It is usually worked on stocking (stockinette) stitch and you use this technique to place a bead on a knit row.

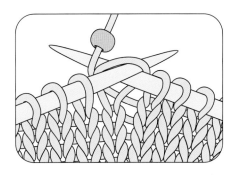

1 Knit to the position of the bead. Put the tip of the right-hand needle into the next stitch, wrap the yarn around it and slide the bead down to the needles.

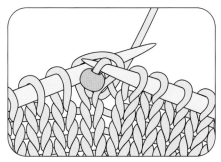

2 Knit the stitch, making sure that as you pull the loop of yarn through, the bead comes with it to the right side of the work.

Knitted-in beading on a purl row

Use this technique to place a bead on the stocking (stockinette) side of the work when working a purl row.

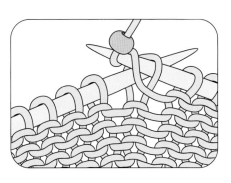

1 Purl to the position of the bead, Put the tip of the right-hand needle into the next stitch, wrap the yarn around it and slide the bead down to the needles.

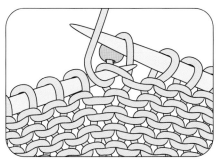

2 Purl the stitch, making sure that as you pull the loop of yarn through, the bead comes with it to the right side of the work.

Wriggling beads

With knitted in beading you will find that the beads will try to wriggle their way through to the back of the work. To help prevent this, before you work the next row push all the beads down so that they are sitting at the bottom of their stitches, then keep an eye on them as you work the next row.

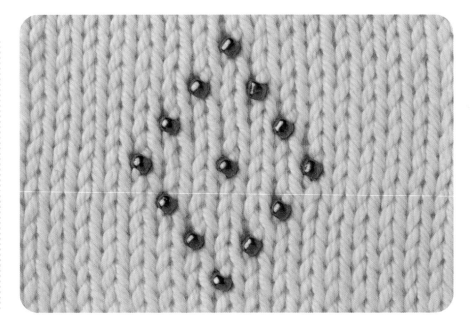

Knitted-in beaded motif.

Beading in different colours

You can take beading one step further and introduce different-colour beads to make a more intricate design. The thing to remember when using more than one colour of bead is that you have to thread them onto the yarn in the right order. The bead that is threaded on last will be the one that is knitted first, so you need to follow the chart backwards. To knit this chart you would have to thread the beads on in the order given below, starting from the top left of the chart.

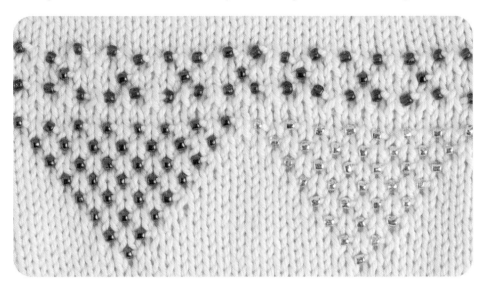

This swatch has been knitted following the chart below.

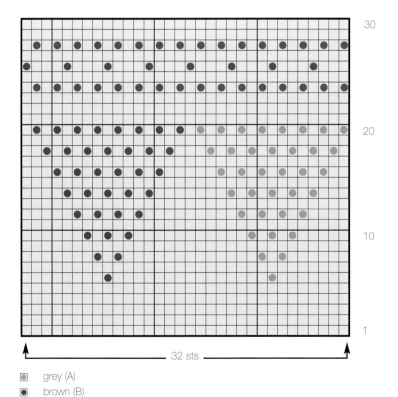

32 sts

◉ grey (A)
◉ brown (B)
◉ red (C)

Thread the beads onto the yarn in the following sequence to knit this chart.

16 C
8 B
16 C
8 B
8 A
7 B
7 A
6 B
6 A
5 B
5 A
4 B
4 A
3 B
3 A
2 B
2 A
1 B
1 A

Sequins on a knit row

Sequins can be placed on knitted fabric using the same technique as for slip stitch beading (page 179). To get the sequins onto the yarn, use a needle and thread as for beading (page 178), but it is better to use a softer yarn, such as a wool-cotton mix, than a pure cotton that is quite firm. This technique shows you how to place a sequin on stocking (stockinette) stitch fabric.

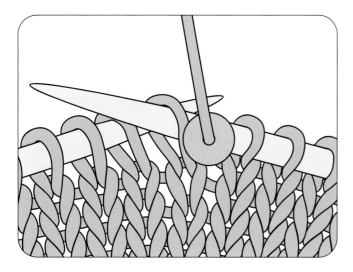

 On a knit row, knit to the position of the sequin. Bring the yarn forward between the needles and slip a sequin down the yarn to sit right in front of the work. Slip the next stitch purlwise (page 50). Knit the next stitch quite tightly, making sure the sequin stays at the front of the work.

Placing sequins

When putting sequins onto stocking (stockinette) stitch fabric, if you purl the stitch immediately following the sequin it will lift the sequin slightly, giving a effect a bit like fish scales.

Sequins on a purl row

Use this technique to place a sequin on reverse stocking (stockinette) stitch fabric.

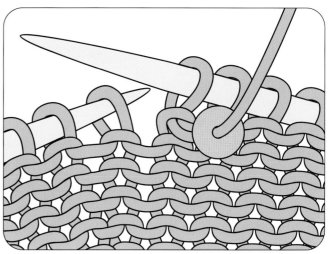

On a purl row, purl to the position of the sequin. Slip the next stitch through the back loop (page 51) and then put it back onto the left-hand needle. Slide a sequin down to sit in front of the needle then purl the twisted stitch in the usual way, keeping the sequin in place.

The sequins overlap a little to fill out the motif.

embroidery

Working embroidery stitches on knitted fabric is generally easy as the stitches and rows act as a grid, helping you to space the embroidery stitches evenly. However, getting the tension of the embroidery right (so that the fabric is not puckered up or the embroidery stitches baggy) can take a bit of practice.

Remember that embroidery will stop knitted fabric stretching, so don't embroider collars or cuffs if you have to stretch them to get the garment on. The embroidery stitches shown here can be used to add detail and colour to a simple project, lifting it to another level.

Swiss darning

Swiss darning resembles knit stitches and can be used to add small areas of colour detail without all the fuss of knitting with several colours. It may also be used to hide a mistake in your colour knitting.

Choosing yarn

For the best results, work Swiss darning in a yarn that is the same weight and texture as that used to knit the project.

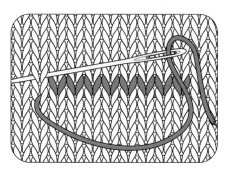

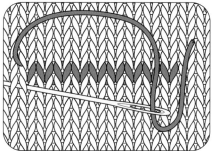

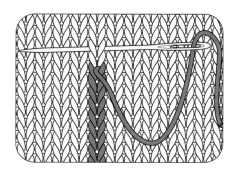

1 To work a horizontal row of Swiss darning, work from right to left across the knitted fabric. Bring the needle through from the back of the fabric at the base of a stitch then take it under the two loops at the base of the stitch above.

2 Put the needle back through to the back of the fabric where it first came out at the base of the lower stitch and take it across to come out at the base of the next stitch to the left. One Swiss-darned stitch is complete.

3 To work a vertical row, work from bottom to top of the knitted fabric. Bring the needle through the base of a stitch and take it under the loops of the stitch above, as before. Take it back through the base of the stitch and the bring it to the front through the base of the stitch above.

Running stitch

The simplest of all the embroidery stitches, running stitch has naïve charm.

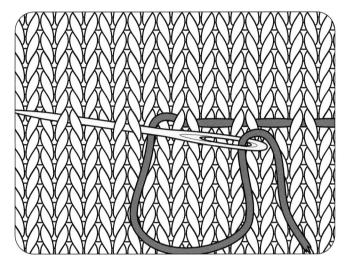

Bring the needle through to the front of the fabric between two stitches. Take it back through the fabric one or two knitted stitches to the left. Repeat, spacing the stitches evenly.

Stem stitch

This is another good stitch for outlining motifs.

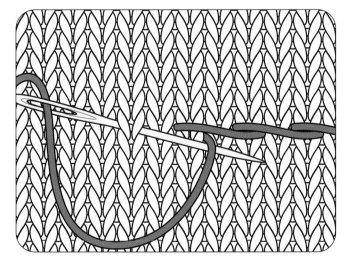

Bring the needle through to the front of the fabric between two stitches. *Take it back through the fabric three knitted stitches to the left. Bring it to the front one knitted stitch to the right of where it last came out, making sure that the tip of the needle goes under the working yarn. Repeat from *.

Backstitch

This is a useful stitch for creating bold outline shapes or for outlining motifs.

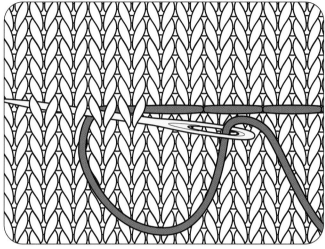

Bring the needle to the front. Take it to the back two knitted stitches to the right. *Bring it to the front two stitches to the left of where it last came out, then down where it last came out. Repeat from *.

Cross stitch

Cross stitches can be worked over different numbers of stitches and rows and in a row, as shown, or individually.

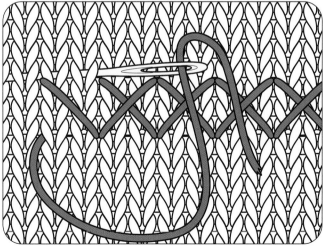

Bring the needle through to the front of the fabric between two stitches and make a diagonal stitch to the right. Bring the needle through the fabric the desired distance to the left of where it last went in and make a second diagonal stitch to complete the cross.

Blanket stitch

This stitch helps stop a knitted edge from curling up. As its name suggests, it's ideal for edging blankets.

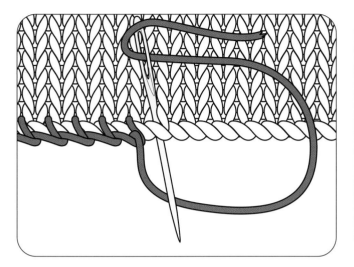

Working from left to right, bring the needle through to the front of the fabric between two stitches, one or two rows up from the edge. *Take it back through the same row, one or two knitted stitches to the right. Bring the needle up under the edge and through the loop of working yarn. Gently pull the stitch taut. Repeat from *.

Colours and textures

You can work embroidery in any yarn, though fluffy yarns, such as mohair, don't produce great results. Experiment with different colours and yarn textures, but remember that the embroidery and knitted fabric must be made in yarns that can be washed and pressed at the same temperature.

Chain stitch

This is a decorative stitch that can be worked in straight or curving lines.

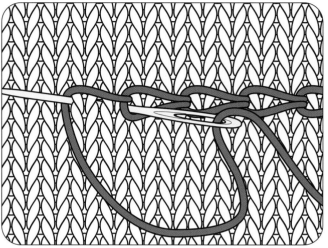

Bring the needle through to the front of the fabric between two stitches. *Take it back through where it came out and make a straight stitch two knitted stitches to the left. Loop the working yarn under the tip of the needle and gently pull the stitch to form a loop. Repeat from *.

Lazy daisy

Several of these stitches, placed as shown, can make a decorative flower embellishment.

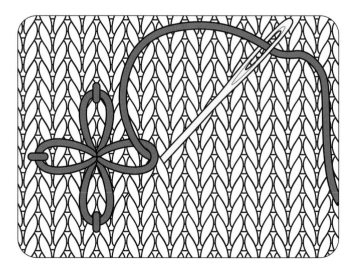

Make a chain stitch (above). Take the needle over the end of the loop and back down where it last came out, making a tiny stitch to hold the loop in place.

Satin stitch

Satin stitch is ideal for covering an area of knit to fill in a motif.

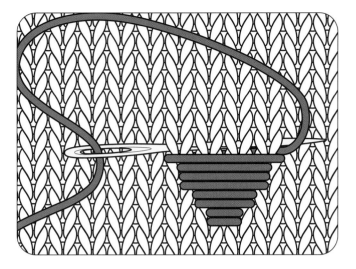

Bring the needle through to the front of the fabric between two stitches. *Take it back through the desired distance to the left, then bring it back up very close to where it last came out. Repeat from *, making sure all the stitches lie flat and close together.

French knot

Another three-dimensional stitch that adds texture to an embroidered design.

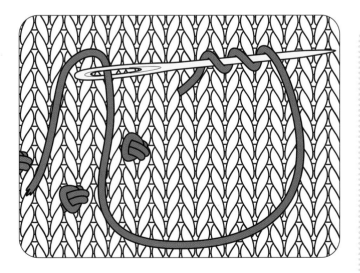

Bring the needle through to the front of the fabric. Wrap the yarn around the needle three times. Press your thumb on the wrapped needle to hold the yarn firmly in place and pull the needle through the wraps. Gently pull the stitch tight and take your needle back through the fabric where it first came through.

Bullion knot

This is a decorative stitch that lends texture to your embroidery.

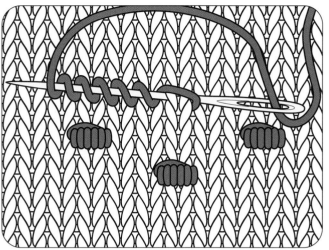

Bring the needle through to the front of the fabric. Put it back into the fabric where it came out and make a short stitch, but do not pull the needle through. Wrap the yarn around the needle five times. Press your thumb on the wrapped needle to hold the yarn firmly in place and pull the needle through the fabric and wraps. Gently pull the stitch tight and take your needle back through the fabric where it first came through.

Starting and stopping

To start embroidery, do not knot the end of the yarn as it will probably just pull through the fabric. Instead, weave the needle and yarn back and forth through a few knitted stitches on the back of the fabric, underneath the area that will be covered by the embroidery stitches. To fasten off after finishing the stitching, either weave in as before or, if the stitch permits, weave the end into the back of the embroidery, being careful not to pull it too tight and so distort the stitching on the right side of the work.

embroidery samplers

These two samplers use stitches and beads in creative ways. Look at how they are worked and then come up with your own embroidery designs.

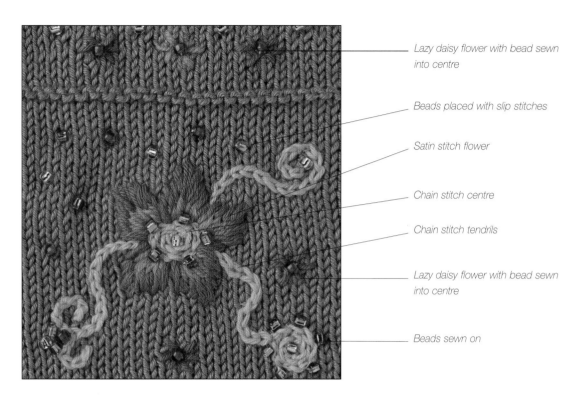

Lazy daisy flower with bead sewn into centre

Beads placed with slip stitches

Satin stitch flower

Chain stitch centre

Chain stitch tendrils

Lazy daisy flower with bead sewn into centre

Beads sewn on

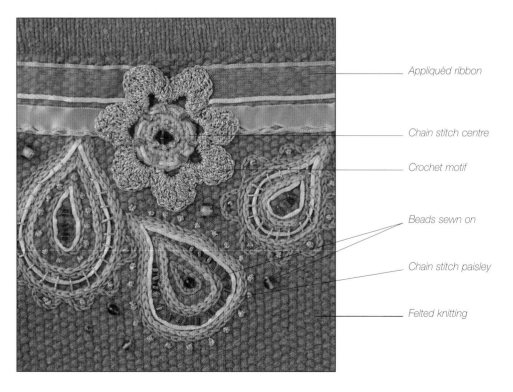

Appliquéd ribbon

Chain stitch centre

Crochet motif

Beads sewn on

Chain stitch paisley

Felted knitting

fringing

Fringing is a great way to embellish a project. It's quick and easy to do and is ideal for decorating jackets, bags and scarves.

Simple fringe

The individual tassels that make up a fringe can be as thick as you wish, just cut as many lengths of yarn as you need, each one being twice the length of the desired fringe, plus a little extra.

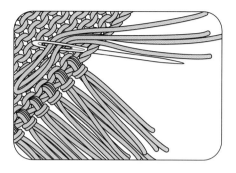

1 Fold the lengths for one tassel in half and put the folded end through a large-eyed tapestry needle. Take the needle and the folded ends of the yarn from front to back through the fabric, just above the edge.

2 Slip the needle off the yarn. Tuck the cut ends through the loop and pull it tight.

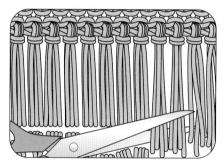

3 Lay the fringe flat (a table fork is great for combing out the strands of yarn). Use scissors to trim the fringe to an even length.

A fringed cast (bound) off edge.

Fluffy fringe

Using a fluffy yarn, such as mohair, for the fringe can look wonderful. Emphasise the fringing by making it in a yarn that contrasts in colour and texture with the yarn used to knit the project.

Knotted fringe

This is an easy way to add elegance to a simple fringe. If you make the fringe long, you can create quite complex knotted designs.

Work a simple fringe (page 189) but space the individual tassels slightly further apart. Split each tassel in half and knot each half to half of the adjacent tassel.

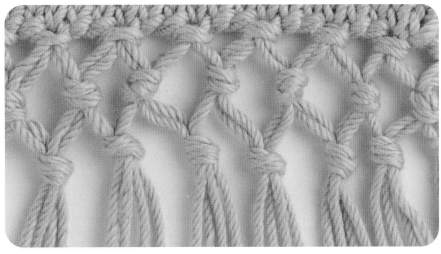

A knotted fringe design.

A fringe decorated with knitting beads.

Beaded fringe

Beads make fringing a little more special and the weight of the beads can help the fringe to drape well.

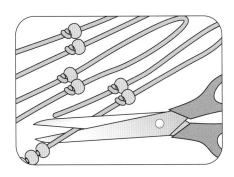

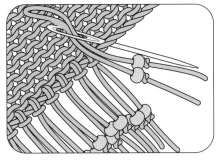

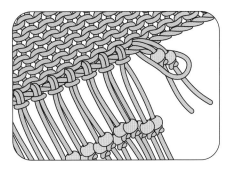

1 Thread the beads onto the yarn as for knitted beading (page 178). Cut the yarn to the lengths required for the fringe, with two beads on each length. Knot each end of each length to stop the beads from falling off.

2 Fold the length in half and put the folded end through a large-eyed tapestry needle. Take the needle and the folded end of the yarn from front to back through the fabric, just above the edge.

3 Slip the needle off the yarn. Tuck the cut ends through the loop and pull it tight. Trim the ends of the fringe.

Unravelled fringe

Unravelled fringing hangs down from the row ends of the work; what would usually be the side edge. So if you were making it for an edging then you would need to work a strip that could be sewn to the hem of the project.

To calculate how many stitches you need to work for the fringe, bear in mind that a stitch will produce a fringe three times its width once it is unravelled. It is always best to work a swatch before casting on for the project.

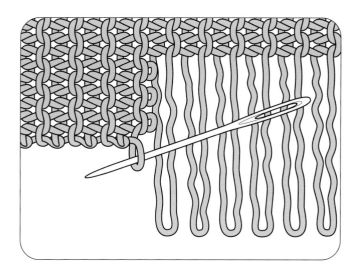

Cast on the required number of stitches for the project, plus the number of stitches needed to make the fringe. Work all the stitches until the knitted fabric is the size you want. On the last row, work the fringe stitches, then cast (bind) off the remaining stitches. Unravel the fringe stitches, using a knitting needle to help free them.

Choosing a stitch

Garter stitch works well with unravelled fringe as the stitch pattern helps prevent the last stitch above the fringe from becoming loose once the fringe is unravelled.

A fringe unravelled from garter stitch.

cords

As ties for hoods and belts or handles for bags, cords are brilliant. There are three main types and the technique you use to make your cord will depend on the look you want to achieve.

I-cord

This is a knitted cord that is strong and smooth.

 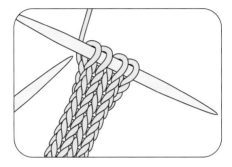 

1. Using double-pointed needles, cast on two stitches and increase (page 74) in each stitch on the first row to make four stitches. Knit the four stitches.

2. Do not turn the knitting, instead, push the stitches back up to the right-hand end of the double pointed needle and hold it in your left hand.

3. Pull the yarn firmly across the back of the work and knit the four stitches again. Continue in this way until the cord is the desired length.

A four-stitch I-cord.

Knit tightly

The first knitted stitch can become a bit baggy as the I-cord grows, so it is important to pull the yarn across firmly in Step 3 and to knit the first stitch tightly.

Twisted cord

This technique makes a cord that resembles rope. You can use as many strands of yarn as you wish, but remember that the thickness will be doubled when the cord is finished. The strands of yarn must be two-and-a-half to three times the desired length of the finished cord.

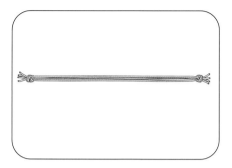

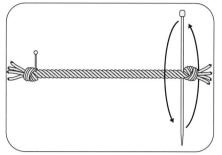

1 Knot the strands of yarn together at each end.

2 Secure one end of the bundle; the easiest way is to ask a friend to hold it. Put a knitting needle through the other end, just in front of the knot. Turn the knitting needle around and around until the cord is twisted so tightly it begins to kink. Take the needle out and hold the end firmly.

3 Bring the knotted ends together and let the cord twist around on itself. Pull firmly on both ends of the twisted cord to smooth out any kinks, then knot the knotted ends together.

A twisted cord.

Plaited cord

Traditional plaiting makes a decorative cord. Use a number of strands of yarn that can be divided evenly by three. Each strand should be about 30 per cent longer than the desired length of the finished cord.

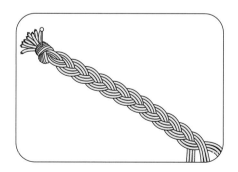

Knot one end of all the strands of yarn together. Pin the knotted end down or ask a friend to hold it. Divide the strands up into a left group, a centre group and a right group. *Move the right group over the centre group, so that the former is now the new centre group. Move the left group over the new centre group, so that the former is now the new centre group. Repeat from * until the plait is the desired length.

A plaited cord.

tassels and pom-poms

These are fun to make, as well as being easy, and can be sewn onto a multitude of projects. Try tassels on the corners of a knitted cushion or the traditional pom-pom on top of a knitted beanie hat. Note that these are not suitable for small babies' clothes as the strands can be pulled out.

Tassels

Make tassels in matching or contrasting yarn to the project they will be attached to.

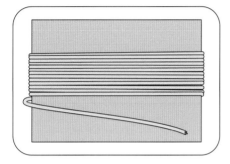

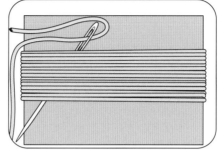

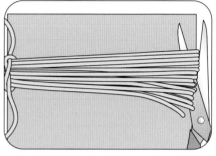

1 Wrap the yarn around a piece of card that is the desired length of the tassel. The more wraps you make, the fuller the head and skirt of the tassel will be.

2 Cut a length of yarn and thread it through a tapestry needle. Slip the needle under the wrapped loops at one end of the card. Pull the yarn halfway through and tie it in a very tight knot around the loops.

3 Using scissors, cut the loops at the other end of the card.

Straight tassels

Try pressing the yarn while it is wrapped around the card before you cut it. This keeps it flat and straight and will help the tassel hang well.

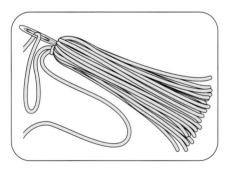

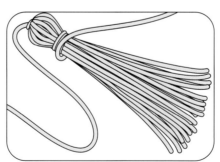

4 Thread one end of the yarn used to knot the loops into a tapestry needle. Take it down through the tassel to where you want to tie off the head.

5 Wrap this end tightly around the strands and knot it to itself to secure the wrapping. Trim the ends of the tassel to an even length. Use the other end of the knotting yarn to sew the tassel to the project.

A yarn tassel.

Poms-poms

There are great pom-pom makers available now which make the task really easy. However, the traditional method using two cardboard circles produces an equally effective result.

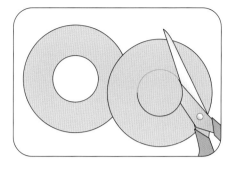

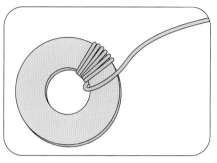

1 Cut two cardboard circles with a circle in the centre of each one. The diameter of the outer circle will determine the diameter of your pom-pom and that of the inside circle will determine how full the pom-pom will be.

2 Hold the two circles together. Wrap yarn around them until the hole in the middle is almost full.

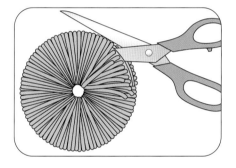

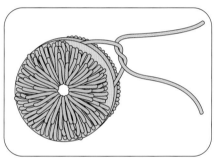

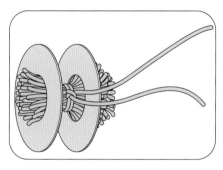

3 Using a pair of pointed scissors, cut the yarn around the outside edge of the card circles.

4 Wrap a length of yarn tightly around the centre of the pom-pom, between the two pieces of card. Tie it as tightly as possible in a knot.

5 Slide or cut the cardboard circles off the pom-pom. Fluff the pom-pom up and trim it to an even ball shape with scissors.

Fluffy yarn pom-poms.

embellishments

felting

Agitating wool yarn in hot soapy water will felt it, as anyone who has accidentally put a cashmere sweater in the hot wash will know. The hot water and soap cause the wool fibres to cling to one another and the more the item is kneaded or rubbed, the more tightly the fibres cling and the more the knitting will felt. Different effects can be achieved by mixing wool yarns, that do felt, and cotton or man-made fibre ones, that don't.

Felting shrinks and thickens knitting, so pieces must be knitted larger and more loosely than usual. Even in experienced hands felting can be a trial and error process, so approach it with caution.

Felting in the washing machine

Put the knitting in a mesh laundry bag to help prevent loose fibres clogging up the filter on the washing machine. If it's a long, narrow item, such as a bag strap, fold it up and safety pin it together. Put an old, lint-free towel in the laundry bag as well to help the felting process. Add a small amount of liquid fabric detergent and set the machine to a 60° wash.

Look through the glass door of the machine every five minutes or so. As soon as the knitted stitches are no longer visible and the fabric looks like commercial felt, spin the water out of the machine.

Rinse the knitting thoroughly by hand in cool water and either spin it gently in the machine or roll it up tightly in a towel and squeeze it. Shape the item with your hands and leave it to dry away from direct heat.

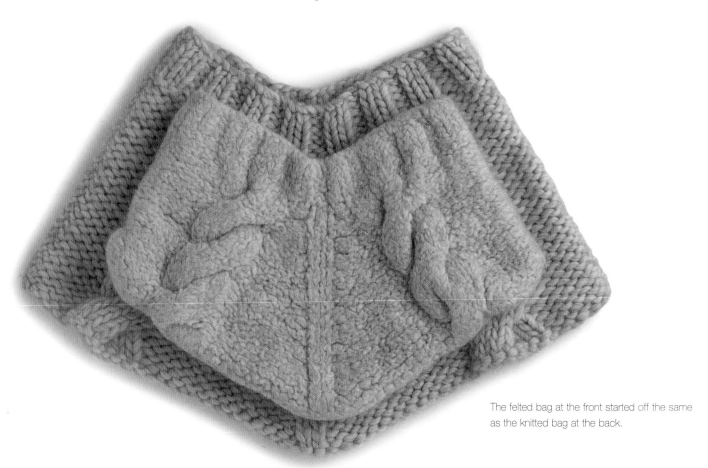

The felted bag at the front started off the same as the knitted bag at the back.

Felting by hand

This is easy to do and it is easier to gauge the results than it is with machine felting, though it can take a while for the knitting to fully felt.

Simply hand-wash the knitting in hot water with plenty of liquid fabric detergent. Rub and squeeze it and you will start to feel and see the fibres felting together. When it is felted to your satisfaction, rinse, shape and dry it as for machine felting.

A felted handbag decorated with crochet and embroidery.

Decorative felting

You can also achieve lovely effects by using objects to stretch the fabric taut so that the stretched areas do not felt while the rest of the fabric does. This example used marbles, but you could try using different-shaped pebbles or nuts, which will produce different-shaped bumps.

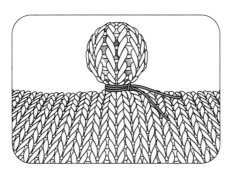

1 Place the marble on the wrong side of the knitted fabric and stretch the fabric over it really tightly. Tie the fabric tightly around the base of the marble with a strong thread.

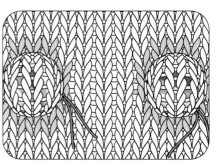

2 Tie in as many marbles as you want there to be bumps. Check that you are happy with the pattern, as once the fabric is felted, it is fixed.

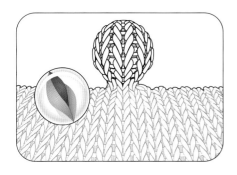

3 Wash the fabric in the washing machine, as described opposite. Using sharp-pointed scissors, snip the threads and remove the marbles to leave bumps of un-felted knitting.

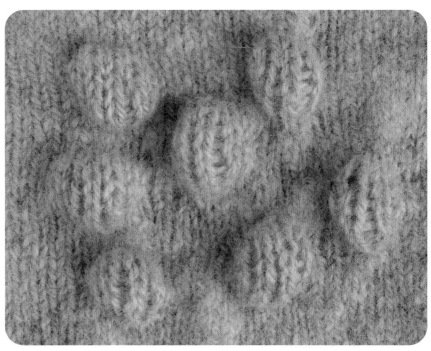

The textural surface of decorative felting.

professional finishing techniques

When you have put time and effort into knitting a project, it is well worth finishing it properly. Some people rush this part of a project and that is always a mistake, as careful finishing does bring rewards in terms of a really professional look.

sewing in ends

The first step in finishing a project is to sew in (or weave in or darn in as it is sometimes known), all the ends of yarn left from casting on, casting (binding) off and joining in new balls.

Cast on and cast (bound) off ends

Thread a tapestry needle with the tail of yarn left over from casting on or casting (binding) off.

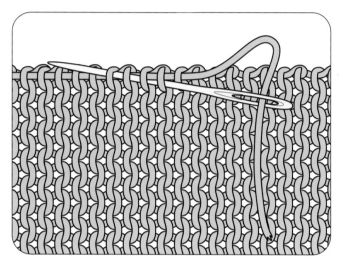 

1 If the edge is not going to be sewn into a seam, then weave the end in and out of a few stitches along the edge of the knitting. Skipping the last stitch, weave it back through the stitches, then trim the end of the yarn tail close to the knitting.

2 If the edge is going to be seamed, then it is neater to weave the end into the seam allowance. To do this, first sew up the seam using the appropriate technique (pages 205–215). Thread a tapestry needle with the tail of yarn and weave it through a few stitches in the seam allowance. Skipping the last stitch, weave it back through the stitches, then trim the end of the yarn tail close to the knitting.

Sewing in ball ends

Once you have sewn up the seams of a project, use the same techniques to sew the tails of yarn left from joining in new balls into the seams or into the edge of the knitting.

Intarsia ends

When you have knitted an intarsia project, you may have a lot of ends to sew in. This can be time-consuming, but you need to do it properly or the knitting will unravel. Sewing in the ends also gives you the opportunity to ease or tighten any irregular stitches at the beginning and end of a motif. Always sew ends into the backs of stitches that are the same colour or you risk the wrong colour showing on the front of the work.

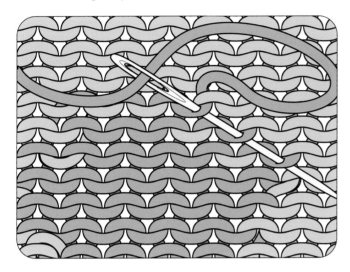

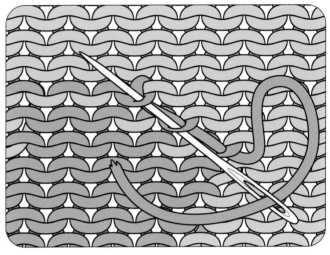

1 Thread a tapestry needle with one end of yarn at a time. Weave the needle into the backs of four to five stitches that are the same colour as the end, making sure that you go though the yarn, splitting it, not under the stitches. This will provide extra friction and help stop the ends working free.

2 Take the needle back through two or three of the same stitches. Pull the fabric slightly to secure the end and trim it close to the knitting.

Sew as you go

If you sew in the ends as you finish each piece of a project then it won't seem like such a huge task when all the knitting is completed.

blocking the knitting

Once you have sewn in all the ends, you are ready to block your knitting. (If you are sewing ends into a seam (page 200), then block the pieces of knitting before seaming them.) Blocking is the careful pinning out of all the pieces on a flat surface to enable you to check the shape and measurements of the finished project. Each piece is then steamed or pressed to smooth the surface and flatten the edges, both improving the look of the knitted fabric and aiding the sewing-up process.

Making a blocking board

You can pin out all the pieces on your ironing board, but if you do a lot of knitting and have learnt how blocking benefits the finished appearance of a project, you may want to make a blocking board.
You will need:

A square or rectangle of board or MDF
Medium-weight wadding the size of the board
Gingham fabric 5cm (2in) larger all round than the board.
Staple gun

Lay the wadding over the board. Lay the fabric over the wadding, making sure that the check pattern is square to the edges. Fold the fabric over to the back of the board and use the staple gun to attach it all around the edges. Do one edge at a time, making sure that the fabric remains smooth and taut across the front of the board.

Pinning out on a blocking board

Lay out the knitted pieces, right side down, using the pattern of the checked fabric to ensure that edges that are supposed to be straight are in fact straight: this is particularly useful when you are working with a piece that is particularly twisted or curled. Pin each piece out, sliding the pins through the edge stitches and into the wadding on the blocking board or ironing board

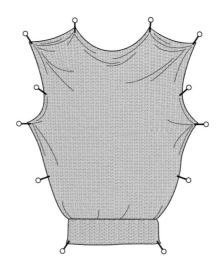

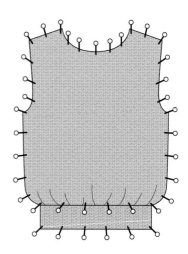

1   This piece is badly pinned and pressing it when it is like this will only make it worse.

2   This is how your piece should be pinned out. As you pin, measure the pieces and if necessary, ease the knitting to fit the required measurements. You can't stretch it too much, but if it has come up slightly small, you may be able to gain some width and length.

Types of fibres

Your next step will depend on the type of fibre you have knitted with. Always check the ball band to see if the yarn fibre can be pressed or not.

If the yarn can be pressed and the knitting is smooth stocking (stockinette) stitch, place a damp cloth on the knitted pieces and press down briefly with a hot iron, taking care not to drag the iron across the work. If it is a delicate yarn, but can be pressed, then hold a steam iron approx 10cm (4in) above the fabric and just steam the pieces.

If the yarn is made from mixed fibres that should not be pressed, simply hold a steam iron fairly close to the surface and steam the pieces.

If the fibre should not be steamed or pressed, then spray the pieces lightly with cold water (a spray gun like the ones you buy for indoor plants is ideal), but do not saturate them. Press the pieces with a dry towel and your hands.

Whichever technique you use, do not remove the pins until the pieces are cold and dry. Unpinning while they are warm and damp is how you are most likely to distort the shape of the knitting.

Putting a garment together

When putting a garment together you would usually do it in the following order, unless stated differently in the pattern you are following.

Sew the front and back pieces together at one shoulder seam first. Then work the neckband as instructed in the pattern. Once that is complete, sew the other shoulder seam. Then you can either sew the sleeves into the armholes and then sew the side seams from wrist to lower hem, or you can sew the body side seams and the sleeve seams then sew the sleeves into the armholes. I always use the latter technique, fitting the sleeve into the completed armhole (pages 218–219). The only time I would put the sleeve into the armhole before sewing up the sides is if it was a drop sleeve or shallow set-in sleeve (pages 216–218) .

Below, you can see how the sleeve head is expected to fit into the armholes.

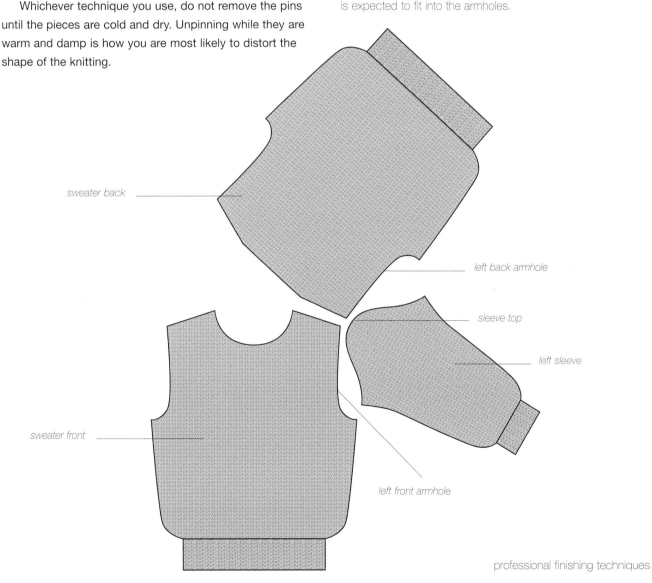

sweater back

left back armhole

sleeve top

left sleeve

sweater front

left front armhole

professional
finishing
techniques

grafting

Grafting is a technique for joining two pieces of knitting together that haven't been cast (bound) off the needles. Grafting forms an almost invisible seam and is particularly useful on shoulders where you want the seam to lie flat. You can graft either by knitting or by sewing; the sewing technique lies slightly flatter than the knitting technique, but the latter can be easier to work. When you have completed the seam, sew in the ends of yarn used (page 200).

Grafting by knitting

With the right sides of the fabric together, hold both needles with the pieces of knitting on in your left hand. Both pieces must have the same number of stitches.

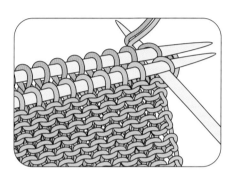

1 Put the tip of right-hand needle into the front of the first stitch on each needle.

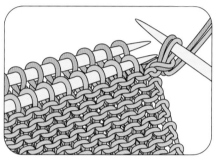

2 Using the tails of yarn from both needles, knit both stitches together.

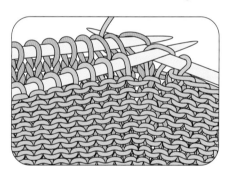

3 Drop one of the tails of yarn. Put the tip of the right-hand needle into the next stitch on each needle and knit them together using the other tail. Cast (bind) off by lifting the first stitch over the second stitch, as if you were casting (binding) off in the usual way (page 54). Using just the one tail of yarn, continue knitting stitches from each needle together and casting (binding) them off until all the stitches have been cast (bound) off.

Fabrics joined by knitted grafting.

Grafting by sewing: stocking (stockinette) stitches to stitches

Both pieces of knitting must have the same number of stitches. Work from right to left across the knitting, slipping the stitches off the needles one at a time once the tapestry needle has gone through them. Thread a tapestry needle with a long length of the yarn used to knit the project (a contrast colour yarn has been used in these illustrations to help you understand the technique).

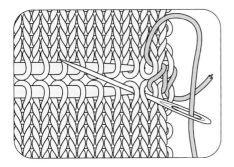
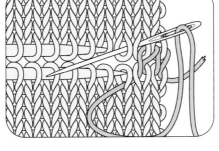
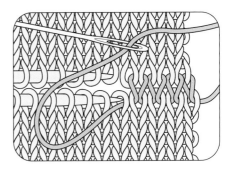

1 Lay the pieces right-sides up on a flat surface with the needles together. From back to front, bring the tapestry needle through the first stitch of the lower piece and then through the first stitch of the upper piece. Take the needle through the front of the first stitch of the lower piece, then from the back, through the second stitch of the lower piece. Go through the front of the first stitch on the upper piece and then through the back of the second stitch on the same piece.

2 Continue in this pattern across the row, taking the tapestry needle through the back and later the front of each stitch in turn.

3 Gently pull the sewn stitches as you work them so that they have the same tension (gauge) as the rest of the fabric.

Altering length

Grafting by sewing is also the technique you would use to alter the length of finished pieces of knitting, rather than unravelling and starting again. Turn to page 254 to see how to work this useful technique.

The first row of dark green is the grafting row.

Grafting by sewing: stocking (stockinette) stitches to row ends

This method is used to join stitches on the needle to a side (row end) edge, for example, a sleeve to an armhole. It produces a more elastic, less bulky seam than mattress stitch (page 210).

Work the stitches on the needle in the same way as for grafting stitches to stitches (page 205). On the side edge, take the needle under one of the loops lying between the first and second stitches. However, as a stitch is wider than it is long, you cannot join one stitch to one row end across the seam and keep it lying flat. Instead, you must periodically take the needle under two loops of the side edge, maybe once in every four grafted stitches: it will depend on the yarn and your tension (gauge).

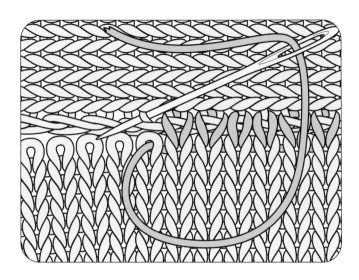

Grafting by sewing: garter stitch

This technique uses the same principles as grafting stocking (stockinette) stitch (page 204), but to keep the stitch pattern correct, one of the pieces of knitting must end on a right-side row and the other on a wrong-side row. The piece finishing with the wrong-side row must be the lower piece.

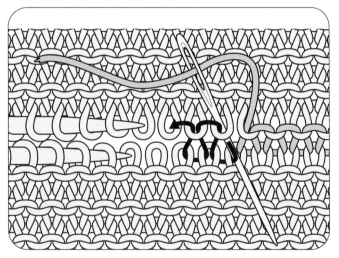

Starting from the right, take the needle in and out of the stitches following the arrow on the illustration. This stitch pattern forms a ridge on the upper piece that will look like a row of garter stitch. Keep the sewn stitches the same tension (gauge) as the knitted stitches for the best result.

Worked well, the grafting row is undetectable.

Grafting by sewing: single rib

This is more complicated than joining stocking (stockinette)
or garter stitch, as you have to keep the stitch pattern
correct to obtain a good result. This technique is used
to join sections of rib that have been worked in the same
direction: for joining ribs worked in the opposite direction,
turn to page 225.

Starting from the right, take the needle in and out of the stitches
following the arrow on the illustration. Be very careful not to twist
any of the stitches and to keep the columns of knit and purl
stitches aligned.

mattress stitch

Also known as ladder stitch, this technique produces an almost invisible seam that is slightly stiffer and bulkier than a grafted seam, but it is a simple technique to work. As mattress stitch is worked row by row on the right side, it is perfect for joining colour work: a touch of magic when piecing stripes together. The other advantage to this technique is that if the yarn you have knitted with has too loose a twist or is too frail to sew up with, you can use another yarn of a similar colour and it won't show. Do not knot one end of the yarn. Instead, leave a tail and when you have completed the seam, sew in the tails at both ends (page 200). The sewing yarn in these illustrations is a contrast colour to help you see how the stitches are made.

Sewing stocking (stockinette) stitches to stitches

This is most commonly used for joining shoulder seams.

Right-sides up, lay the two pieces to be joined side by side.

Thread a tapestry needle with a long length of yarn.

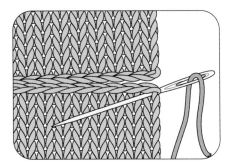

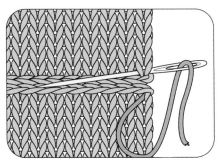

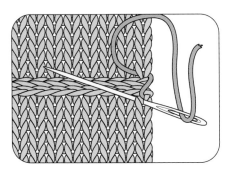

1 From the back, bring the tapestry needle up through the first stitch in the lower piece of knitted fabric.

2 Take the needle under both loops of the same stitch on the other piece, so that it emerges between the first and second stitches.

3 Go back into the lower piece where the needle first came out and take it under one loop, so that it emerges between the first and second stitches.

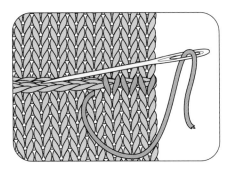

4 Take the needle under both loops of the second stitch on the upper piece, then under both loops of the second stitch on the lower piece. Continue in this way. When you have sewn about 5cm (2in) of the seam, gently pull the stitches up to close the seam.

Two cast on edges joined with mattress stitch.

Pinning pieces

Use safety pins to loosely pin the pieces of fabric together before you start sewing. This will help you keep the rows and/or stitches aligned.

Sewing stocking (stockinette) stitch row ends to row ends

This technique will usually be used when sewing up side seams. Here it is shown worked half a stitch in from the edges, but you can work a whole stitch in if you prefer (or if your edge stitches tend to be baggy). Right-sides up, lay the two pieces to be joined side by side. Thread a tapestry needle with a long length of yarn.

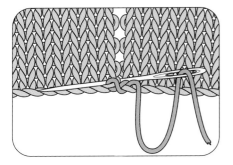 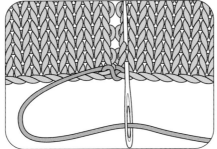 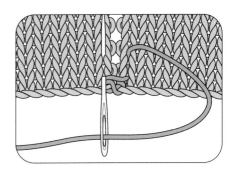

1 To start the seam, bring the needle from the back of the right-hand piece through the centre of the first stitch of the first row. Take it across to the other piece and, from the back bring it through the first stitch. Take it back to the first piece and, again from the back, bring it through where it first came through. Finally take the needle through the back of the first stitch on the left hand piece and pull tight the figure-of-eight you have made.

2 Take the needle across to the right-hand piece and, from the front, take it through the middle of the first stitch and under the bar of yarn that divides that stitch from the one above. (If the knitted fabrics are both all one colour, and so precise matching is not important, you can take the needle under two stitch bars at a time.)

3 Take the needle across to the left-hand piece and, from the front, take it through the middle of the first stitch and under one (or two) bars. Continue up the seam in this way, zigzagging between the two pieces and picking up the same number of stitch bars on either side. When you have sewn about 5cm (2in) of the seam, gently pull the stitches up to close the seam and then continue.

Pull gently

When you are working mattress stitch, on either stitches or row ends, do not pull the yarn too tightly or the seam will be very stiff. You also risk breaking the yarn and having to unpick the seam and start again.

If these pieces of knitting were the same colour, the join would be invisible.

Sewing stocking (stockinette) stitch row ends to stitches

This is a combination of the techniques for sewing stitches
to stitches (page 208) and row ends to row ends (page 209).

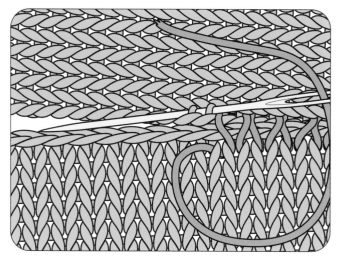

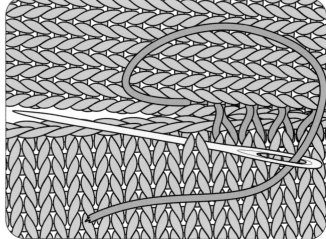

1 On the row end edge, take the needle under two bars
of yarn.

2 On the stitch edge, take the needle under both loops of
each stitch.

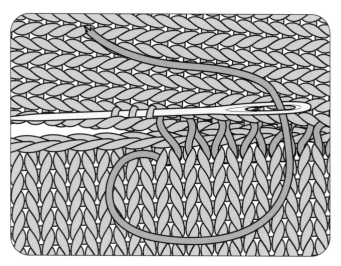

3 However, as a stitch is wider than it is long, on
approximately every third stitch through the row end edge,
take the needle under three bars instead of two.

Row ends joined neatly to stitches.

Sewing reverse stocking (stockinette) stitch fabric

If reverse stocking (stockinette) stitch is the right side of the work, then use this technique to sew the seams.

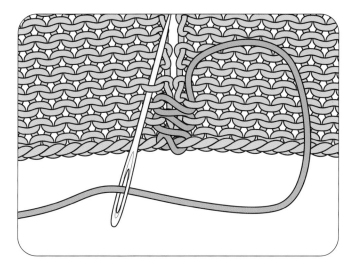

Work in exactly the same as for joining stocking (stockinette) stitch row ends to rows ends (page 209), but always work under only one bar at a time.

The slight break in the pattern is inherent to this type of seam.

Sewing single rib

The magic of mattress stitch on single rib is that you can take half a stitch from each side to make one whole stitch. This keeps the rib pattern continuous and the seam becomes almost invisible. Both pieces of knitting must start and end with the same stitch, usually a knit stitch.

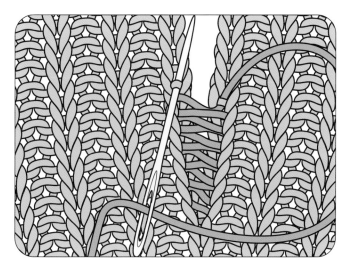

Bring the needle up the centre of the first knit stitch on each side and work as for joining stocking (stockinette) stitch row ends to rows ends (page 209).

A half stitch on each of the light and dark pieces makes one full stitch.

Reverse seam

If you want to make the seams a design feature of the project, consider working a reverse seam so that the edges of the knitting show on the right side of the work.

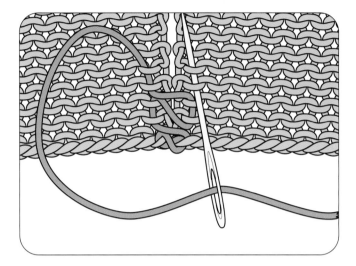

Place the pieces of knitting to be joined on a flat surface, wrong sides up. Work the seam as for sewing stocking (stockinette) stitch row ends to row ends (page 209). The edges will push out onto the right side of the project.

A visible seam looks best if the edges of the pieces are neatly knitted.

Edge stitches

If you work a garter stitch selvedge (page 52) on the edges of the knitting the reverse seam will be even more decorative.

Backstitch seam

This is the stitch most commonly used for joining knitting. It can sometimes make a bulky seam and it can be difficult to match patterns as backstitch is worked on the wrong side of the fabric. However, for plain stocking (stockinette) stitch it is a strong, fairly quick stitch to work. Always pin the pieces together before you start to sew.

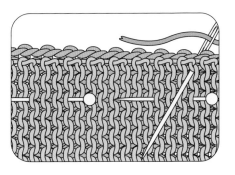

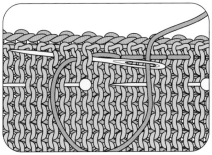

1 Work the backstitch about one knitted stitch in from the edge. Starting on the right, bring the needle through both layers of fabric from the back to the front.

2 Take the needle back through the fabrics about one knitted stitch back from where it last came out and bring it back through to the front about one knitted stitch in front of where you started. Continue along the seam in this way to the end.

Flat seam

A flat seam is achieved by using overstitch. This seam is good for joining a button band, collar or some welts, especially with moss (seed) or garter stitch edgings. Look carefully at the edge of moss (seed) and garter stitch and you will see a series of regularly spaced bobbles: it is these that will be stitched together.

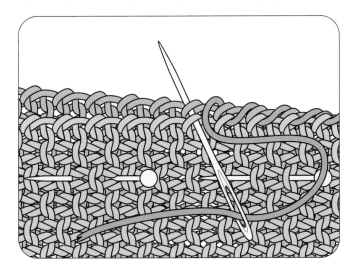

Starting at the back of the work on the right, bring the needle through the same bobble on the edge of both pieces of fabric and pull tight. Take the needle over the top of the edges of the fabric and, from the back, go though the next bobbles on the edges. Continue along the seam, going through each pair of bobbles in turn.

A flat seam has no bulk and, as the name suggests, lies flat.

professional finishing techniques

crochet seams

Crochet can be used for joining two pieces of either knitted or crocheted fabric. The seams are neat, but can be bulky.

Slip stitch seam

This is just like working slip stitch in crochet (page 280).

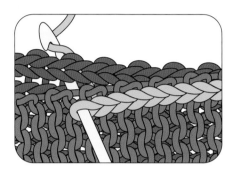

Hold the two pieces to be joined right sides together. From the front, put the crochet hook through both pieces, one stitch in from the edge. Catch the yarn and pull a loop through on the hook. Go through the layers once more, pull a second loop through and pull this loop through the first one on the hook. Continue along the seam in this way.

A slip stitch seam joining row ends to row ends.

Single (double) crochet seam

This can be worked on two cast on or cast (bound) off edges. Worked on the right side of the project it makes a decorative seam.

Put the hook through aligning inside stitch loops on the cast (bound) off edges of both pieces. Wrap the yarn around the hook and pull a loop through. Repeat on the next pair of stitch loops. *Wrap the yarn around the hook and pull a loop through both loops on the needle. Take the hook under the next two stitch loops of the edges and pull a loop through. Repeat from * along the seam.

A single (double) crochet seam joining stitches to stitches.

Two-needle crochet seam

It is also possible to crochet off the stitches while they are still on the knitting needles. This is a quick and neat way of joining two pieces of knitting.

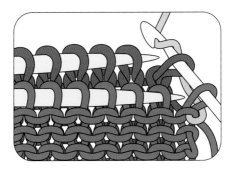  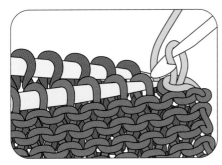

1 With the stitches on the needles and the pieces to be joined right sides together, put the hook knitwise into the first stitch on each needle, dropping them off the needles as you do so. Wrap the yarn around the hook.

2 Pull a loop through both loops on the hook. Put the hook into the next stitch on each needle, slipping them off the needles, and wrap the yarn around the hook.

3 Pull a loop through all three loops on the hook. *Put the hook through the next stitch on each needle, wrap the yarn around the hook and pull it through all three loops on the hook. Repeat from * across all the stitches.

A two-needle crochet seam joining stitches to stitches.

Hook size

Use a hook that is the same size as the needles used. A larger hook can be difficult to push through the stitches without stretching them.

sewing in sleeves

Sewing in sleeves can be a tricky part of putting a garment together. The best technique to use will depend on which type of sleeve head you have to work with.

Sewing in a drop sleeve

A drop sleeve has no shaped sleeve head and the body it is being sewn to has no armhole shaping. The most important thing when sewing in a drop sleeve is to get it positioned correctly. First, you must sew up the shoulder seam.

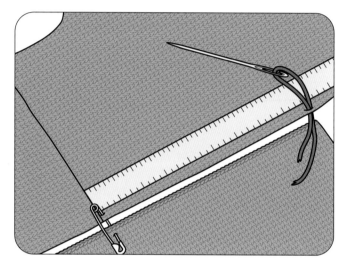 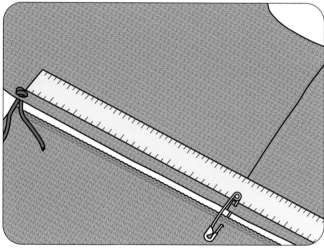

1 Using a safety pin, pin the centre of the sleeve to the shoulder seam. Smooth one side of the sleeve out flat next to the front body and place a marker on the body at the edge of the sleeve. Measure the distance from the shoulder seam to the marker.

2 Measure across from the shoulder seam on the back body and place a marker to match the first one. Using the technique for sewing row ends to stitches (page 210), sew the sleeve in place.

Measuring sleeves

With this style of sleeve you can knit the body and sew it up first. Try the body on and then you can measure for the perfect sleeve length.

Knitting in a drop sleeve

An extremely neat way to join a drop shoulder sleeve to the body is to knit off the sleeve along the side edge of the sweater. Do not cast (bind) off the sleeve, just leave the stitches on a needle.

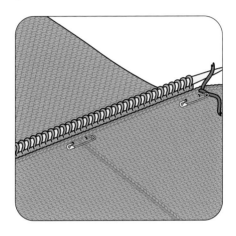

1 Following Step 1 of Sewing in a Drop Sleeve (opposite), position the sleeve correctly. Safety pin the right sides of the sleeve and body together.

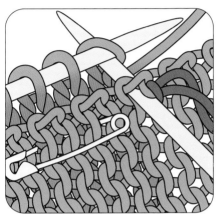

2 Pass a knitting needle, held in your right hand, through the body under the edge stitch and into the first stitch of the sleeve stitches.

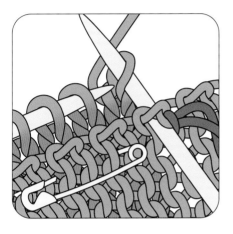

3 Using matching yarn, knit the stitch off the left-hand needle.

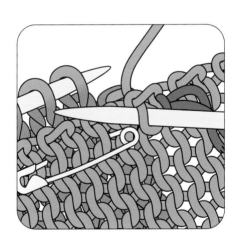

4 Using the tip of the right-hand needle, bring the stitch through the side edge of the body.

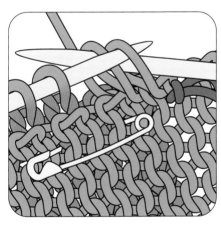

5 Repeat Steps 2–4 with the next stitch on the left-hand needle. Lift the first stitch on the right-hand needle over the second one to cast (bind) off the first stitch.

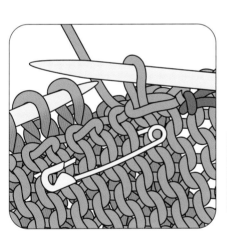

6 Continue in this way across all the stitches to complete the seam.

Shallow set-in sleeve

This type of sleeve has a slightly shaped sleeve head and the garment body has matching shaped armholes. Join the shoulder seams of the body first.

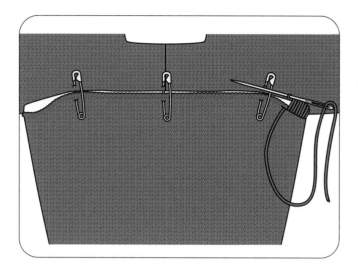

Fold the sleeve in half to establish the centre point and safety pin this to the shoulder seam. Pin the sleeve into the armhole shaping, as shown. Using the technique for sewing row ends to stitches (page 210), sew the sleeve in place.

Set-in sleeve

This type of sleeve has a fully shaped sleeve head and the body has fully shaped armholes. First of all, sew up the sleeve and side seams. Turn the body inside out and have the sleeve right side out.

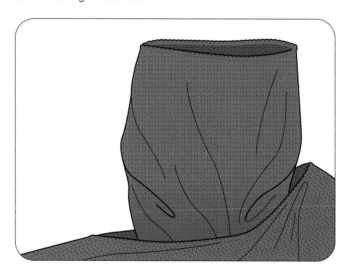

1 Slip the sleeve into the armhole.

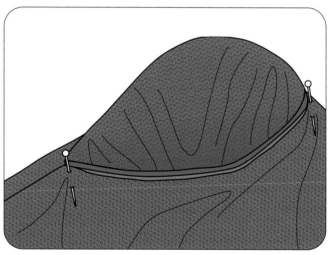

2 Pin the side seam to the sleeve seam. Fold the sleeve in half to establish the top of the sleeve head and pin this to the shoulder seam.

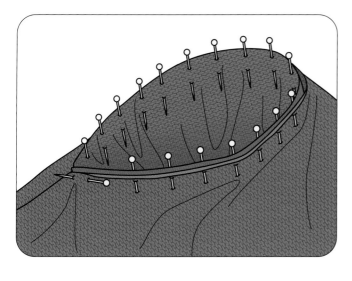

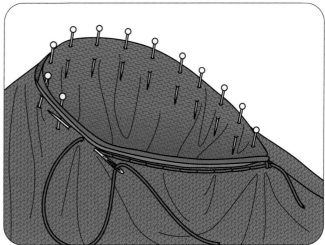

3 Pin the rest of the sleeve in place, matching the shapings.

4 Using backstitch (page 213), sew the sleeve in place.

Puffed sleeve

This type of sleeve has a fully shaped sleeve head with a wide top that is gathered up and the body has fully shaped armholes. Sew up the sleeve and side seams. Turn the body inside out and have the sleeve right side out.

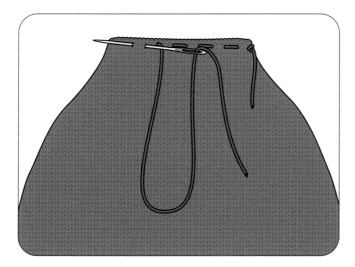

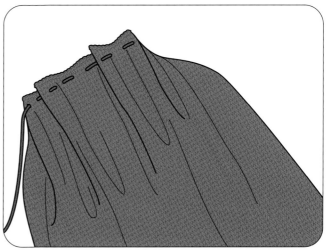

1 Thread a tapestry needle with the yarn used to knit the garment. Work a straight line of running stitch (page 185) across the wide, straight top of the sleeve.

2 Pull up the running stitch to gather the sleeve head up to the correct width. Follow the instructions for Set-in Sleeve (opposite) to fit and sew the sleeve to the body.

professional finishing techniques

collars and neckbands

Collars and neckbands can be difficult things to master and can also make or break the final appearance of the garment. You can make a neckband or collar and sew it into place, or you can pick up stitches around the shaped neckline and then knit the collar or neckband to suit.

Sewing on a collar

Lay the body and collar flat, with the right side of the garment facing up and the wrong side of the collar facing up.

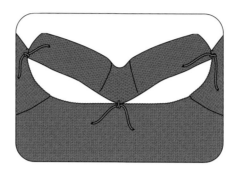

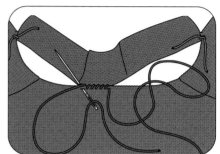

1 Fold the collar in half to establish the centre point and tack this to the centre of the back neck. Tack the collar into place at the front edges.

2 Thread a tapestry needle with enough yarn to sew on the whole collar, but don't knot the end. Start sewing the collar on at the centre back by pulling the needle and half the yarn through the body, one stitch in from the edge. Using slip stitch, sew one side of the collar in place, securing the end on the inside edge. Thread the needle with the tail of yarn left at the centre back and sew the other side of the collar to match.

Sewing on a neckband

You can attach a neckband by sewing, too. Pick up stitches (opposite) around the neck and work the neckband. Do not cast (bind) off, but leave the stitches on a length of scrap yarn.

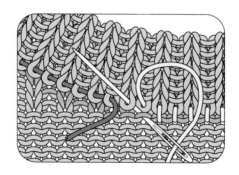

Slip stitch the neckband in place by taking the yarn through the stitches on the needle, one at a time, and then under the stitch loops of the last stitches of the garment body.

Picking up stitches

How many of you have followed pattern instructions that say, 'Pick up and knit 46 stitches along left side of neck', and when you have 46 stitches on your needles you are still 4cm (1½in) from the end of the neck? Usually this is because you are trying very hard to eliminate any holes and have picked up too many stitches in some areas. It's not a bad thing to have too many stitches, as long as you keep a note of how many extra there are and decrease to the right number on the first row of rib. Also, if you have five extra stitches on one side of the neck, try and make sure you have the same number extra on the other side. If you don't have enough stitches on the needles and have already reached the end of the neck, it could be that you are using the incorrect edge stitch (page 52).

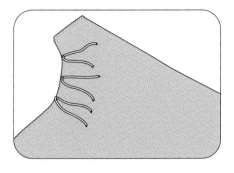

1 Before you start picking up stitches, divide the edge you are going to pick up along into evenly sized sections. Mark these with loops of contrast yarn. Divide the number of stitches to be picked up by the number of sections you have marked out and you will know how many stitches to pick up in each section.

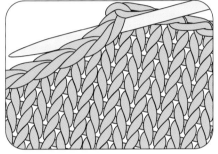

2 Put the tip of a needle into the first row, in the space between the edge stitch and the next stitch.

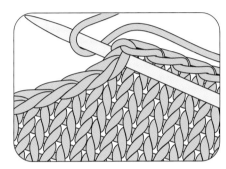

3 Wrap the yarn around the needle and pull the loop through on the tip of the needle. Pick up one stitch from each row in this way.

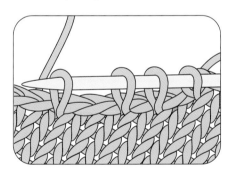

4 As the stitches you are picking up are wider than the rows you are picking up from, after every third picked-up stitch, skip one row space.

5 If, when you pick up a stitch you have a hole lying below it or the stitch is very loose, slip the stitch onto a spare needle and knit into the back of it. This will help to close the gap.

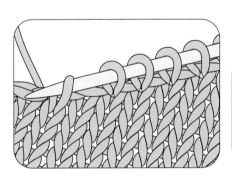

6 When you get to the part of the neck where you will knit the stitches left on the holder at the front of the neck, it can be quite a jump from the stitch picked up from the last row. I find it's best to pick up a stitch from one of the vertical stitches to make the neckband fit evenly around the curve.

professional finishing techniques

front bands

A cardigan or jacket has two front bands, one with the buttonholes in (page 233–236), and one that you sew the buttons to (page 237). There are four main techniques for attaching front bands and designers have different preferences as to which to use.

Picking up stitches

This is the technique I prefer for working front bands as it gives the neatest edge. As the band is knitted out from the front edge, the rows run at right-angles to the rows of the body fabric.

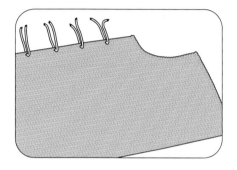 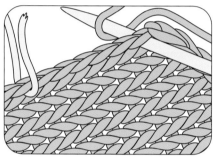 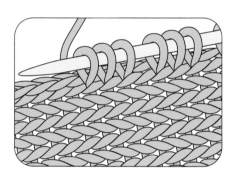

1 Divide the front edge into equal-sized sections and mark them with loops of contrast yarn. Divide the number of stitches to be picked up by the number of sections you have marked out and you will know how many stitches to pick up in each section.

2 Put the tip of a needle into the first row, in the space between the edge stitch and the next stitch. Wrap the yarn around the needle and pull the loop through on the tip of the needle. Pick up one stitch from each row in this way.

3 In order to keep the correct tension (gauge), pick up three stitches from consecutive rows and then miss one row.

Checking tension (gauge)

If the bands are quite long it can be difficult to judge whether your tension (gauge) is too tight when you are knitting on straight needles. To solve this, pick up the stitches on a circular needle. Work a couple of rows then lay the needle flat and spread the stitches out to check tension (gauge).

Sewn on bands from the wrong side

With this technique, the bands are knitted separately and then attached to the body of the cardigan, so the band rows run in the same direction as those of the body.

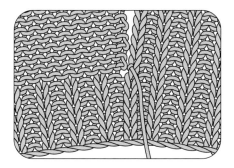

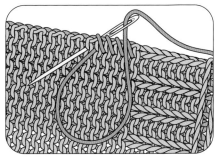

1 When knitting the garment, increase by one stitch (page 74) on the front edge of the garment and on the inner edge of the band. These stitches will be taken into the seam allowance.

2 Working on the wrong side, sew the band to the body using a flat seam (page 213). Stretch the bands slightly when you are sewing them on: tensioning them a little in this way prevents them going baggy when the cardigan is worn.

Matching bands

Usually a pattern will tell you to knit the bands to a certain length. When you have knitted the first one to the right length, count the number of rows you have worked and knit the same number for the second band.

Sewn on bands from the right side

To make this technique as simple as possible, it is best to increase by one stitch on the front edge of the garment and on the inner edge of the band. If the bands are to be knitted in garter stitch, as here, work the extra stitch on the body as a garter stitch selvedge (page 52).

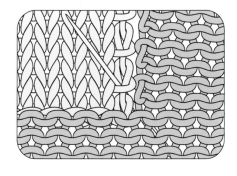

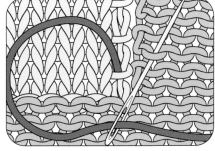

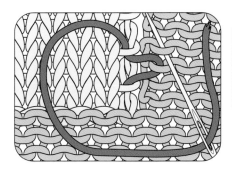

1 Lay the pieces side by side and, stretching the band slightly, safety pin it into place. Thread a tapestry needle with yarn and bring the needle up from the back through the centre of the first stitch of the selvedge.

2 From the front, pick up the centre of an aligning stitch of the band.

3 Continue in this way, pulling the stitches taut as shown in mattress stitch (page 208).

professional finishing techniques

Knitted in bands

It is possible to knit the band on to the
garment as you work it.

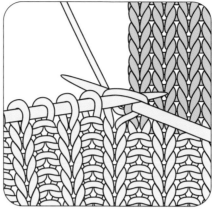

1 When working the left front band,
cast on the number of stitches
required for the band and rib one row,
stopping before the last stitch, which must
be a purl stitch. With the yarn at the front,
put the right-hand needle into the purl
stitch and also pick up one stitch purlwise
(page 50) from the edge of the garment.

2 Purl the two stitches together (page
78) and turn the work. Slip the first
stitch knitwise (page 50) and rib back
along the row. Continue to work the whole
band in this way.

3 When working the right front band,
cast on the number of stitches
required for the band and rib one row,
stopping before the last stitch, which must
be a knit stitch. With the yarn at the back,
put the right-hand needle into the knit
stitch and also pick up one stitch knitwise
from the edge of the garment.

4 Knit the two stitches together
(page 78) and turn. Slip the first
stitch purlwise and rib back along the
row. Continue to work the whole band in
this way.

Joining bands together

If the garment does not have a separate collar and the bands themselves simply extend around the neck, then they will need to be joined and a bulky seam is not what you want at the back of your neck. Garter stitch bands can be grafted with the usual technique (page 206), but if the bands are ribbed then, as they have been worked in different directions, you need to use the following method. This method can be used to join any sections of rib worked in opposite directions.

Centre back seam

The seam must be precisely at the centre back of the neck, so measure the bands carefully and pin them in position to check before joining them. While you are joining one side of the bands, put point protectors on the needles holding the other stitches to prevent them falling off.

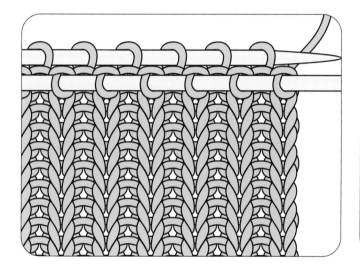

1 Slip the knit stitches and purl stitches of each band onto separate double-pointed needles. You will have four needles in total, two on each piece of rib.

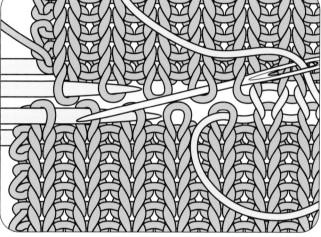

2 Right sides up, graft the knit stitches together as shown for stocking (stockinette) stitch (page 205), making sure the grafted stitches are kept quite loose. Be careful to keep the stitches in the correct order as you graft them.

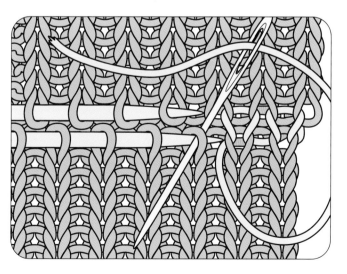

3 Turn the work over so the wrong side is facing up and repeat the process.

hems

Hems are always thought of as being at the bottom of a garment, but you can use these techniques to create neckbands, waistbands and cuffs and to finish off the tops of bags, as well as to make professional-looking hems. A garment hem is worked at the beginning of the project piece if you are working from the lower edge up.

Plain hem

This is the simplest type of hem and will be neatest if the hem stitches are worked on needles one size smaller than those used to knit the main part of the garment.

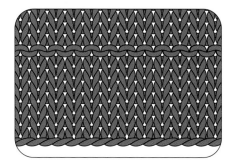

Cast on the number of stitches needed for the project and work in stocking (stockinette) stitch for the required depth of the hem. Then work a reverse stocking (stockinette) stitch row: knit the row if it should be purled or vice versa. This is the fold row and will be visible on the bottom edge of the project. Continue to work the rest of the project in stocking (stockinette) stitch. When the knitting is complete and the project sewn up, fold up the hem along the reverse stocking (stockinette) stitch row and sew it in place (page 231).

A folded and sewn plain hem.

Picot hem

This is a pretty edging that is used a lot in baby knitwear designs.

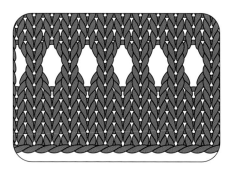

Cast on the number of stitches required and work the required depth of the hem in stocking (stockinette) stitch, finishing on a wrong side row. On the next row, work k2tog, yfwd (pages 78 and 100) across the row. Then finish the piece in stocking (stockinette) stitch. Fold up the hem along the eyelet row and sew it in place (page 231).

When the hem is folded up along the eyelet row, it creates a subtly scalloped edge.

Knitted-in hem

This technique allows you to knit in the hem before finishing the project piece. It is the best technique to use if the project is being knitted in the round (pages 120–122) or if there are no side seams, as the double-thickness hem will make any seams bulky.

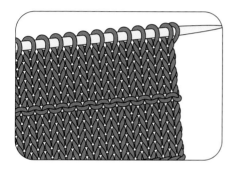 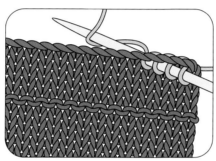 

1 Cast on the number of stitches required and work as for a Plain Hem (opposite). Work the rows above the reverse stocking (stockinette) stitch fold row until they are the same depth as the hem below it, ending with a wrong-side (purl) row.

2 Using another needle of the same size, pick up and knit (page 127) one stitch from every cast on stitch. When you have worked across the row, the tip of the needle must be pointing in the same direction as the needle holding the garment stitches.

3 Fold the hem so that the wrong sides are together and hold the needles together in your left hand. Using a third needle, knit the corresponding stitches from each needle together. Continue the rest of the garment in the usual way.

A knitted-in hem from the front.

The hem section was knitted in a contrast colour.

facings

Facings are basically hems worked vertically, usually to make a front edging for a jacket or cardigan instead of knitting front bands (pages 222–224). To make the fold row for a facing you have to use a knit or slipped stitch so that the fabric will fold smoothly. The facing is worked at the same time as the project piece.

Garter stitch edge

This technique produces a knobbly edge along the fold, similar to a Plain Hem (page 226).

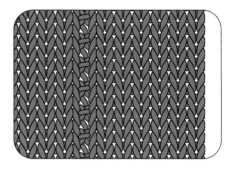

Cast on the required number of stitches, plus one stitch for the fold row and as many as are needed to make the facing the required depth. No matter whether the row is knit or purl, knit the fold stitch on every row. When the knitting is completed, fold the facing along the fold row and sew it into place (page 231).

A folded and sewn facing showing the knobs of the garter stitch edge.

Slip stitch edge

The edge of the fold will be smooth if you use this technique.

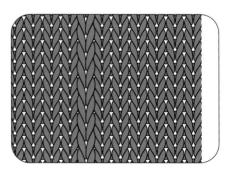

Cast on the required number of stitches, plus one stitch for the fold row and as many as are needed to make the facing the required depth. On a piece of stocking (stockinette) stitch, slip the fold stitch purlwise on the right side of the work and purl it on the wrong side. When the knitting is completed, fold the facing along the fold row and sew it into place (page 231).

The slipped stitches show along the front edge of the facing.

Picked up facing

You can pick up stitches along the edge of the piece (page 127) and knit a hem sideways to make even more of a feature of the facing.

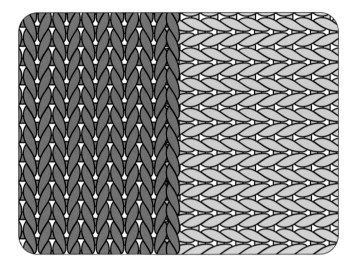

Pick up the number of stitches required. Work the band to the depth required, then work a reverse stocking (stockinette) stitch row as for a Plain Hem (page 226). Continue working for the depth of the hem then cast (bind) off loosely. Fold the facing along the fold row and sew it into place (page 231).

The stitches of the facing run in the opposite direction to those of the body of the garment.

Replacing a ribbed edge

If you are following a pattern and are replacing the recommended ribbed edging with a hem or facing, remember that stocking (stockinette) stitch does not draw in in the way rib does. Therefore, you may need to decrease the number of stitches cast on or picked up.

Mitred facing

If the piece you are knitting has both a hem and a facing, then you need to create a mitre so that when the hem and facing are folded over they do not overlap to make an ugly, bulky corner. This technique produces a hem and facing that are the same depth.

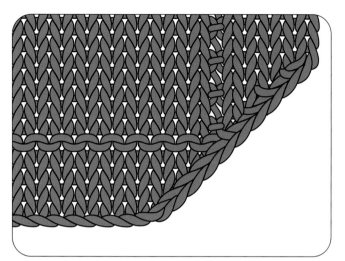

A folded and sewn mitred facing.

First, decide how many rows deep the hem will be, for example, five rows. Cast on the required number of stitches for the lower edge of the project, less five (or the number of rows you want your hem to be). Increase one stitch on the front edge on every row so that when you reach the hem fold row, you have the right number of stitches. On the hem fold row, increase by one stitch to make the facing fold row. Work the project piece, increasing by one stitch at the front edge on every row for the first five rows (or the number of rows worked for the hem). Continue working the piece straight. When the knitting is complete, fold in the hem and facing and sew them in place (page 231).

Working buttonholes in facings

Remember that when working buttonholes (pages 233–236) in a garment that has a facing, you need to make identical buttonholes on both side of the fold line. When the facing is sewn in place, it is best to work blanket stitch (page 186) around the buttonholes, stitching through both layers of fabric, to make it easier to button up the garment.

Contrast colours

A lovely touch is to work the facings or hems for a garment in a different colour yarn. On a jacket you will see the contrast colour when the front is open and on a flared skirt there will be flashes of colour when you walk. Working the turning row in the contrast colour as well gives a more visible accent.

Sewing hems and facings in place

For a professional finish, you need to make sure that the stitching isn't visible. Fold the hem or facing along the fold row. Make sure that the edge stitches line up with the backs of the body stitches along the appropriate row and pin the hem or facing in place. On lightweight fabrics use whipstitch and on bulkier fabrics, use herringbone stitch, which is less liable to stretch. Here the sewing yarn is shown in a different colour to make the techniques easier to see, but you should thread a tapestry needle with the same yarn used to knit the project, or one in the same colour if the project yarn has a very loose twist or is to frail to sew with.

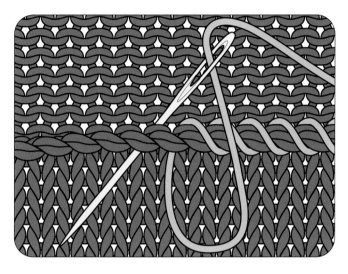

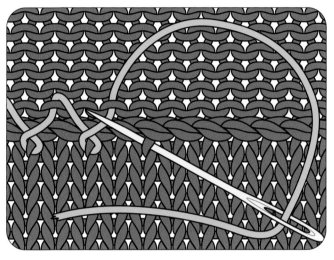

For whipstitch, take the tapestry needle from top to bottom under the loop of the back of a stitch on the body and then through the cast on edge of the hem. Don't pull the stitching too tight and repeat along the row on every stitch.

For herringbone stitch, work from left to right across the hem. Take the tapestry needle from bottom to top under the loop of the back of a stitch on the body. From right to left, take it through the right-hand loop of a stitch just under the cast on edge. Repeat across the hem until it is sewn in place.

placing buttonholes and buttons

Placing buttonholes and buttons correctly is a vital part of the overall appearance of the finished project. The spacing is important yet many designs will just tell you something like: 'Place one buttonhole 1cm (½in) from the top and one buttonhole 1cm (½in) from the lower edge, with the remaining six spaced evenly between them'. This sounds very simple, but you must do it properly to achieve a neat result.

Vertical button band

If the bands are knitted in the same direction as the body, then use this technique to place the buttons and the buttonholes.

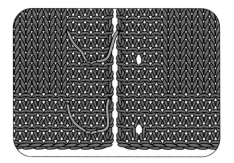

Knit the button band and sew it to the garment piece. Lay the band flat without stretching it.

Measure and mark with a thread the positions of the buttons 1cm (½in) from the lower edge and neck edge. Measure the space between the threads and divide it by seven. Put a pin into the button band at each measured division to place the six buttons. Count the number of rows between the pins, making sure that they are equal. When the placing is correct,

mark each position with a thread. Knit the buttonhole band to match. If the buttonholes are horizontal and worked over one row (pages 233–234), then work the counted number of rows between each buttonhole. If the buttonholes are horizontal but worked over two rows (page 235), then add an extra row for each buttonhole. Vertical buttonholes (page 236), should begin one or two rows (depending on the size of the button) below the marker on the button band and end one or two rows above it.

Picked up button band

Pick up stitches and work the button band. Once you have worked out the spacing for the buttons, you can pick up and work the buttonhole band to match.

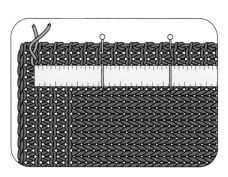

If you have picked up and knitted the button band it is better to calculate how many stitches there should be between the buttonholes. Once you have worked out the spacing, mark the positions of the buttons on the button band using pins.

Example
You have picked up 100 stitches for the button band.
You need eight buttons in total.
The first button is three stitches from the top, the last button is three stitches from the bottom and each buttonhole is worked over two stitches.

Taking away the stitches used for these two buttonholes leaves 90 stitches and six buttonholes.
12 stitches are for buttonholes, so this leaves 78 stitches.
Dividing 78 by the seven spaces needed gives you 11 stitches between buttonholes with 1 stitch left over, which should be placed between the lowest buttonhole and the next one up.

making buttonholes

Choosing how to work the buttonholes will depend on how big the buttons are. The eyelet technique (below) is very quick and neat, but the size of the buttonhole is dictated by the sizes of the yarn and needles. The two-row buttonhole technique (page 235) is the most versatile, as you can cast (bind) off as many or few stitches as you need in order to make the buttonhole the right size. Look out for the special technique that will eliminate the unsightly bar you usually get in a two-row buttonhole – your buttonholes will be revolutionised!

Eyelet buttonhole

This is a great technique for working small buttonholes and so is often used on children's clothes that only require little buttons.

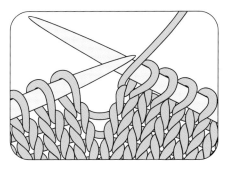

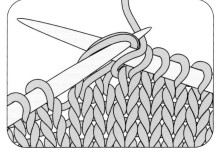

1 On a knit row, work to the position of the buttonhole and bring the yarn forward (page 100) to make a new stitch.

2 Work the next two stitches together (page 78) to maintain the original stitch count.

This technique produces round buttonholes.

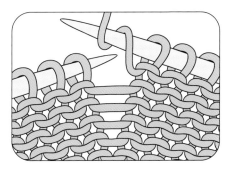

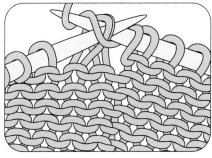

3 On a purl row, work to the position of the buttonhole and make a stitch by bringing the yarn round the needle (page 102).

4 Work the next two stitches together (page 78) to maintain the original stitch count.

Larger eyelet buttonholes

To make a larger eyelet, wrap the yarn around the needle twice (page 101). If the band is rib or moss (seed), use the appropriate yarnover depending on whether the stitch before is knit or purl (pages 100–103). Knit or purl the next two stitches together so that the following stitch can worked the right way to maintain the pattern.

Horizontal buttonhole over one row

This buttonhole is larger than an eyelet buttonhole (page 233), but is still worked over just one row. It is a little trickier to work than a two-row buttonhole (opposite).

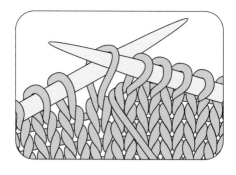

1 Work to the position of the buttonhole. *Bring the yarn forward (page 100) and slip the next stitch purlwise (page 50).

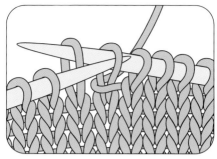

2 Take the yarn back, slip the next stitch purlwise, use the left-hand needle to pass the wrapped stitch over the top of the stitch just slipped. Repeat from * until you have cast (bound) off the number of stitches required.

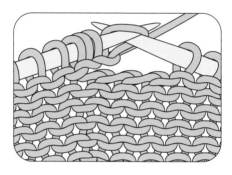

3 Turn the work. Using the cable cast on technique (page 28), cast on the required number of stitches plus one extra. Bring the yarn to the side of the work facing you.

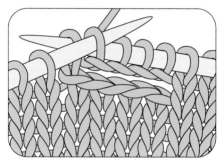

4 Turn the work so that the right side is now facing you and the yarn is at the back. Slip the next stitch from the left-hand needle onto the right-hand needle. Using the tip of the left-hand needle, pass the extra stitch on right-hand needle over the top of the slipped stitch. Work to the end of the row.

Measuring for buttons

The size of the buttonhole you work will depend on the size of the buttons you choose. A pattern may give a specific button size but if it doesn't you will have to measure. Lay the button on a completed part of the knitting and count the number of stitches it covers. Make the buttonhole two stitches smaller, as they do stretch over time.

A three-stitch one-row buttonhole.

Horizontal buttonhole over two rows

This is the most commonly used buttonhole on adult garments.

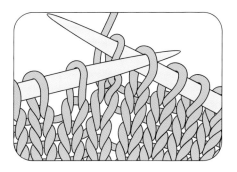

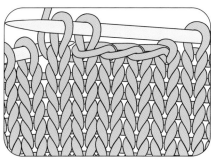

1 On the first buttonhole row, work to position of the buttonhole. Work two stitches and lift the first stitch over the second one to cast (bind) off one stitch (page 54).

2 Continue casting (binding) off the required number of stitches. Work to the end of the row.

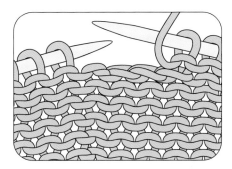

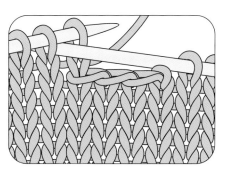

3 On the next row, work to the cast (bound) off stitches.

4 Turn the work and put the tip of the right-hand needle between the first two stitches on the left-hand needle.

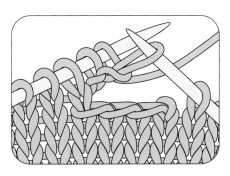

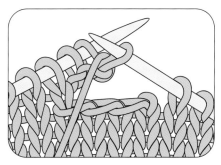

5 Using the cable cast on technique (page 28), cast on the number of stitches required. For the last cast on stitch, pull the loop through onto the right-hand needle.

6 Before placing the last stitch on the left-hand needle, bring the yarn forward between the two needles to the front of the work, then put the stitch on the left-hand needle. Turn the work back and complete the row. Bringing the yarn forward in this way will prevent an unsightly loop in the buttonhole.

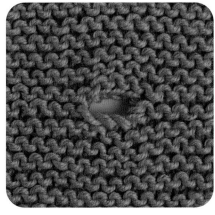

A two-row buttonhole in garter stitch.

Vertical buttonhole

Always have a minimum of two stitches either side of
a vertical buttonhole to reduce the risk of it stretching.

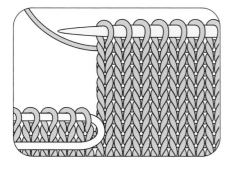 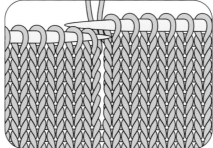 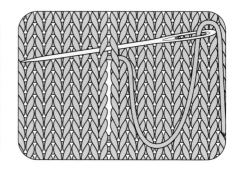

1 On the right side of the work, work
to the position of the buttonhole.
Slip the remaining stitches onto a holder.
Turn the work and work on these stitches
for the required number of rows for the
buttonhole, finishing with a right side row.
Do not cut the yarn.

2 Join another ball of yarn to the
stitches on the holder and, using a
third needle, work one row less than the
first half of the buttonhole. With the needle
holding the stitches of the first half in your
right hand, knit across the stitches of the
second half of the buttonhole.

3 Using the ends of yarn at the top
and bottom of the buttonhole,
stitch across the top and bottom to
reinforce them and then sew in the ends
(page 200).

A vertical buttonhole over four rows.

The right-sized buttonhole

As with a horizontal buttonhole, to work out the
size lay the button on the fabric, count the rows
and make the buttonhole two rows smaller.

Knitted loop

**An alternative way of fastening a button is to work a loop to
slip over it.**

Using the cable method (page 28), cast on as many stitches as
required and on the next row, cast (bind) them off again (page
54). Fold the loop in half and, using the tails of yarn from casting
on and off, neatly sew the ends to the inside of the front edge of
the garment.

A knitted loop can be as large or small as is needed to fit over the button.

buttons

Buttons can make or break a garment, so spend time choosing the perfect ones for your project. If you can't find what you need, you can make your own (pages 238–240).

How to sew a button on

If you sew on a button incorrectly and too loosely, this can damage the fabric it is sewn to and distort the front bands, which will look unsightly. If the garment is knitted in a fine weight yarn you should use this yarn to sew on the buttons. If the yarn is too thick, then use a sewing thread in a matching colour.

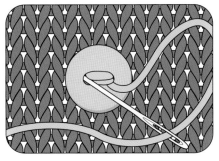

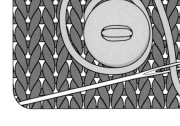

1 Thread a sewing needle with thread or yarn and knot one end. Sew the button in place, coming through the holes or shank several times.

2 Bring the needle through to the front of the fabric, but not through the button. Wrap the yarn a few times around the button stitches, between the button and the right side of the work. Take the needle to the wrong side of the work and secure and cut the thread.

Washing buttons

Make sure the buttons are washable or you must take them off for laundering and sew them back on when the garment is dry. Check wooden buttons particularly, as they are often not washable.

professional finishing techniques

making buttons

Sometimes it is hard to find a button that suits your yarn or garment. In these instances there are buttons that you can make from the yarn used to knit the project. If the yarn is chunky but is made up of several firm plies, then you can untwist it to create single-ply, fine yarn that can be used to make buttons.

Dorset buttons

To make these you need a curtain ring the size you want the finished button to be. You can make the buttons in one or more colours of yarn.

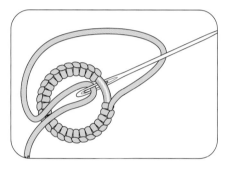 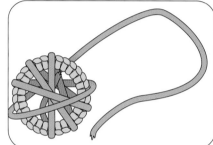 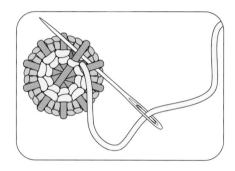

1 Using a length of yarn and a tapestry needle, cover the curtain ring by working blanket stitch all around it. Work over the starting tail of yarn to secure it as you go.

2 Wind the yarn tightly over the ring a few times to create a spider web effect. Oversew the centre of the web a couple of times and secure the yarn with a loop knot.

3 Bring the needle from the back to the front between the spokes, close to the centre of the web. Work backstitch over the spokes, working around and around until the ring is full of stitching. Fasten off the yarn with a few stitches through the back.

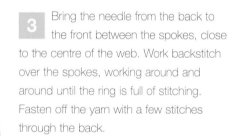

A Dorset button worked in three different colours of yarn.

Knitted bobble button

You can use a knitted bobble as a button as long as you are using quite a substantial yarn. You could stuff the bobble with more of the same yarn to make it a little firmer.

Using needles a size smaller than those used to knit the project, cast on three stitches. Knit one row. On the next row, increase into the first and last stitch (page 74), turn and knit all five stitches. Continue to increase on every alternate row as set until the bobble is as large as required. On the next row, decrease the stitches by k2togtbl (page 80), knit to last two stitches k2tog (page 78). Continue to decrease as set on every alternate row until you are left

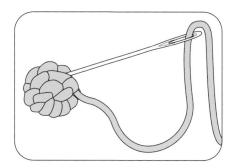

with three stitches. Cast (bind) off. Sew a small running stitch (page 185) around the edge of the knitting and pull it up tightly to make a bobble. Secure the end of the yarn with a few backstitches through the base of the bobble where they won't show.

A bobble button in yarn to match the project.

Covered button

You can buy these great self-cover buttons in various sizes. Using needles a size smaller than those used to knit the project, knit a square slightly bigger than the button itself. Fold the knitting over the top of the button and,

following the manufacturer's instructions, make up the button. You can embroider the knitted square before making up the button or knit it in a different stitch pattern to the rest of the garment.

A reverse st st button on st st fabric.

Sewing in elastic

If you want to have elastic around the waistband of a skirt you would usually make a hem (page 226) and then thread the elastic through it. However, if the yarn is bulky, this will make a lumpy, unsightly waistband. In this instance it is better to use herringbone stitch to hold the elastic in place.

Measure the elastic, overlap the ends and sew them together, making sure the elastic isn't twisted. Pin the loop of elastic in place on the wrong side of the garment. Using a herringbone stitch (page 231) and

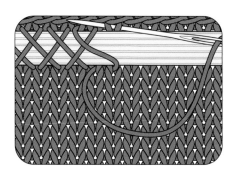

the yarn that the garment is knitted in, sew the elastic in place by working into every alternate stitch and trying not to pull too tightly, as this will make the fabric pucker.

This technique is neat and easy to work.

Zip fastening

When using a zip to close a garment it's always worth buying the zip at the same time as the yarn so that you get one the right colour and length.

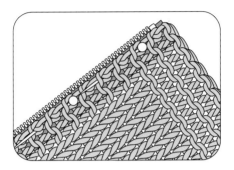

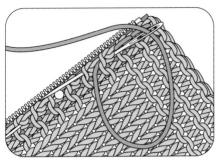

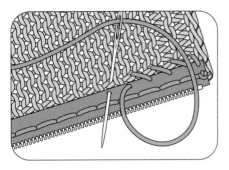

1 Open the zip and pin it in place, with the edge of the garment as close to the teeth as possible.

2 Using a sharp-pointed embroidery needle and the yarn used to knit the garment, sew the zip in place. Work on the right side and use small backstitches, making them as invisible as possible.

3 On the wrong side, slip stitch the zip tape to the back of the garment, making sure you sew through the backs of the stitches so that no stitching is visible on the front.

Facing for a zip

As a garment may often be worn unzipped or partly open, the inside of the zip tape will show, so it's a good idea to knit a simple facing to cover it and give the project a really neat finish.

Using the yarn the garment has been knitted from, work a strip of knitted fabric approximately 2.5cm (1in) wide and as long as the zip. You could work the strip in stocking (stockinette) stitch or moss (seed) stitch. Slip stitch it in place over the zip tape using sewing thread to match the yarn and stitching as neatly and invisibly as possible.

A zip sewn to moss (seed) stitch borders.

A moss (seed) stitch facing on the inside of the garment, covering the zip tape.

lining a jacket

If you have knitted a beautiful jacket, you may want to take the time to line it as this will help the knitted fabric keep its shape. Buy the lining at the same time as the yarn so that you get a good colour match. Choose a good-quality, lightweight lining that will fold and is soft: knitted fabric has a lot of movement so something soft will enhance its drape.

Fabric lining

Before you cut out the lining pieces, carefully block all the pieces of knitting (page 202).

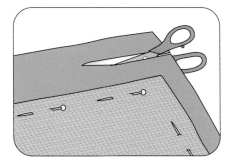

1 Pin the knitted pieces onto the lining, making sure that they are perfectly flat and not stretched at all. Cut out around the pieces, allowing 2.5cm (1in) for seam allowances.

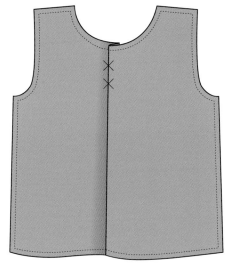

2 To gain extra movement in the body, allow 5cm (2in) extra in width across the back piece and make a pleat at the back of the neck.

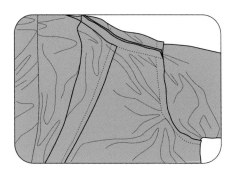

3 Using a sewing machine, make up the lining up in the same way as the knitted pieces. Press under the seam allowances around the hems, neckline, cuffs and front edges.

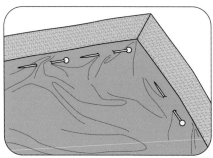

4 Slip the lining into the jacket, with the wrong side of the lining facing the wrong side of the knitted jacket. Pin the lining in place.

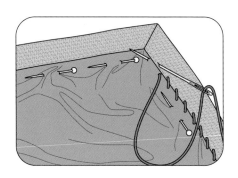

5 Slip stitch the lining into the jacket using matching thread.

Knitted lining

You may wish to consider a knitted lining. This works well when all the welts and sleeves on the garment are worked in doubled yarn, for example, two strands of 4-ply, and the body is made in just single 4-ply yarn. Knit another body in a contrasting-colour 4-ply yarn and slip stitch it into the main body as a lining.

Shoulder pads

Shoulder pads can improve the line of a jacket, but it is sometimes impossible to find the right colour and size for your project. Using matching yarn, you can make your own in the perfect size.

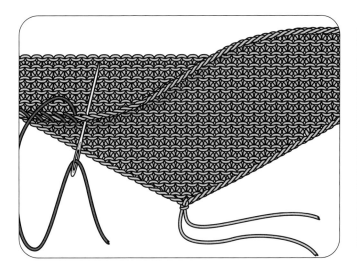

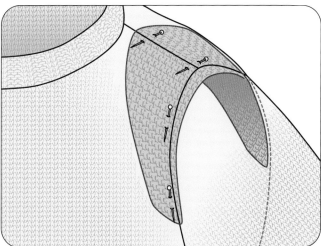

1 If you use garter stitch and doubled yarn, you can usually get the thickness you need without actually padding the knitted piece. Cast on two stitches and increase at each end of every alternate row (page 78) until the required width is reached: an average garment needs a pad about 17cm (6¾in) wide. Work straight for 5cm (2in) and cast (bind) off loosely. Fold the cast (bound) off edge back on itself, level with the end of the increasing, and slip stitch it in place.

2 Tack the pad in position and try on the garment to make sure it is the perfect place. Stitch the pad to the shoulder and armhole seams in just a few places.

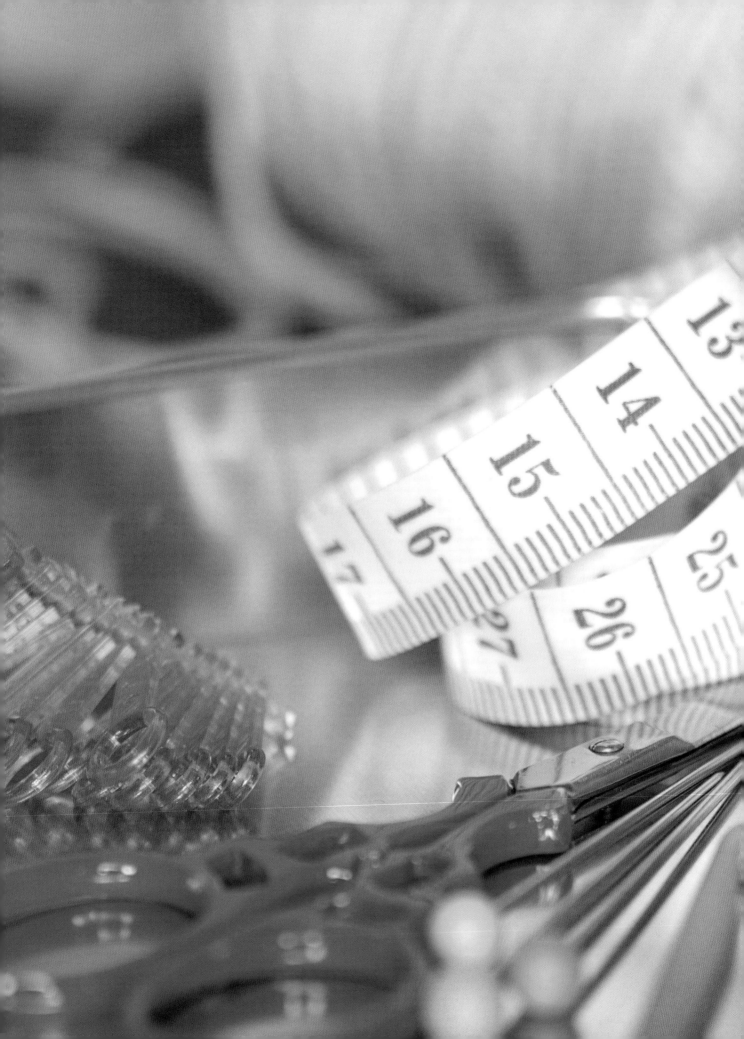

troubleshooting

Now you have learned to knit, you need to learn how to correct the mistakes you will make. Don't feel despondent about this – the best knitters get it wrong from time to time and there is little that can't be fixed, though the sooner you spot the mistake, the easier and quicker it is to put it right.

dropped stitches

When a stitch drops off a needle while you are knitting, the most important thing is not to panic: just keep the work still to stop it unravelling further. Keep a safety pin pinned to the top of your knitting bag, so that it is handy for emergencies, and slip this through the loop of the dropped stitch to hold it while you get to the right position in the row to pick it up. If the stitch has dropped down by just one row, so that there is just one loose horizontal strand with it, then use the 'one row down' technique. If it has dropped by several rows, turn to page 248.

One row down on a knit row

If you have dropped a stitch and only noticed after you have knitted a few more, unravel the stitches (page 249) until you get to the one before the dropped stitch.

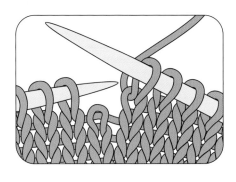

1 Make sure that the loose horizontal strand between stitches is behind the stitch that has been dropped.

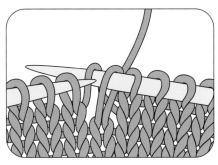

2 Put the tip of the right-hand needle into the front of the dropped stitch and under the horizontal strand behind it.

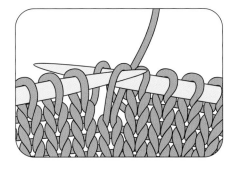

3 Put the tip of the left-hand needle into the back of the dropped stitch, which is being held on the right-hand needle, and lift this stitch over the horizontal strand. The strand has become the picked-up stitch.

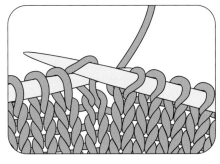

4 Put the tip of the left-hand needle into the front of the picked up stitch and slip it onto the left-hand needle ready to be knitted as part of the row you are on. The dropped stitch has been picked up.

The right direction

If you have to turn the work to pick up a stitch, when you are ready to start knitting again make sure that the working yarn is attached to the last stitch on the right-hand needle. If it is on the left hand needle you will be knitting in the wrong direction, a surprisingly easy thing to do.

One row down on a purl row

On a purl row, the principle is the same but you are working from the other side of the knitted fabric.

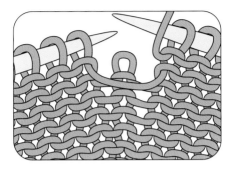

1 Make sure that the loose horizontal strand between stitches is in front of the dropped stitch.

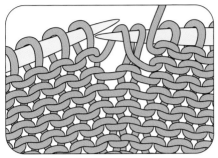

2 Put the tip of the right-hand needle into the back of the dropped stitch and then under the loose horizontal strand.

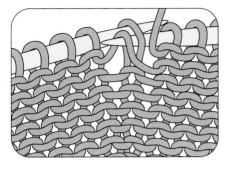

3 With the tip of the left-hand needle, lift the dropped stitch up and over the horizontal strand. The strand has become the picked-up stitch.

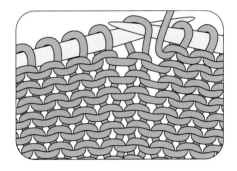

4 Put the tip of the left-hand needle into the front of the picked up stitch and slip it onto the left-hand needle ready to be purled as part of the row you are on. The dropped stitch has been picked up.

Multiple rows down on a knit row

If you have worked several rows before you notice the dropped stitch, or if it has fallen down a few rows before you have had a chance to put a safety pin through it, you will need this technique and a crochet hook. Knit to the stitch before the dropped one.

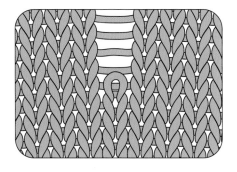

1 Make sure the loose horizontal strands are lying behind the dropped stitch.

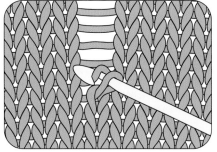

2 Put the crochet hook into the front of the dropped stitch and under the first horizontal strand. Pull the strand through. This strand has now become the stitch and you have picked it up by one row. Continue in this way, picking up all the strands in turn, until you have reached the top. Put the tip of the left-hand needle into the front of the picked up stitch and slip it onto the left-hand needle ready to be knitted as part of the row you are on. The dropped stitch has been picked up.

Multiple rows down on a purl row

The technique on a purl row is a little bit trickier. Purl to the stitch before the dropped one.

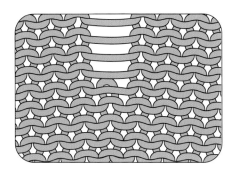

1 Make sure the loose horizontal strands are lying in front of the dropped stitch.

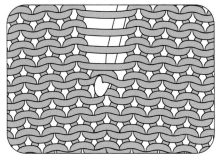

2 From the other side of the work, put the crochet hook into the dropped stitch and under the first strand. Pull the strand through the stitch. Continue in this way, picking up all the strands in turn, until you have reached the top. Put the tip of the left-hand needle into the front of the picked up stitch and slip it onto the left-hand needle ready to be purled as part of the row you are on. The dropped stitch has been picked up.

Picking up the strands

The illustrations show the stitches either side of the dropped stitch pulled apart, so you can see the horizontal strands. If you have knitted a few rows before noticing the dropped stitch, the stitches will have closed up and the strands will not be so visible. But they are there and you can pick up the stitch rather than having to unravel down to it.

unravelling work

Sometimes you have to unravel the work to correct a mistake. This can be heart-breaking, but it is still better than ignoring the mistake, finishing the project and then never wearing it because the mistake shows. If the mistake is just a few stitches back, unravel stitch by stitch. If it is a few rows back, then you will have to pull out the rows down to the mistake then pick up the stitches again.

Unravelling stitch by stitch on a knit row

To unravel just a few knit stitches, use this technique.

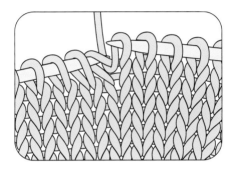

Put the tip of the left-hand needle into the front of the first stitch below the first stitch on the right-hand needle. Let the stitch drop off the right-hand needle and pull the yarn free. Continue in this way until you reach the mistake.

Stitch by stitch on the purl side

The same principle applies when unravelling on a purl row.

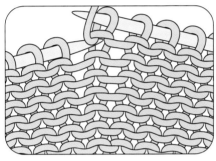

Put the tip of the left-hand needle into the front of the first stitch below the first stitch on the right-hand needle. Let the stitch drop off the right-hand needle and pull the yarn free. Continue in this way until you reach the mistake.

Unravelling several rows

If you have knitted a few rows before you spot the mistake, then it would take too long and be too boring to unpick each row stitch by stitch.

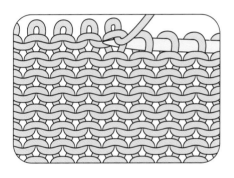

Take the knitting off both needles and slowly pull out yarn, unravelling stitches, until you reach the row with the mistake. Hold the knitting in your left hand and a needle in your right. Put the tip of the needle into the first stitch below the unravelled loops and pull the yarn free. Continue until all the stitches are back on the needle.

Unravelling to a thread

If you have to unravel several rows and you are worried about going down further than the right row, use this technique. It takes a bit more time, but it is safe.

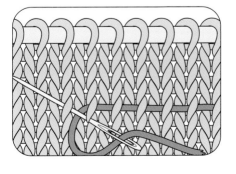

Thread a tapestry needle with a contrast colour yarn. Slip the needle through the

right-hand (front) loop of each stitch in the row below the one with the mistake in. This yarn is now holding all the stitches safely, so you can take the knitting off both of the needles and pull out the yarn until you reach the marked row. Slip the stitches onto a needle, making sure they are not twisted (page 250), and pulling out the contrast yarn as you go.

twisted stitches

Stitches, whether they are knit or purl, should always sit on the needle with the right-hand (or front) loop (as you look at the knitting) coming over the front of the needle. If the left-hand (or back) loop is over the front of the needle, then the stitch is twisted. When you have unravelled several rows (page 249), you may find that when you put the stitches back onto the needle they become twisted. If you were to knit or purl a twisted stitch it would show quite clearly in the finished fabric. If you haven't unravelled your work but have a twisted stitch on your needle anyway, this could be caused by winding the yarn around the needle the wrong way when working a stitch. Check your techniques for knit and purl stitches (pages 38–43) to make sure you are making them the right way.

On a knit row

You may not notice the twisted stitch until you come to knit it, when it will be very obvious.

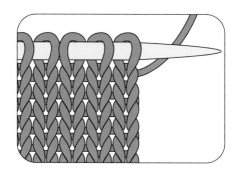

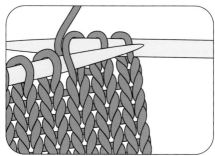

1 Here, you can see that the third stitch from the tip of the needle is twisted.

2 Knit to the twisted stitch then knit it through the back loop (page 51). This will turn it around the right way.

On the purl row

Use the same technique to correct a twisted purl stitch.

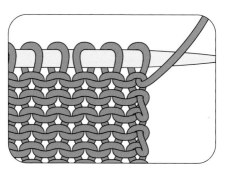

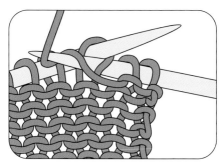

1 Again, the third stitch from the tip of the needle is twisted.

2 Purl to the twisted stitch then purl it through the back loop (page 51). This will turn it around the right way.

incomplete stitches

Incomplete stitches are usually caused when you are knitting or purling a stitch and you wrap the yarn around the needle but fail to bring it through the stitch. You need to keep an eye out for these, as it is easy to work both parts of the incomplete stitch and so inadvertently increase by one stitch.

Incomplete stitches on a knit row

The incomplete stitch was made on the previous purl row. It looks a bit like a yarnover (page100–103) followed by a slip stitch (page 50).

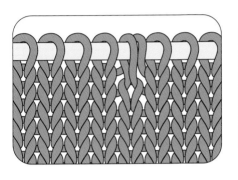

1 Here, the fourth stitch from the right is incomplete.

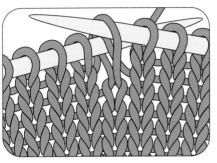

2 Knit to the incomplete stitch. Put the tip of the right-hand needle into the back of the 'slipped' stitch on the left-hand needle. Lift this over the 'yarnover' and off the needle. The stitch has been completed and is ready to be knitted in the row you are working.

Incomplete purl stitches

The incomplete stitch was made on the previous knit row. Again, it looks a bit like a yarnover followed by a slip stitch.

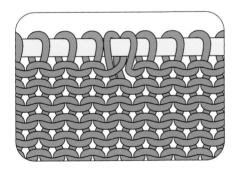

1 Here, the fourth stitch from the right is incomplete.

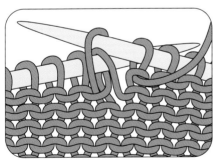

2 Purl to the incomplete stitch. Put the tip of the right-hand needle into the front of the 'slipped' stitch on the left-hand needle. Lift this over the 'yarnover' and off the needle. The stitch has been completed and is ready to be purled in the row you are working.

uneven knitting

Various things can cause your knitting to look uneven in different ways. As a novice knitter, it is common for knitting to be slightly uneven, but as you perfect your techniques this should disappear. If it doesn't then you need to check the following elements.

Different-sized stitches

Are your stitches all different sizes? There are three main reasons why this could be.

Look at how you are holding your needles (pages 36–37). If you have to let go of the needles when wrapping the yarn around the needle, the work could be slipping and this will make the stitches uneven.

Holding the yarn in your right hand correctly (pages 36–37) will determine the tension (gauge) you are getting. If you keep letting go of the yarn then the tension (gauge) could become inconsistent. Similarly, if the finger that is holding the yarn is not close to the needle and stitches, the tension (gauge) could be inconsistent.

Are your stitches being held too far down the left-hand needle, causing you to stretch the stitches to get them off of the needle? Keep nudging the stitches to be worked up towards the tip of the needle to prevent stretching them.

Ridges across the work

Do you have ridges across your knitted fabric? If they are evenly spaced then either your knit or purl row is loose; usually it is the purl row. You may be noticing that when you come to knit a row the stitches are a bit loose so you knit tightly to compensate, but this just makes the problem worse.

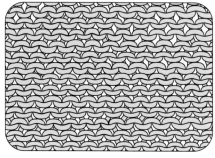

The best and easiest solution is to go back to basics and practise your purl (or knit) technique (pages 38–39). Time spent doing this will be rewarded with more even knitting.

A sure way to eliminate the problem is to work your looser row on a smaller needle. For example, if the pattern asks for 4mm (US 6) needles and your loose row is the purl row, then cast on and knit the first row with 4mm (US 6) needles. Now set one needle aside and pick up a 3.75mm (US 5) needle. Purl the next row with the smaller needle in your right hand. When knitting the next row, the larger needle will be in your right hand.

Uneven rib

Having the last stitch in each section of a rib larger than the others is quite a common problem on multiple stitch rib patterns (page 47).

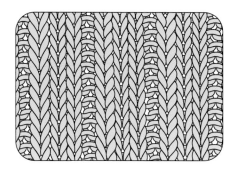

Here, you can clearly see that the last knit stitch is larger than the previous two. To fix this, when knitting the offending stitch, knit into the back of it. When purling the same stitch, wrap the yarn clockwise rather than anticlockwise around the needle.

Single ridge

A single ridge across the work could be the result of the knitting having been left for a while on the needles at that row, causing the stitches to stretch. If you do have to set a project aside for a while, always unravel (page 249) the last row worked when you start it again.

slanting work

You might find that one edge of your knitting is longer than the other edge, or that the whole piece is slanted, almost as if it were knitted on the bias (page 145).

One long edge

In this illustration you are looking straight at the knitting, not looking at it from the left. The left edge is longer than the right, making the perspective look odd.

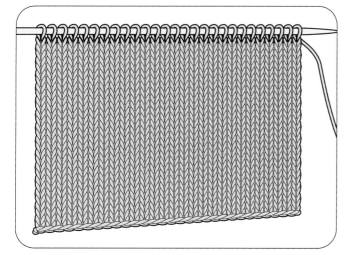

The most common cause of this problem lies at the start of the purl row; make sure you tighten your yarn a little more on the first stitch of the purl rows to correct it.

It can also occur when you finish a knit row and are about to start a purl row. When you have finished the last knit stitch, make sure you take the yarn to the back of the work before you turn the work ready for the purl stitch. This usually tightens the stitch and corrects the problem.

Blocking

Small differences in length can be corrected when blocking the piece (page 202). Use more pins than usual and ease the piece to the right shape.

Slanted fabric

If your piece of work slants along both edges, then there are two probable causes.

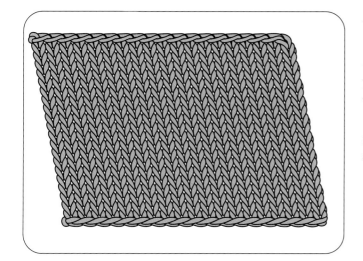

The most likely cause is the construction of the yarn. If it has been twisted too tightly, then knitting with it makes the work slant in this way. However, this can usually be spotted when you knit the tension (gauge) square, before you make the whole project.

If you are working in a stitch pattern, sometimes it is the pattern that causes the slant, especially if you are using lace stitches (pages 100–103) and twists (pages 94–95).

troubleshooting

altering length

If you have knitted the whole garment, then discovered it is too long or too short, you can rectify this without having to unravel the work and knit the piece again.

Lengthening a garment

This can be useful if a child has had a major growth spurt and you would like them to get more wear out of the garment you have knitted for them. It is always best to lengthen a garment just above the ribbing.

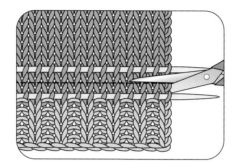

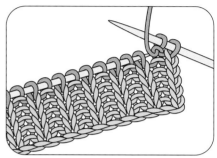

1 Thread a knitting needle through the stitches at the top of the ribbing, putting the needle through the right-hand (front) loop of every stitch. Thread another needle through a row about four rows above the first needle. Now comes the scary bit! Cut across the fabric between the two needles and unpick the yarn to each needle.

2 Work the extra length required onto the needle holding the rib, working any shaping that is required at the same time. When you have worked the additional length needed, graft the two pieces together (page 205).

Shortening a garment

You can shorten a garment by as much as you need using this technique. Firstly, work out how many rows you need to take out of the knitting.

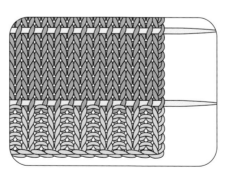

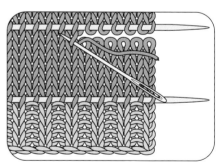

1 Thread a knitting needle through the stitches at the top of the ribbing, putting the needle through the right-hand (front) loop of every stitch. Thread another needle through the row at the top of the section you need to remove.

2 Cut the first stitch of the row below the upper needle and then unpick the stitches using a tapestry needle. Unravel the rows down to the needle at the top of the ribbing. Graft the two pieces together (page 205) with the unravelled yarn. Alternatively, re-knit the rib, working down from the upper needle.

correcting colour and cables

If you have worked a colour pattern or a cable design and only spotted a mistake once the knitting is finished, the idea of unravelling the work is so depressing. However, you can sometimes fix the problem without taking that drastic step.

Correcting colour work

If you have knitted an all-over Fair Isle pattern, this is how you can correct a mistake in the colour stitches.

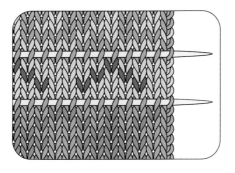

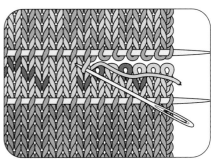

1 Find a single-colour row above the mistake. Thread a needle through the stitches of the row above this single-colour one, putting the needle through the right-hand (front) loop of every stitch. Thread another needle through the row below the mistake.

2 Cut a stitch on the single-coloured row and unpick the stitches across the row.

Practise first

If you do need to use this technique, practise it on a tension (gauge) swatch before correcting the project. As you unpick the stitches, keep trimming the tail of unpicked yarn short to prevent it snagging and tangling.

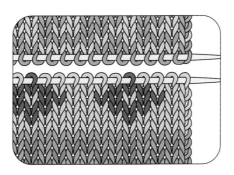

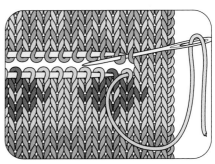

3 Unravel the stitches back to the lower needle. Work the correct pattern until you reach the row below the single-colour one.

4 Using the single colour, graft the two pieces together (page 205). The pattern is now corrected.

Correcting a cable

Another common mistake is to cross a cable the wrong way in an Aran design. This technique is a good way of correcting the twist, but work it carefully to prevent the knitting unravelling further than you want it to.

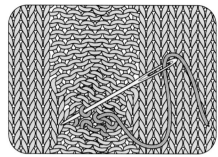

1 Carefully cut the centre stitch of the cable where it crosses. Unpick the stitches, leaving the ends of yarn loose on either side.

2 Lift up the lower stitches, which will become the top stitches. From the wrong side, graft the original stitches together (page 205). The cable is now corrected. Sew in the ends (page 200).

mending snags and holes

If you are unlucky enough to catch your sweater and pull out a stitch, or even tear a hole, don't despair, it can be mended.

Snags

The golden rule is never, never cut off a snag. The stitches will just unravel and before you know it there will be a big hole in your knitting. Firstly, just try gently stretching the fabric with your hands to see if the snag can be eased back into the fabric.

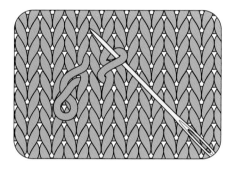

1 If stitches either side of the snag have been pulled tight, use a tapestry needle to re-shape them and take the excess yarn back into the fabric. Gently pull each stitch in turn, working back and forth across the row until the snag has disappeared.

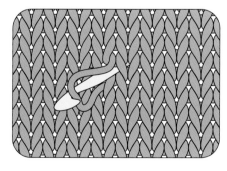

2 If you still have a loop, bring this to the wrong side using a crochet hook. Weave the loop into the back of the work in the same way as you would weave in an end (page 200).

Holes

When you have finished a project, don't just put any left over yarn into your stash. Keep some of it in a safe place so that if you do make a small hole in the project, you can repair it.

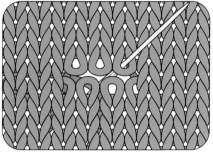

1 Thread a tapestry needle with the yarn the project was knitted in. Coming from the back, bring the needle through the centre of the stitch to the top right-hand side of the hole. Take the needle under the two loops of the stitch above, as you would in Swiss darning (page 184). Take it through to the back and then back through the centre of the first loose stitch loop.

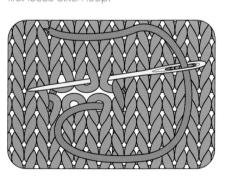

3 To work the next stitch, bring the needle through the next two stitches at the top of the hole.

2 Put the needle through the tops of two stitches at the bottom of the hole. Pull the yarn through to make a new stitch, making sure that it is the same size as one lying next to it. The technique is very similar to grafting (page 205).

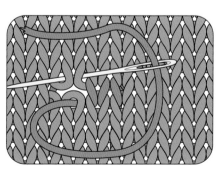

4 Continue working across the hole, mending one stitch at a time. Weave the ends in at the back of the work (page 200) when the hole is mended.

care of knitwear

Having spent time and money making a knitted project, it makes sense to look after it properly. If you keep a knitting journal, stick the ball band into it with your project notes as it will be useful when you come to launder the garment later on. If you don't keep a journal, try to keep the ball band, with a piece of the project yarn tied around it, in a safe place.

Washing

If the ball band says you should dry clean the yarn, then this is what you should do. If it states hand-washing as the cleaning method, then I usually wash the piece by hand but put it in the washing machine for a short spin, as holding a lot of water in the fabric for too long can damage or discolour it. I put the knitting in a wash bag and put a couple of old (but clean) towels in the machine with it so that it doesn't get thrown around the whole drum and so possibly stretched.

Bear in mind that the technique of felting (page 196) is based on washing your knitting at the wrong temperature!

Pressing

Always check your ball band to tell you if the yarn can be pressed or not. If it can be pressed and the knitting is smooth stocking (stockinette) stitch, place a damp cloth over the knitting and press with a hot iron, taking care not to drag the iron across the work. Some people just hold a steam iron about 10cm (4in) above the fabric and steam the pieces.

If your yarn contains mixed fibres, do not press it. Simply hold a steam iron fairly close to the surface and steam it. If you cannot press the yarn, then you can choose to spray it lightly with cold water (the spray guns used for indoor plants are ideal for this), but do not saturate it. Press the fabric smooth with a dry towel and your hands. You can actually felt your knitting by using too hot a temperature on wool yarn.

Storing

Care of your knitwear goes beyond washing and pressing into proper storage. Never store knitwear in plastic covers and always store it clean, as moths are attracted to dirt and oils. Chemical and natural moth repellents can be bought and it's worth using them if you are storing knitwear away for the whole summer. Fold your sweaters as shown here.

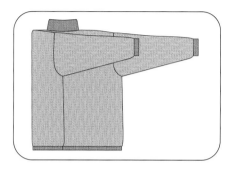

1 For a light to medium-weight sweater, place the sweater face down and fold the side seam to the centre of the back.

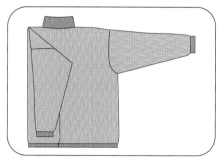

2 Fold the sleeve down and then fold the other side in the same way.

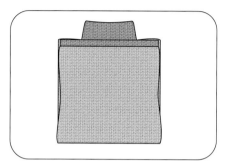

3 Fold the hem up to the shoulders.

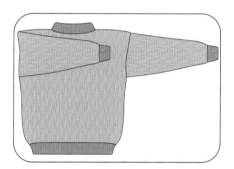

4 For a heavier-weight garment, place the sweater face down and fold one sleeve into the centre of the back.

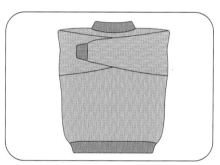

5 Fold the other sleeve over in the same way.

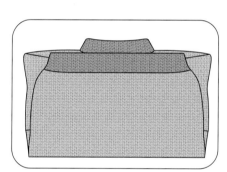

6 Fold the hem up to the shoulders. This way of folding gives you quite a wide garment to store, but it is fairly flat so you can store several sweaters on top of each other.

Hanging knitwear

Heavy knits shouldn't be hung as their own weight will stretch them. Fine knits should be hung on padded clothes hangers to prevent the hanger stretching the shoulder and creating a bump.

designing and adapting patterns

On a simple level, knitwear design is just working out the mathematics of shapes. When you understand how this is done, adapting patterns becomes easier and you feel more confident doing it, rather than just hoping that the project you are knitting is going to work out. The examples used in this chapter are garments, as they tend to be the most complex projects.

designing a garment

When designing your own garment you have the freedom to use any yarn you choose or even mix fibres together to make your own version of a yarn (page 21). You may be a spinner, in which case this chapter is a must for you.

Checking your tension (gauge) (page 18) is an element that everybody wants to, or does, miss out at the beginning of a pattern but to adjust or design a project it is essential.

Calculating stitches and rows for a square

Knit a tension (gauge) square in the yarn of your choice. You can use whatever texture you would like, but make sure the tension (gauge) square is knitted in the same stitch as the project. If you plan to have texture only on part of the garment, then you need to refer to page 275 to see how best to do this.

Once you have a finished tension (gauge) square, measure it (page 18) and establish how many stitches and rows there are to 10cm (4in). Always count any half stitches or rows as they do add up when the figures are multiplied up for a whole garment.

As an example I am going to use a tension (gauge) of 20 stitches and 28 rows to 10cm (4in) square. Divide those numbers by 10 (4) to find out how many stitches and rows there are to 1cm (1in): in this instance there are 2 (5) stitches and 2.8 (7) rows.

Using this information you can calculate the number of stitches you would need to cast on and the number of rows you would need to work to knit a square of the size shown right.

To calculate the number of stitches:
15 (6) x 2 (5)= 30 stitches
To calculate the number of rows:
25 (10) x 2.8 (7) = 70 rows

Knit your own tension (gauge) square, work out the stitches and rows per centimetre (inch) and then work out how many stitches and rows you would need to make the square shown right.

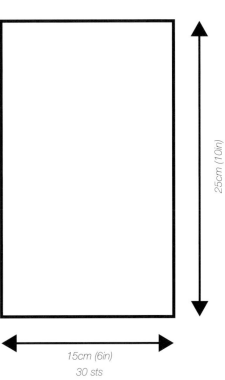

25cm (10in)

15cm (6in)

30 sts

Calculating stitches and rows for a symmetrically shaped piece

For a shaped piece of knitting, you have to work out how many decrease or increases you need to work.

Increase calculations

If you were increasing instead of decreasing you would work the sums in exactly the same way, but start out with the smaller measurement and add increase rows to get to the larger one.

You need to work out how many stitches to cast on, how many you want to end up with and so how many you need to decrease by. Then you need to know how many decrease rows there will be and at what intervals they will occur.

To calculate the number of stitches to cast on to make the piece shown right:
15 (6) x 2 (5) = 30 stitches

To calculate the number of stitches you want to end up with:
8 (3) x 2 (5) = 16 stitches (Round odd numbers up to an even number to produce symmetrical decreases).

To calculate the number of stitches you need to decrease by:
30 - 16 = 14 stitches

To calculate the number of decrease rows there will be:
For symmetry you decrease at both ends of the row, so you will need to work 7 decrease rows.

To calculate intervals of decrease rows:
25 (10) x 2.8 (7) = 70 rows
Divide the number of rows by the number of decrease rows
70 ÷ by 7 = 10. You will decrease every 10 rows. (If the number had a fraction you would need to round up or down to a whole number.)

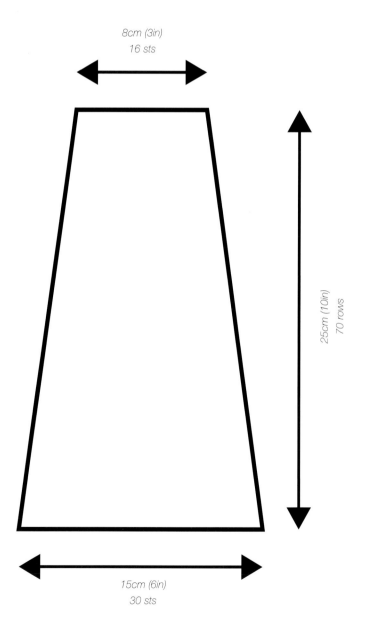

8cm (3in)
16 sts

25cm (10in)
70 rows

15cm (6in)
30 sts

designing and adapting patterns

Calculating stitches and rows for an asymmetrically shaped piece

If the shaping was only required on one side of the piece of work, then the calculations are slightly different.

To calculate the number of stitches to cast on to make the piece below:
15 (6) x 2 (5)= 30 stitches
To calculate the number of stitches you want to end up with:
4 (1$^{1}/_{2}$) x 2 (5) = 8 stitches (Round fractions up to a whole number).
To calculate the number of stitches you need to decrease by:
30 - 8 = 22 stitches
To calculate the number of rows to you must work:
20 (8) x 2.8 (7) = 56 rows
To calculate intervals of decrease rows:
56 ÷ 22 = 2.5. You will decrease every 2 rows. As you cannot decrease on fractions of a row, you must round up or down. Here, we are rounding down so the piece will be slightly shorter than planned. If you need the piece to be an exact length then you would need to plot out the decreases on graph paper (page 267).

4cm (1½in) 8 sts

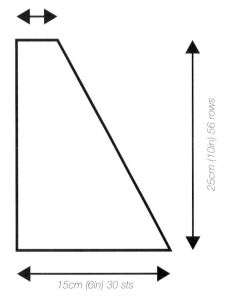

25cm (10in) 56 rows

15cm (6in) 30 sts

Calculating stitches and rows for a garment

Now you understand the basics of calculating stitches and rows, try out your mathematics on an actual garment shape. Here, you have basic shapes with all the measurements required to work out the stitches and rows needed to make your own sweater. Using the calculations on pages 262–264, have a go at working through the measurements to calculate the number of stitches and rows required for each piece. (The answers are at the bottom of the page).

Using the calculations on pages 262–264

Practice patterns

Practice drawing out garment shapes and photocopy those you are happy with for future use.

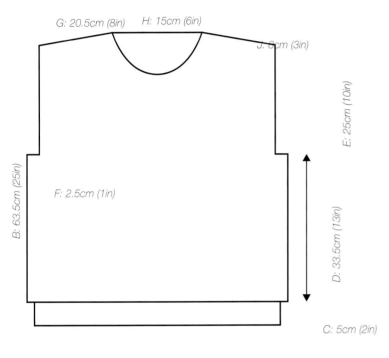

G: 20.5cm (8in)   H: 15cm (6in)
J: 8cm (3in)
E: 25cm (10in)
B: 63.5cm (25in)
F: 2.5cm (1in)
D: 33.5cm (13in)
C: 5cm (2in)
A: 61cm (24in)

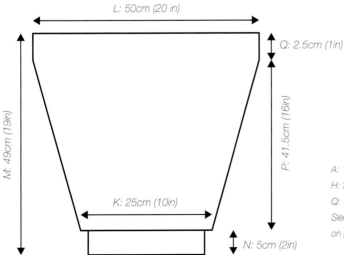

L: 50cm (20 in)
Q: 2.5cm (1in)
M: 49cm (19in)
P: 41.5cm (16in)
K: 25cm (10in)
N: 5cm (2in)

Tension: 20 sts and 28 rows to 10cm (4in)

Body
A:
B:
C:
D:
E:
F:
G:
H:
J:

Sleeve
K:
L:
M:
N:
P:

Sleeve increases
From __ sts to __ sts over __ rows.

A: 122 sts, B: 178 rows, C: 14 rows, D: 94 rows, E: 70 rows, F: 55 sts, G: 41 sts, H: 30 sts, J: 22 rows, K: 50 sts, L: 100 sts, M: 138 rows, N: 14 rows, P: 116 rows, Q: 7 rows.

Sleeve increases: 100 sts to 50 sts ÷ 2 = 25 increases. 116 rows ÷ 25 = 4.64. Plot on graph paper or try decreases on alternate 4th and 5th rows.

designing and adapting patterns

Graphing out a garment

Once you have worked out the stitches, rows and increases and decreases you must draw out the garment on graph paper to double check your calculations and make sure all the increases and decreases work out symmetrically. You can use ordinary graph paper, not knitter's graph paper (page 155) to do this on.

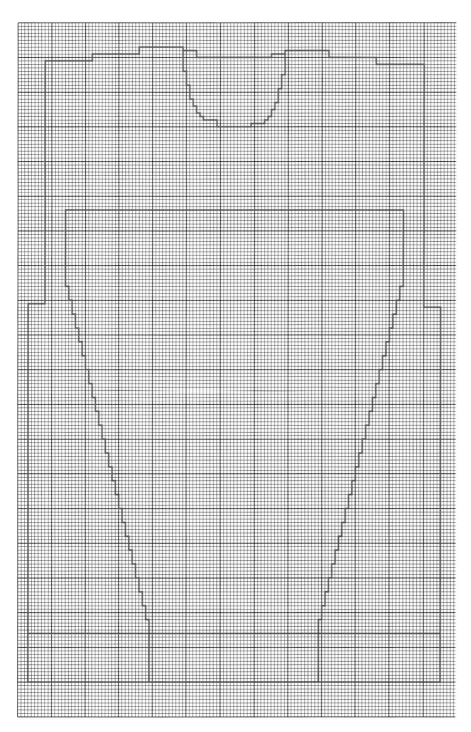

Here, you can see the garment shapes from page 265 plotted out on graph paper to give you an idea how they should look. To save space, the sleeve is plotted inside the body shape. If you have made an error in your calculations it will often show up when you are plotting out the garment, as a piece will be oddly shaped.

designing and
adapting patterns

shaping

As well as the overall shape of the garment, you need to be able to work out shaping for specific areas. When working out curved shapes on graph paper, draw the curve in pencil and then draw over it in pen, translating the curve into squares. For symmetrical curves, draw one side and translate it, then copy the translation for the other side.

Waist shaping

The principles used to work out the stitches and rows for a simple garment (page 265) also apply to a shaped garment. Here is a garment shaped before and after the waist. Calculate how many decreases need to be worked over how many rows before the waist; how many rows must be worked straight at the waist; how many increases need to be worked over how many rows after the waist. (The answers are at the bottom of the page.)

Tension: 20 sts and 28 rows to 10cm (4in)

A:
B:
C:
D:
E:
F:
Decreases: from __ sts to __ sts over __ rows.
Increases: from __ sts to __ sts over __ rows.

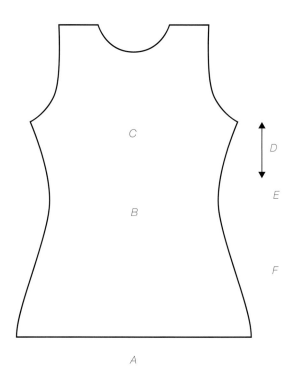

Neck shaping

To plot the neck shaping, first plan the shoulders and the back neck stitches. The width of the lowest part of the front neck is usually about a third of the number of stitches on the back neck. Plot this width on the graph paper at the desired depth of the neckline. Draw a curved line on one side, joining the front neck to the shoulders. Translate this into squares on the graph paper, then copy this translation for the other side of the neck.

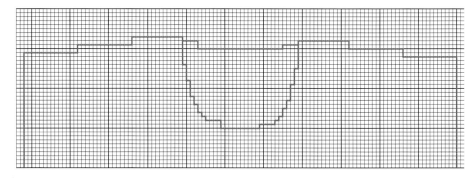

A: 81 sts, B: 61 sts, C: 81 sts, D: 28 rows, E: 14 rows, F: 64 rows.

Decreases: 81 sts - 61 sts = 20 sts. 20 ÷ 2 = 10 decreases. 64 ÷ 10 = 6.4. Plot on graph paper or try decreases on every 6th row.

Increases: 10 increases needed to get back to 81 sts but over 28 rows. 28 ÷ 10 = 2.8. Plot on graph paper or try decreases on alternate 2nd and 3rd rows.

Armhole shaping

Sometimes you need to treat this separately on another drawing, as shown here.

The general rule is that the curve inwards under the arm from the side seam covers the same distance as the curve up before you work straight to the shoulder, as indicated by the arrows on the illustration below.

The armhole then needs to be plotted onto graph paper to create a smoothly curved pattern you can follow.

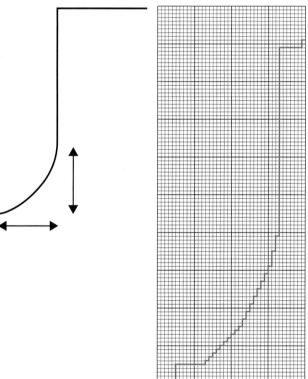

Fitted sleeve shaping

When designing a more fitted garment, you will require a more fitted sleeve head.

On a sleeve you firstly need to establish the number of stitches you have after all the increases. Then you decrease the same number of stitches as for the first two rows of the back and front armhole shaping.

You then calculate how deep the sleeve head has to be: this is usually two-thirds of the armhole depth. For example, if the armhole is 15cm (6in) deep, then the sleeve head should be 10cm (4in) deep (C).

Plot the position of the top of the sleeve head on the chart and allow approximately 8cm (3in) in width for the top of the sleeve cap (B). Draw a curved line to join one edge of the sleeve cap to the underarm decreases and translate that into squares on the graph paper. Copy the translation to plot the other side of the sleeve head.

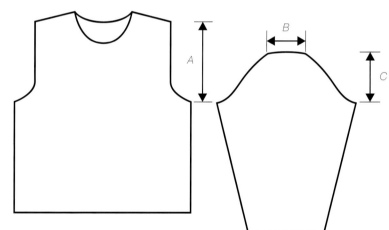

Taking measurements

You can always take the measurements of a favourite garment in your wardrobe and make a working drawing from them that you can then translate onto graph paper. Another place to get measurements from as a starting point is a dress-making pattern.

altering a pattern

When working from an existing pattern you need to be able to extract the information you need to make the alterations required.

Extracting information from a pattern

You need to know what the original measurements are that the pattern knits up to before you can alter them.

Some patterns have diagrams that show you measurements for elements such as the width, length, sleeve length, which are always a helpful start. If your pattern doesn't have a diagram then you need to make one. You don't have to be an artist, this is a working drawing that only you are going to see. Even if there is a diagram, you may need to add measurements to it to get all the information you need.

To do this, read through the pattern and note down as much detail as necessary. You will need to extract elements such as the depth of the armhole, the back neck measurement and the shoulder measurements.

You will need to know the pattern tension and in this sample pattern it is 22 sts and 30 rows to 10cm (4in), which is 2.2 (5.5) sts and 3 (7.5) rows to 1cm (1in). These are the measurements used in the calculations below. The first size is referred to throughout, but the same principles apply for any size.

The length and width are given on the diagram, but the body is shaped and you need to know the lengths of the shaped areas. You have to go from 97 sts to 85 sts which is a loss of 12 sts, but you decrease at both ends of the row, so 6 decrease rows. The first decrease row is the 13th row then there will be 5 more sets of 6 rows, which equals 43 rows. 43 ÷ by 3 = 14cm (5¾in).

There are then 7 rows straight: 7 ÷ by 3 = 2.5cm (1in).

Then increase back up to 93 sts, which is only an increase of 8 sts so makes 4 increase rows, which equals 19 rows. 19 ÷ 3 = 6cm (2½in).

Continue straight until back measures 32cm (12¾in). 32 - 14 - 2.5 - 6 = 9.5cm (3¾in) of straight knitting. You are now able to recalculate those measurements or alter them as needed.

The armhole is 18cm (7in) long.

For the width of the back neck, always look at the shoulder shapings; here it tells you to cast off 31 sts. 31 ÷ 2.2 = 14cm (5¾in).

SIZE

8	10	12	14	16	18	20	22	
To fit bust								
82	87	92	97	102	107	112	117	cm
32	34	36	38	40	42	44	46	in

YARN
Details of yarn
Number of balls x 50gm

NEEDLES
1 pair 3¼mm (no 9) (US 5) needles

TENSION
22 sts and 30 rows to 10 cm measured over stocking stitch using 3¼mm (US 5) needles.

BACK
Using 3¼mm (US 5) needles cast on 97 [101: 105: 111: 119: 125: 131: 139] sts.
Beg with a K row, work in st st, shaping side seams by dec 1 st at each end of 13th and every foll 6th row until 85 [89: 93: 99: 107: 113: 119: 127] sts rem.
Work 7 rows, ending with RS facing for next row.
Inc 1 st at each end of next and every foll 6th row until there are 93 [97: 101: 107: 115: 121: 127: 135] sts.
Cont straight until back meas 32 [32: 31: 34: 33: 35: 34: 36] cm, ending with RS facing for next row.
Shape armholes
Cast off 4 [5: 5: 6: 6: 7: 7: 8] sts at beg of next 2 rows.
85 [87: 91: 95: 103: 107: 113: 119] sts.**
Dec 1 st at each end of next 3 [3: 5: 5: 7: 7: 9: 9] rows, then on foll 3 [3: 2: 2: 3: 3: 2: 4] alt rows.
73 [75: 77: 81: 83: 87: 91: 93] sts.
Cont straight until armhole meas 18 [18: 19: 19: 20: 20: 21: 21] cm, ending with RS facing for next row.
Shape back neck
Next row (RS): K21 [22: 23: 25: 25: 27: 29: 30] and turn, leaving rem sts on a holder.
Work each side of neck separately.
Dec 1 st at neck edge of next 4 rows.
17 [18: 19: 21: 21: 23: 25: 26] sts.
Work 1 row, ending with RS facing for next row.
Shape shoulder
Cast off.
With RS facing, rejoin yarn to rem sts, cast off centre 31 [31: 31: 31: 33: 33: 33: 33] sts, K to end.
Complete to match first side, reversing shapings.

FRONT
Work as given for back to **.**
Divide for neck
Next row (RS): K2tog, K40 [41: 43: 45:

49: 51: 54: 57] and turn, leaving rem sts on a holder.
Work each side of neck separately.
Dec 1 st at armhole edge of next 2 [2: 4: 4: 6: 6: 8: 8] rows, then on foll 3 [3: 2: 2: 3: 3: 2: 4] alt rows **and at same time** dec 1 st at neck edge of 2nd and every foll 9 [9: 7: 7: 6: 6: 4: 2] alt rows, then on every foll 4th row until 17 [18: 19: 21: 21: 23: 25: 26] sts rem.
Cont straight until front matches back to shoulder cast-off, ending with RS facing for next row.
Shape shoulder
Cast off.
With RS facing, rejoin yarn to rem sts, K2tog, K to last 2 sts, K2tog.
Complete to match first side, reversing shapings.

SLEEVES
Using 3¼mm (US 5) needles cast on 53 [53: 55: 55: 57: 57: 59: 59] sts.
Beg with a K row, work in st st, shaping sides by inc 1 st at each end of 7th [7th: 7th: 7th: 7th: 7th: 5th: 5th] and every foll 8th [8th: 8th: 8th: 8th: 8th: 6th] row to 59 [69: 67: 77: 77: 87: 89: 69] sts, then on every foll 10th [10th: 10th: 10th: 10th: -: -: 8th] row until there are 77 [79: 81: 83: 85: -: -: 91] sts.
Cont straight until sleeve meas 43 [43: 44: 44: 45: 45: 44: 44] cm, ending with RS facing for next row.
Shape top
Cast off 4 [5: 5: 6: 6: 7: 7: 8] sts at beg of next 2 rows.
69 [69: 71: 71: 73: 73: 75: 75] sts.
Dec 1 st at each end of next 5 rows, then on every foll alt row to 29 sts, then on foll 3 rows, ending with RS facing for next row.
23 sts.
Cast off 4 sts at beg of next 2 rows.
Cast off rem 15 sts.

MAKING UP
Press as described on the information page.
Join both shoulder seams using back stitch, or mattress stitch if preferred.
Lace trim
Using 3¼mm (US 5) needles cast on 30 sts.
Row 1 (RS): sl 1, K3, (yfwd, K2tog) 7 times, yfwd, K2.
21 sts.
Row 2: Knit.
Row 3: sl 1, K6, (yfwd, K2tog) 6 times, yfwd, K2.
22 sts.
Row 4: Knit.
Row 5: sl 1, K9, (yfwd, K2tog) 5 times, yfwd, K2.
23 sts.

Row 6: Knit.
Row 7: sl 1, K12, (yfwd, K2tog) 4 times, yfwd, K2.
24 sts.
Row 8: Knit.
Row 9: sl 1, K23.
Row 10: cast off 4 sts, K to end.
20 sts.
These 10 rows form patt.
Cont in patt until trim, when slightly gathered, is long enough to fit up centre front, from cast-on edge to base of V neck, and around entire neck edge, ending after patt row 10 and with RS facing for next row.
Cast off.
Using photograph as a guide, sew lace trim in place.
See information page for finishing instructions, setting in sleeves using the set-in method.

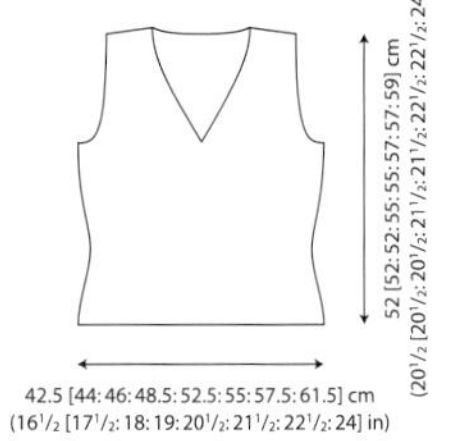

To alter sleeve length you need to know how many stitches you start with and end up with before shaping the top. Here, you start with 53 sts. 53 ÷ 2.2 = 24cm (9½in).

After all the increases there are 77 sts. 77 ÷ 2.2 = 35cm (14in). You can now make the alterations you need or work in the yarn of your choice.

Altering length

This is an easy alteration to make, though where you add the length depends on the style of the garment.

If a garment is straight-sided, then the length needs to be added or decreased between the top of the welt and the bottom of the armhole (A).

If the garment is shaped, you need to work out where you require the alteration. Unless you are completely happy with the shaping and just want the hem to be lower, it is usually best to add or subtract length between your waist and the nape of your neck (B). Measure yourself (page 70) then decide on the finished measurement of the garment. You will then have to re-calculate either the decreases and increases (page 265).

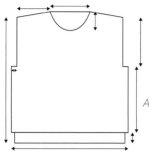

Altering width

On a plain garment this is very easy, but on a patterned one – either colour or texture patterning – it can be trickier. First of all you need to establish how much width in centimetres (inches) you need to either gain or loose.

Work out the tension (gauge) of your fabric and calculate how many stitches there are to 1cm (1in) (page 262). Work out how many stitches to gain or loose by multiplying the number of centimetres (inches) you want to alter by the number of stitches per centimetre (inch). This is all you need to do if the garment is plain in design, but if there is a pattern you may have to look at pattern repeats and adjust the stitches accordingly. Think of the patterns as panels and increase or decrease stitches between them.

Once you have calculated the number of stitches you need to add or remove, and if the alteration isn't too much, you can usually work the armhole shapings as the pattern tells you, making sure you have added or taken away the number of stitches you have adjusted by at every stage. When it comes to the shoulders and back neck, it is best to distribute the extra or fewer stitches equally across them, taking the same number away from each shoulder and the neck, as shown right.

Adding stitches

If you are adding extra stitches to make a plus size, measure the width of your back from shoulder to shoulder, as you will often find that you don't need the extra width across your shoulders. In this instance you will need to decrease more stitches at the armholes so that the shoulder seams don't hang down over your shoulders, making you look wider than you actually are.

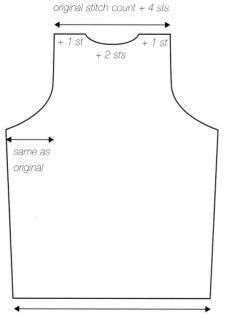

original stitch count + 4 sts

+ 1 st   *+ 1 st*

+ 2 sts

same as original

original stitch count 52 sts + 4 sts: 2 sts on each side

designing and adapting patterns

Altering sleeve length

First of all establish the length of sleeve you require. If possible, it is best to knit the front and back of the garment, tack them together and try it on. You then know exactly where the armhole is going to fall and you can measure from the armhole to the cuff.

Once you have the length, work out how long the cuff is going to be and take this measurement off the overall length. You now need to re-calculate the decreases for the sleeve (page 265), keeping the armhole and sleeve top the same as the pattern.

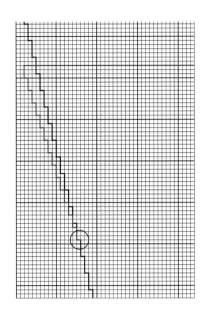

Altering a neckline

Necklines are sometimes the deciding factor as to whether you like the sweater or not. I have had many knitters say to me, 'I would love to make that sweater but I don't like the high neck', or, 'I would like to make this cardigan but would prefer one with a collar rather than a crew neck'. What they often don't realise is that whether the sweater has a crew neck or a turtle neck, the same neckline lies underneath. Here are some examples of what you can achieve by simply knitting the actual neckband differently, but keeping the neck shaping instructions given in the pattern.

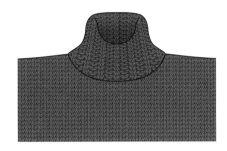

The four neckbands on this page all sit on top of a basic crew neckline. For this polo neck, you pick up stitches as you would for a crew neck, but continue in rib until the fabric is long enough to fold over.

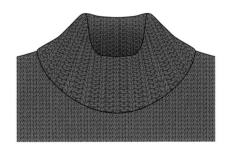

To work a cowl neck, pick up stitches as for a crew neck. Work half the length of the neckband in rib, then change to larger needles and rib until the fabric is long enough to fold over.

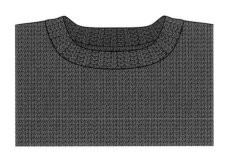

To work a classic crew neckband, simply pick up the stitches and work 4cm (1½in) in rib.

For a collar, start picking up the stitches at the centre front. Work backwards and forwards in your chosen stitch until the collar is the desired length.

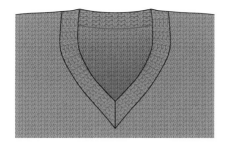 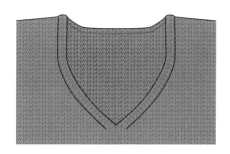 

These three necks are based on a simple V neckline. For this traditional V-neck, pick up stitches and work in rib. The stitches are mitred at the front point using the tight inner corner technique (page 143).

This more contemporary V-neck is worked in the same way, but without the mitred shaping at the front.

For a V-neck with a rolled edge, pick up stitches and work a few rows in rib. Change to stocking (stockinette) stitch for a few more rows, then cast (bind) off loosely. The stocking (stockinette) stitch section will roll over the rib section.

However, if the neck is too wide, or perhaps not wide enough, then you will need to do more than alter the neckband. The width of the neck is determined by the width of the back neck. Plot the pattern neck shapings onto graph paper (page 268) and then determine how you want to alter them. It's worth measuring

something that fits you well around the neck as well as measuring the drop of the neck. Plot the new neck shapings on the same graph paper using a different colour pen. You then need to re-calculate how many stitches to pick up around the neck.

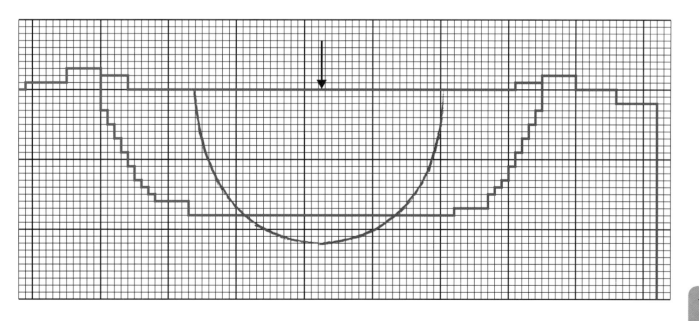

designing and adapting patterns

designing with colour and texture

Designing with colour

When designing with colour you need to think of the balance of colours used and the placement of the patterns. A starting point is to decide on the width of a border. Draw the pattern onto graph paper and then plot it accurately to make a chart you can knit from. If it is a repeat pattern, plot out one repeat then copy it.

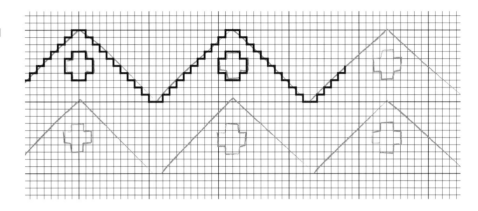

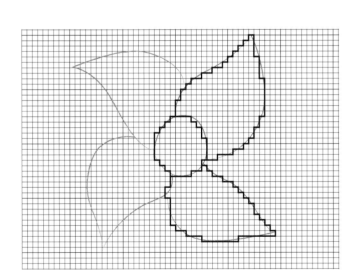

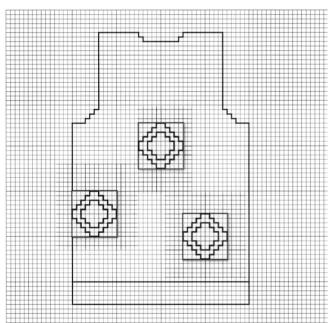

Chart a motif in the same way, drawing out the shape you want and then translating that into squares to make a chart. This is particularly important if you are designing a curving, flowing shape rather than a geometric one.

To decide how to position motifs on a garment, graph out the body shape you require. Graph out the individual motifs, cut them out and place them on the graphed body so you can see how they will look. When you are happy with the positions, either stick the cut out motifs in position, or copy them onto the graphed body.

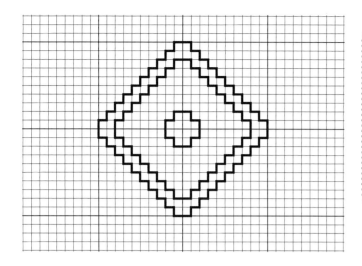

Colour motifs

When designing colour motifs you must remember that a knitted stitch is not square (page 154). Chart the motif onto knitter's graph paper if need be and then copy it onto squared graph paper to chart it onto a plotted garment shape.

Another way of using colour in a design is to use it as an accent. Consider knitting pocket linings in a contrast colour (pages 128–129), or choose a different colour for the garment welts and neckband (page 221). You don't have to add much to enliven an otherwise plain pattern.

Designing with texture

Unfortunately, you can't just choose a plain sweater pattern and knit it in rib or put a cable onto it.

As most textures have a different tension (gauge), you will need to calculate the extra stitches required to make up the width. This also applies to the other way around, too. If you like the shape of a textured garment but knit it plain, it will knit up too big. Always do a tension (gauge) for the texture you plan to work with and re-calculate the number of stitches you will need (page 265).

If the texture you want to use isn't an all-over pattern, or consists of several different stitches – for example, in an Aran design – you will need to swatch each texture and map out how they will be laid out on the garment in the same way you would for the placing of colour motifs (opposite). Bear in mind that when sampling for an Aran you will need to work at least half of the garment to make sure it will be the right width.

How much yarn will you need?

There isn't an easy way of instantly working out how much yarn you are going to need for a project.

If you are faced with the dilemma of standing in a scrumptious yarn shop a long way from home and have fallen in love with a particular yarn, then you can get an idea of how much you might need by looking at existing designs the shop has for that yarn. You may not like the designs, but it will give you an idea of how much you can knit from one ball of the yarn. Some yarns are great and actually tell you on the ball band what the average requirement is for a garment in that yarn.

Always buy at least one ball more than you think you will need; there is little worse than running out of yarn just before you finish a project and not being able to go back for more. Any leftovers can always join your stash (every knitter's secret source of joy and guilt) and get used in a smaller or multi-yarn project.

If you are able to buy just one ball of yarn and go back for the rest, then you can calculate your needs properly. Firstly, you must knit a 10cm (4in) square piece of fabric, making the measurements as precise as possible. Either weigh this swatch or unravel it and measure how much yarn you have used.

You then have to calculate how many 10cm (4in) squares will fit into the surface area of the garment you want to make. Multiply that number by the length or the weight of the swatch and you have the amount required in either weight or length. The ball band should tell you both the weight of the ball and the length of yarn in a ball, so you can then calculate how many balls you will need.

designing and adapting patterns

crochet for knitting

In this chapter I don't aim to teach you everything there is to know about crochet, as this is a knitting manual. However, it is becoming more popular for designers to put crocheted edgings and motifs on garments and I am often asked to show people how they can do this, too. So here you will find the basic crochet stitches, plus some decorative techniques, to enable you to expand your knitting horizons.

getting started

Crochet uses just one hook and the yarn, so as a knitter you shouldn't find the techniques difficult to master. Practise all the stitches on spare yarn before you start adding crochet to a knitted fabric, though it is easy enough to pull the crochet stitches out if you make a mistake.

Holding the hook and yarn

As with knitting, everybody will have their own way of holding the crochet hook and if you are just learning to crochet, don't get too hung up about holding it properly.

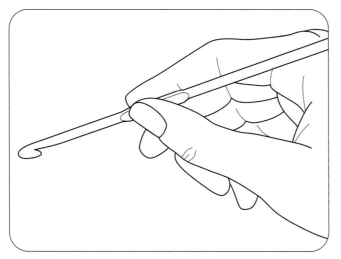

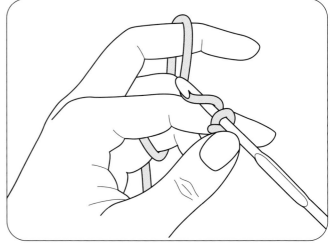

1 Hold the hook in your right hand, holding it like a pen. Grip it lightly with finger and thumb on the flat section (if there is one) of the handle. If you are left-handed, hold it the same way, but in your left hand.

2 The other hand has to hold the yarn and for crochet it always feeds from the left. This can be difficult if you haven't used your left hand for holding yarn before. Wrap the yarn around your little finger to keep it in position and then bring it up over your second and index fingers. Left-handers should try holding the yarn in their right hands.

Holding the chain

As the chain grows, hold it with your left thumb and index finger just under the hook to help control the tension (gauge) of the stitches.

Slip knot

You need to make a slip knot on the hook in order to start work. With crochet it is important for the slip knot to tighten by pulling the tail end of the yarn rather than the ball end.

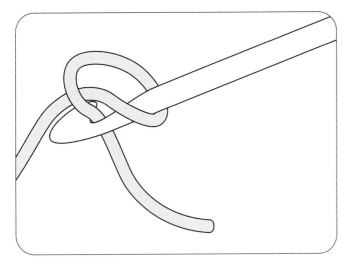

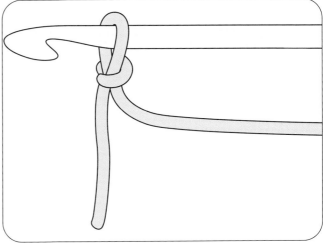

1 Lay the tail end of the yarn over the ball end to make a loop. Put the hook through the loop and pull a loop of the tail end through.

2 Pull the tail end of the yarn until the loop fits snugly around the hook.

crochet stitches

Crochet looks scary to novices, but actually all the stitches have the same action, it is just the number of times you go though the loops that decides which stitch you make. The different stitches are of different heights and the varying heights of the stitches are used to create the decorative designs.

Chain stitch

Chain stitch is the first crochet stitch you need to learn.
It is used in a similar way to the cast on row of knitting.

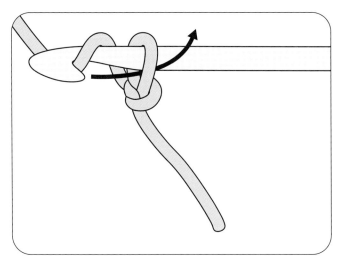

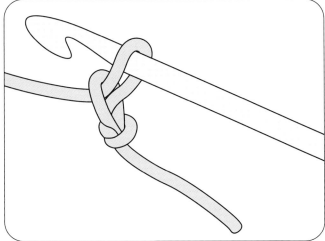

1 With a slip knot on the hook, wrap the yarn over the hook in an anticlockwise direction.

2 Pull the wrapped yarn through the stitch on the hook, forming a new loop. Tighten the loop on the hook, but not too tightly. Repeat this action until you have made as many chains as required.

Slip stitch (ss) [slip stitch (sl st)]

Slip stitch is the shortest of the crochet stitches and is mainly used to travel over a number of stitches without gaining any height. It is also used to join circles when working in a round (page 286).

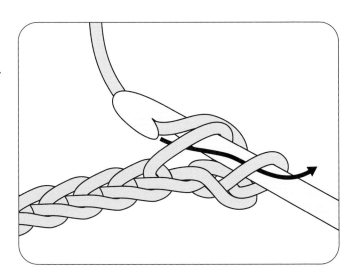

1 Put the hook into the stitch where the slip stitch is required: it is shown here working into a chain. Wrap the yarn around the hook and draw a loop through both of the stitches on the hook.

Double crochet (dc) [single crochet (sc)]

For this stitch you draw the loop through one stitch and then
through two.

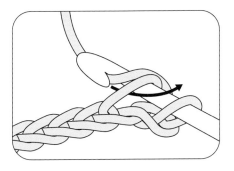 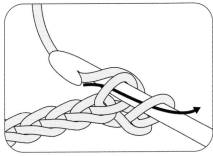 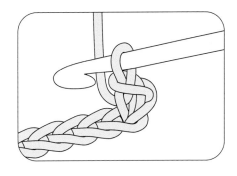

1 Put the hook into the stitch where
the double crochet is required: it is
shown here working into a chain. Wrap
the yarn around the hook and draw a loop
through the first stitch on the hook. There
are two loops on the hook.

2 Wrap the yarn around the hook
again and this time draw the loop
through both stitches on the hook. There
is one loop on the hook.

3 One double (single) crochet has
been made.

Dc (sc) crochet fabric.

Htr (hdc) crochet fabric.

Half treble (htr) [half double crochet (hdc)]

This stitch involves wrapping the yarn around the hook
before putting the hook through a stitch, rather like a
yarnover (pages 100–103) in knitting.

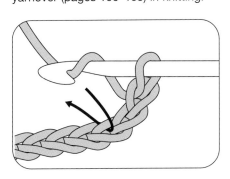 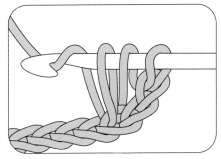 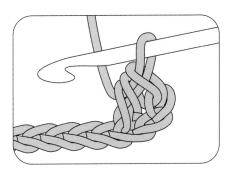

1 Wrap the yarn around the hook
before putting it into the stitch. Put
the hook into the place needed: if you are
working along a chain, it would be the
third chain from the hook.

2 Wrap the yarn around the hook
again and draw a loop through the
first stitch on the hook. There are three
loops on the hook.

3 Wrap the yarn around the hook
for a third time and draw a loop
through all three stitches on the hook.
One half treble (half double crochet) has
been made.

Treble (tr) [double crochet (dc)]

Here you wrap the yarn around the hook four times in total to make one stitch.

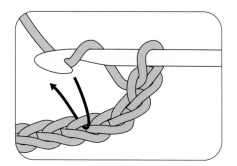

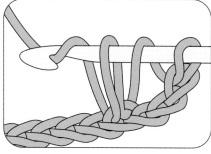

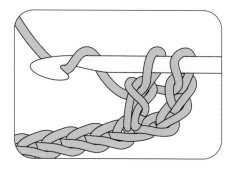

1 Wrap the yarn around the hook before putting it into the stitch. Put the hook into the place needed: if you are working along a chain, it would be the fourth chain from the hook.

2 Wrap the yarn around the hook again and draw a loop through the first stitch on the hook. There are three loops on the hook.

3 Wrap the yarn around the hook for a third time and draw a loop through the first two stitches on the hook. There are two loops on the hook.

4 Wrap the yarn around the hook for a fourth time and draw a loop through the remaining two stitches on the hook. One treble (double crochet) has been made.

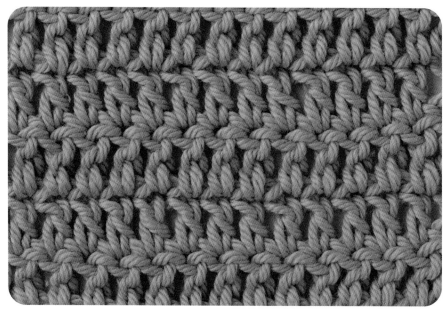

Tr (dc) crochet fabric.

 Following patterns

Don't try to follow a crochet pattern to start with, just practise going in and out of stitches and then go on to a pattern when you feel a little more confident.

Double treble (dtr) [treble (tr)]

Five separate wraps around the hook are needed to make this stitch.

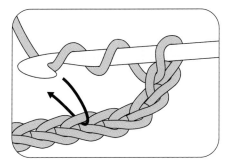

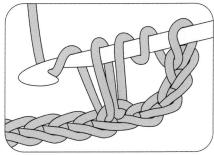

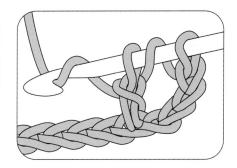

1 Wrap the yarn around the hook twice before putting it into the stitch. Put the hook into the place needed: if you are working along a chain, it would be the fifth chain from the hook.

2 Wrap the yarn around the hook again and draw a loop through the first stitch on the hook. There are four loops on the hook.

3 Wrap the yarn around the hook for a third time and draw a loop through the first two stitches on the hook. Wrap the yarn around the hook for a fourth time and draw a loop through the next two stitches on the hook. There are two loops on the hook.

4 Wrap the yarn around the hook for a fifth time and draw a loop through the remaining two stitches on the hook. One double treble (treble) has been made.

Placing the hook

When you are working a stitch into a chain, always put the hook under the upper loop of the chain. If you are working into a previous stitch, turn to page 288 to see where to place the hook.

Dtr (tr) crochet fabric.

Triple treble (trtr) [double treble (dtr)]

After the first multiple wrap, you repeat an action four times to complete this stitch.

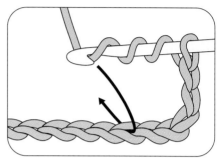  

1 Wrap the yarn around the hook three times before putting it into the stitch. Put the hook into the place needed: if you are working along a chain, it would be the sixth chain from the hook. Wrap the yarn around the hook and draw it through the first loop on the hook.

2 Wrap the yarn around the hook and draw a loop through two stitches on the hook.

3 Repeat the last step three more times till one stitch remains on the hook. One triple treble (double treble) has been made.

Trtr (dtr) crochet fabric.

Tension (gauge)

If you are struggling to keep the tension (gauge) of your crochet even when holding the yarn in your left hand, try holding the yarn in your right hand, as for knitting the English way (page 36).

Crochet along a knitted edge

Most often you will use crochet to work a decorative border along the edge of a piece of knitted fabric. The number of knitted stitches left between each stitch the hook is put into will vary depending on both the size of the knitted stitches and the crochet pattern you are working, but the principle is always the same. The technique is shown here with double (single) crochet worked into every stitch.

Double (single) crochet across stitches

This is how you would add a crochet border to the cast on or cast (bound) off edge of a knitted fabric.

Corners

If you need to work around a corner, especially if you were working around the edge of a blanket, you would need to work three double (single) crochets into the same stitch to turn the corner neatly.

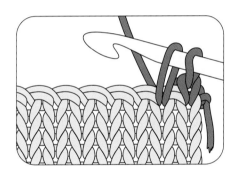

1 Put the hook into the top of the knitted stitch, wrap the yarn around the hook and draw a loop through. Repeat on the following knitted stitch, so you have two crochet stitches on the hook.

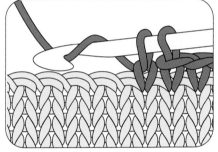

2 Wrap the yarn around the hook again and draw a loop through both crochet stitches. One double (single) crochet has been made. Repeat the steps across the edge.

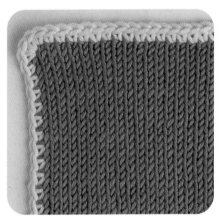

Dc (sc) edge on stocking (stockinette) stitch.

Double (single) crochet across row ends

Here you can see the same technique being worked across the row ends of knitted fabric.

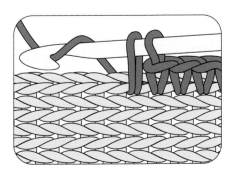

Work exactly the same way as for across stitches, making sure that the edging is lying flat and not too fluted or pulled in.

rows and rounds

Crochet is worked in two basic ways, back and forth in rows or round and round in circles. From a knitter's point of view, working in rows will be the technique you probably use most often to add borders to projects. However, working rounds allows you to make circular motifs that can be appliquéd to knitting to great effect.

Working in rows

When working in rows you usually start by making a chain – which works like a cast on row in knitting – and then you work into the chain in the stitch required. The stitch you are about to use will determine which chain you put the hook into first.

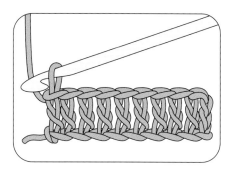

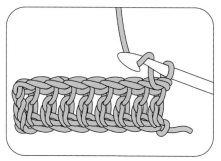

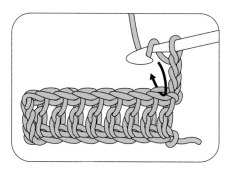

1 If you were working a double (single) crochet (page 281) you would need to start in the second chain from the hook to enable the stitch to stand upright. Subsequent double (single) crochet stitches are worked into every chain stitch.

2 At the end of the row you need to turn the work. Before you start the next row you have to make a turning chain. This will enable the first stitch on the next row to stand upright. If you don't work turning chains you will end up with badly shaped edges.

3 The length of the chain depends on the stitch you are about to use: the turning chain will count as one stitch of the row. Here are the numbers of chains you need to make for the turning chain at the end of a row to accommodate different stitches.

Double (single) crochet = 2 chain
Half treble (half double crochet) = 2 chain
Treble (double crochet) = 3 chain
Double treble (treble) = 4 chain
Triple treble (double treble) = 5 chain

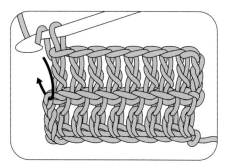

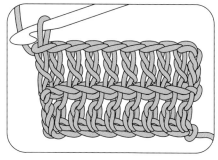

4 When you have worked across the whole row you must do the last stitch into the top of the previous turning chain, as shown here.

5 You are now ready to work the turning chain for the next row. The stitches in all rows should stand upright and the edges should be neat and straight.

Rows worked in coloured stripes.

Working in the round

For crochet motifs and to make lovely corsages you would need to work in the round.

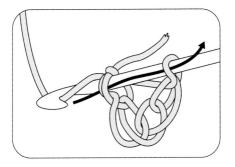

1 Make a chain of three or more stitches and join them together using a slip stitch (page 280) into the very first chain.

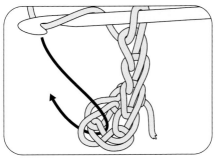

2 To start the first round, you must make a starting chain, for exactly the same reasons and in exactly the same way as you make a turning chain on rows (opposite). Always put the hook into each chain on the first round.

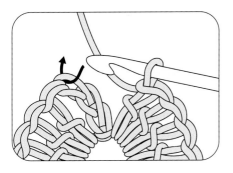

3 When you have completed your round you will slip stitch into the top of the starting chain, as shown here, to join the round.

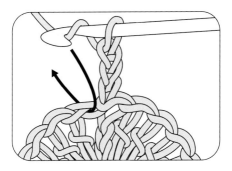

4 When working subsequent rounds you will need to increase in order to make the motif lie flat. Therefore, the pattern will tell you to make a number of stitches into the same stitch of the previous row.

A circular medallion.

placing the hook

When I learnt to crochet, the hardest part was to understand where to put the hook to make the stitches. However, there are actually only two places it can go to create most patterns.

Under a loop

There are two loops at the top of each stitch in the previous row or round you have worked. The pattern may ask you to work into the front or the back loop, depending on the effect you are creating or the stitch being worked.

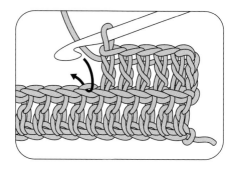

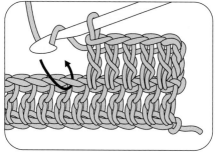

1 Here the hook will be put through the back loop.

2 In this illustration you can see that it will be put through the front loop.

Placing the hook

As you can see from the illustrations on the left, the look of the fabric is affected by where you place the hook. If the text does not say where to place the hook, then put it under both loops of the stitch.

In a chain space

The chain space means the space made by making a chain. When you are asked to work into a chain space you place your hook right under the chain and not into any loops.

If you look at the base of the shells making up the second row of the crochet, you can see that the stitches wrap right around the tops of the shells in the previous row. This is because the hook was put into the top of the lower shell, under the chain, not through its loops.

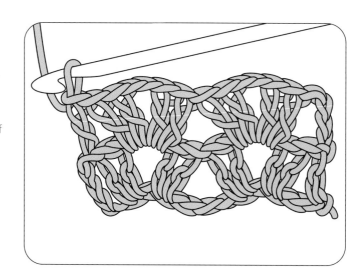

changing yarn

As with knitting, unless a crochet project is very small you will need to join in a new ball of yarn at some point. You will also need to join in new yarn if you are changing colours.

Joining in new yarn to start in the middle of a row

If the pattern has asked you to fasten off and begin again in a different place, use this technique.

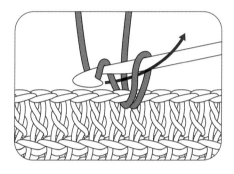

Put the hook through the stitch and draw a loop through, then just start working the stitch. After working the next few stitches, weave in the tail end to secure it.

Joining in new yarn to continue a pattern

When joining in new yarn because the ball has run out and you need to continue in the same colour, use this technique. (The new yarn is shown here in a different colour so that you can easily see what is happening.)

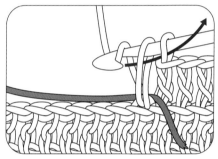

1   When you have about 30cm (12in) of the old yarn left, lay the tail of the new yarn across the tops of the stitches and work the next few stitches over it, trapping it into the work.

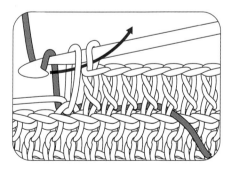

2   When wrapping the yarn around the hook to complete a stitch, wrap it around the new yarn instead of the old yarn. Work the next few stitches over the tail of old yarn, trapping it into the work.

Changing colour

A different technique is needed to join in a new colour yarn. It is shown here on double (single) crochet, but the principle is the same for all stitches.

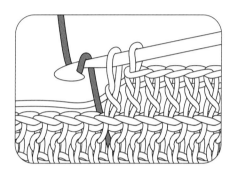

1   Work to the stitch before the colour change. Work the next stitch in the old colour, but stop at the last step with two loops of yarn on the hook. Wrap the new colour yarn around the hook and draw a loop through the two stitches on the hook to complete the stitch.

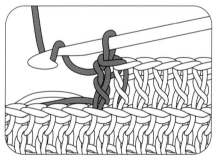

2   When you have worked the next stitch in the new shade you will see that there is a neat colour change: if the previous stitch had been completed in the old colour, that colour would have 'bled' over into the top of the new colour stitch. Sew the ends in when the crochet is complete.

increasing and decreasing

You can increase and decrease stitches in crochet to create shapes. Increasing is very simple, but there are various techniques for decreasing.

Increasing

The technique is shown here in double (single) crochet, but it is the same for all stitches.

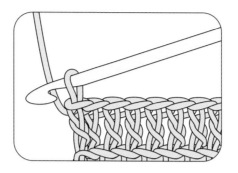

Simply work two stitches into the top of one stitch of the previous row. You can work more than two stitches into one, see Groups of Stitches (opposite).

Decreasing

Essentially you simply work stitches together to decrease. Here the techniques are shown with different numbers and types of stitches.

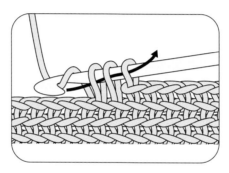

1 To make two double (single) crochet stitches into one, put the hook into the next stitch, wrap the yarn around the hook and draw a loop through. Repeat this step into the next stitch so that there are three stitches on the hook.

2 Wrap the yarn around the hook again and draw a loop through all three stitches. You have made two stitches into one and so decreased by one stitch.

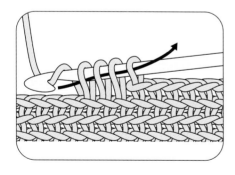

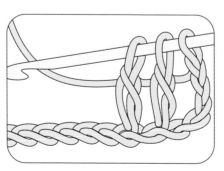

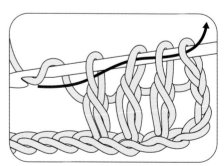

3 To make three double (single) crochet stitches into one, work as above, but repeat into the next two stitches. Wrap the yarn around the hook and draw a loop through all four stitches. You have decreased by two stitches.

4 To decrease other stitches, work in the same way, working the number of stitches to be decreased plus one and then drawing a loop through all the stitches. Here, two trebles (double crochets) are being worked together.

5 In this illustration, three trebles (double crochets) are being worked together.

decorative techniques

There are many different decorative stitches that can be incorporated into your designs, but here are just two that you may find useful.

Groups of stitches

Multiple stitches can be worked into single ones to make decorative shapes from stitches, as well as for decreasing. This is where you will see how different heights of stitches can be useful.

A group can consist of, for example, one double (single) crochet, three trebles (double crochets) and one double (single) crochet all worked into the same stitch to make a fan shape.

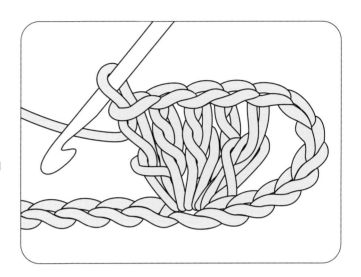

Popcorns

Popcorns are similar to bobbles in knitting and can look great in edging designs.

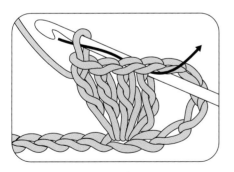

1 Work four double (single) crochets into the same stitch. Take the hook out of the working loop and from front to back put it behind the first stitch worked and through the working loop again.

2 Draw the loop behind the stitches until it appears at the front, then make a slip stitch (page 280) to complete the popcorn.

Crochet motifs

Decorative crochet motifs, such as popcorns and medallions, can be made and then appliquéd to knitted fabric. Use a tapestry needle and yarn to match the motif to sew it on.

samplers

If you can master all of the techniques on the previous pages you will have a good grounding in most things that will be asked of you when making a crocheted edging or motif.

Here are some examples of edgings for you to practise with.

Frilled edging

Lacy border

Double (single) crochet border

With RS facing rejoin yarn at base of one seam, 1ch (does not count as a st) work one round of dc evenly around entire hem, working an even no of sts and ending with a ss into first dc to join.

Next round (RS facing): 4ch, (counts as 1tr and 1ch), (1tr, 1ch) 3 times into front loop only of dc at base of 4ch, (1ch, 1tr) 3 times into back loop only of same dc, 1tr into back loop of same dc, *miss 1dc, (1tr, 1ch) 4 times into front loop only of next dc, (1tr, 1ch) 3 times into back loop only of same st, 1tr into back loop of same dc, rep from * to last dc, miss last dc, ss into 3rd dc of 4ch at beg of previous round. Cut yarn and pull through the st left on the hook to fasten off.

With RS facing rejoin yarn at base of one seam, 1ch (does not count as a st) work one round of dc evenly around entire hem, working an odd no of sts. Turn.

Row 1 (WS facing): 3ch (counts as first tr), 1tr into each dc to end, turn.

Row 2: 4ch (counts as 1tr and 1ch), miss first 2 sts *1tr into next tr, 1ch, miss 1tr, rep from * to last st, 1tr into top of 3ch at beg of prev row, turn.

Row 3: 3ch (counts as 1st tr), itr into first ch sp, *1tr into next tr, 1tr into next ch sp, rep from * to last st, 1tr into top of 3ch at beg of prev row, turn.

Row 4: 1ch (does not count as st), 1dc into first st, *miss 2tr, {3tr, 3ch and tr} into next tr, miss 2 tr, 1dc into next tr, rep from * to end, working dc at end of last rep into top of 3ch at beg of previous round. Cut yarn and pull through the st left on the hook to fasten off.

With RS facing rejoin yarn at base of one seam, 1ch (does not count as a st) work one round of dc evenly around entire hem. Turn.

Next row (WS facing): 1ch, *1dc into each of next 2dc, 3ch, 1dc into next dc, rep from * to last dc, 1dc into last dc. Cut yarn and pull through the st left on the hook to fasten off.

Arches border

Shell border

Picot edging

With RS facing rejoin yarn at base of one seam, 1ch (does not count as a st), work one round of dc evenly around entire hem, making sure that the final no of sts is a multiple of 7 + 1 and ending with a ss into first dc to join.

Next round (RS facing): 3ch (counts as a tr), miss 1dc, 1tr into each dc to last st, ss into first dc of previous round.

Round 2: 1ch, 1dc into each of first 2 tr, *7ch, miss 4 tr, 1dc into each of next 3 tr. Repeat from * to end of last rep, ss into first dc of previous round.

Round 3: 1ch, 1dc into each of first 2dc, *7dc into 7ch sp, 1dc into each of next 3dc. Repeat from * to end of last rep, ss into first dc of previous round.

Round 4: 7ch (counts as 1dtr, 3ch), miss 4dc, 1dc into each of next 3dc, *7ch, miss 7dc, 1dc into each of next 3 dc, repeat from * to last 4dc, 3ch, 1dtr into last dc, ss to 4th ch of 7ch.

Round 5: 1ch, 3dc into 3ch sp, *1dc into each of next 3dc, 7dc into 7ch sp, repeat from * to end, working 3dc into last ch sp, ss into 1st dc. Cut yarn and pull through the st left on the hook to fasten off.

With RS facing rejoin yarn at base of one seam, 1ch (does not count as a st) work one round of dc evenly around entire hem, making sure that the final no of sts is a multiple of 7 plus 1 and ending with a ss into first dc to join.

Next round (RS facing): 3ch (counts as a tr), miss 1dc, 1tr into each dc to last st, ss into first dc of previous round.

Round 2: 1ch, 1dc into each of first 2 tr, *7ch, miss 4 tr, 1dc into each of next 3 tr. Repeat from * to end of last rep, ss into first dc of previous round.

Round 3: 1ch, 1dc into each of first 2dc, *7dc into 7ch sp, 1dc into each of next 3dc. Repeat from * to end of last rep, ss into first dc of previous round.

Round 4: 7ch (counts as 1dtr, 3ch), miss 4d, 1dc into each of next 3dc, *7ch, miss 7dc, 1dc into each of next 3 dc. Repeat from * to last 4 dc, 3ch, 1dtr into last dc, ss to 4th ch of 7ch.

Round 5: 1ch, 3dc into 3ch sp, *1dc into each of next 3dc, 7dc into 7ch sp, repeat from * to end, working 3dc into last ch sp, ss into 1st dc. Cut yarn and pull through the st left on the hook to fasten off.

With RS facing rejoin yarn at base of one seam, 1ch (does not count as a st) work one round of dc evenly around entire hem, working an even no of sts and ending with a ss into first dc to join.

Next round (RS facing): 1ch (does not count as a st) 1dc into first dc *3ch, 1ss into same place as last dc **1dc into each of next 2 dc, rep from * to end, finishing last rep with **, 1dc into last dc, ss into first dc of previous round. Cut yarn and pull through the st left on the hook to fasten off.

Using crochet

Tension (gauge) squares from previous projects are perfect for practising crochet edges. Experiment with yarns that are different weights and textures to the knitting yarn.

conversions

Needle sizes

There are three systems of sizing needles and this table gives you the equivelent sizes across all three systems.

Metric	US	old UK and Canadian
25	50	–
19	35	–
15	19	–
10	15	000
9	13	00
8	11	0
7.5	11	1
7	10½	2
6.5	10½	3
6	10	4
5.5	9	5
5	8	6
4.5	7	7
4	6	8
3.75	5	9
3.5	4	–
3.25	3	10
3	2/3	11
2.75	2	12
2.25	1	13
2	0	14
1.75	00	–
1.5	000	–

Weights and lengths

You can use either the metric or imperial system of measurement but do not use both in one project or you will confuse yourself.

grams	=	ounces x 28.35
ounces	=	grams x 0.0352
centimetres	=	inches x 2.54
inches	=	centimetres x 0.3937
metres	=	yards x 1.0936
yards	=	metres x 0.9144

Yarn standards

The Yarn Council of America have a system of categorising yarns that you may find useful. It provides a guide only and you should always use the tension (gauge) and needle size given in a pattern you are following.

yarn weight symbol	yarn category names	recommended metric (US) needle size	tension (gauge) range in stocking (stockinete) stitch over 10cm (4in)
0 LACE	4-ply, 10-count crochet thread (fingering)	1.5–2.25mm (000–1)	33–40 sts
1 SUPER FINE	4-ply, sock, baby (fingering)	2.25–3.25 (1–2)	27–32 sts
2 FINE	Light-weight DK, baby (sport)	3.25–3.75mm (3–5)	23–26 sts
3 LIGHT	DK (light-weight worsted)	3.75–4.5mm (5–7)	21–24 sts
4 MEDIUM	Aran (worsted, afghan)	4.5–5.5mm (7–9)	16–20 sts
5 BULKY	Chunky (craft, rug)	5.5–8mm (9–11)	12–15 sts
6 SUPER BULKY	Super-chunky, (bulky, roving)	8mm and larger (11 and larger)	6–11 sts

glossary

A

Abbreviations Short versions of words and phrases used in *knitting*.

Aran Types of *knitting stitches* and techniques named after a group of islands off the coast of Scotland where these *stitches* are thought to have originated.

B

Ball band The paper wrapper around a ball of *yarn*.

Bias *Knitted fabric* with slanted edges.

Blocking The process of pinning out and finishing *knitted fabric*.

Blocking board A special board for *blocking knitting* on.

Bobbins Small bundles of *yarn* used when *knitting* with different colours; a purchased holder for winding small amounts of *yarn* onto.

Button band The knitted band down the centre front of a cardigan or jacket to which the buttons are sewn.

Buttonhole A hole in the *buttonhole band* through which buttons are put to fasten a cardigan or jacket.

Buttonhole band The knitted band down the centre front of a cardigan or jacket into which the *buttonholes* are worked.

C

Cable A type of *Aran* stitch made by moving groups of *stitches* across one another using a cable *needle*.

Cable needle A small double-pointed needle used in *Aran* knitting.

Carrying yarn The process of looping and anchoring a *yarn* not in use up the side or across the back of a piece of *knitted fabric*.

Casting (binding) off The process of securing the knitted *stitches* to prevent the fabric from unravelling.

Casting on The process of making the first row of *stitches* of a project.

Changing colours The action of changing from one colour of *yarn* to another in *colour knitting*.

Chart A drawing on graph paper that replaces all or part of a written *pattern* with coloured blocks or symbols denoting which *stitches* or colours of *yarn* are to be used where.

Chevron A 'V' or inverted 'V' made by *increasing* and *decreasing* stitches.

Circular knitting *Knitting* either on a *circular needle* or on four or five *double-pointed needles*.

Circular needle A *knitting needle* with two pointed metal or wooden ends joined by a flexible cord that is usually made of plastic or nylon; used for *circular knitting*.

Collar A style of *neckband* on a garment.

Colour knitting Knitting with more than one colour of *yarn*.

Continental techniques Methods of holding the *yarn* and *needles*, *casting on*, *knitting* and *purling* that are popular in Continental Europe.

Contrast colour A secondary colour of *yarn* in a *colour knitting* project; a *yarn* that is a different colour to the *main yarn* or *project yarn*.

Crochet A fabric made by intertwining loops of *yarn* or thread with a *crochet hook*; the action of making this fabric.

Crochet hook A small hook used to make *crochet fabric*.

Cross stitches A type of *Aran* stitch made by crossing individual *stitches* over one another.

D

Decreasing The process of reducing the number of *stitches* on the *knitting needle*.

Dorset button A type of button made by stitching and winding *yarn* around a metal or plastic ring, named after the English county in which these buttons are thought to have originated.

Double-pointed needles *Knitting needles* with a point at both ends; used for *circular knitting*.

Drop sleeve A sleeve with a straight top edge, without a *sleeve cap*, that does not need to be fitted into armhole *shaping* in the body of the garment.

E

Edge stitches The first and last *stitches* of a *row* of *knitting*; *stitches* worked to make a *selvedge*.

F

Facing A piece of *knitted fabric* that is sewn to the opening edge of a garment and turned to the inside to make a neat finish; a piece of *knitted fabric* that covers the tape of a zip fastener.

Fair Isle A type of *colour knitting*.

Felting The process of washing *knitted fabric* made from *wool yarn* to turn it into felt fabric.

Fibres Filaments of animal, vegetable or man-made material that are spun to make *yarn*.

Finishing techniques The methods used to sew up and otherwise complete a *knitting* project.

Flare A *knitted fabric* that widens by *increasing* or *decreasing stitches*.

Front bands The *button band* and *buttonhole band*.

Front loop The loop of a *stitch* that lies in front of the *knitting needle* as you look at it.

Fully fashioning The technique of using *increasing* and *decreasing* as a feature in a knitted project.

G

Garter stitch A *knitted fabric* made by *knitting* every *stitch* and every *row*.

Gathers A *knitted fabric* that is puckered by *increasing* or *decreasing stitches*.

Gore A shaped piece in a *knitted fabric* that widens or narrows it.

Grafting Techniques used to join pieces of *knitted fabric* without sewing.

Graphing The process of drawing out a planned *knitting* project on graph paper.

Gusset A shaped piece in a *knitted fabric* that allows for free movement; a piece that enlarges or gives a three-dimensional aspect to a knitted project.

H

Hem The edge (usually the lower edge) of a *knitted fabric* that is folded over and sewn for a neat finish.

Holding needles and yarn The techniques used to hold the *knitting needles* and *yarn* in the correct positions for *knitting*.

I

I-cord A yarn cord made by *knitting* in a specific way.

Incomplete stitch A *knit* or *purl* stitch that was not worked properly and has left two loops of yarn over the *knitting needle* instead of one.

Increasing The process of adding to the number of *stitches* on the *knitting needle*.

Inset pocket A pocket that has just a visible opening with the lining being sewn to the back of the *knitted fabric*.

Intarsia A type of *colour knitting*.

J

Joining in yarn The process of attaching a new or different-coloured ball of *yarn* to a piece of *knitting* being worked.

K

Knit The most basic of the *stitches* used in *knitting*; the generic term used to describe the action of making *knitted fabric*.

Knitted fabric A fabric made from only *knit stitches*, only *purl stitches* (very rarely), or any combination of the two; a fabric made by *knitting*.

Knitter's graph paper Special graph paper with rectangular boxes that accurately reflect the shape of a *knit* or *purl* stitch.

Knitting A generic term for a *knitted fabric* and the action of making it, whether the *stitches* used are *knit* or *purl*.

Knitting needle A stick, usually made from wood, metal or plastic, that is used to *knit* with.

L

Lace *Knitted fabric* with holes in a pattern to create an open-work design.

Left The left side of a knitted garment as you are wearing it, not as you are looking at it.

Left-hand needle The *knitting needle* held in the knitter's left hand.

M

Main colour The primary colour of *yarn* in a *colour knitting* project.

Mattress stitch A sewing stitch used to sew pieces of *knitted fabric* together, producing a very neat and often undetectable seam.

Meterage (yardage) The length of *yarn* in a ball in metres (yards).

Mitre A neat corner produced by working angles on the two pieces to be joined so that they lie flat against one another.

Moss (seed) stitch A knitted *stitch pattern* made by alternating *knit* and *purl stitches*.

N

Neckband A knitted piece that finishes off the neckline of a garment.

Needle Usually refers to *knitting needles*, but can refer to the tapestry needle or knitter's sewing needle used to sew up a project.

P

Panel knitting A style of *knitting* that involves working and joining separate panels to create a *knitted fabric*.

Patch pocket A pocket made by sewing a separate piece of *knitted fabric* to the front of a garment.

Pattern The written instructions for making a knitted project; the design made by a combination of *knit* and *purl* stitches or by using different-coloured *yarns*.

Pattern repeat A small section of a design that is repeated to make up the full design.

Pattern terminology Standard phrases that are used to desribe specific actions or sequences in written *patterns*.

Picking up stitches The technique used to make new *stitches* that are attached to a finished piece of *knitted fabric*.

Picot edge A series of small points that make a decorative edging.

Ply/plies Thin strands that are twisted together to make *yarn*.

Project yarn The *yarn* a project was knitted with.

Purl The other *stitch* (other than *knit stitch*) used in *knitting*.

R

Reverse stocking (stockinette) stitch A *knitted fabric* made by working alternate rows of *knit* stitches and *purl* stitches; the reverse side of *stocking (stockinette) stitch* fabric.

Rib A knitted *stitch pattern* made by alternating *knit* and *purl stitches*.

Right The right side of a knitted garment as you are wearing it, not as you are looking at it.

Right-hand needle The *knitting needle* held in the knitter's right hand.

Right side The side of a *knitted fabric* that will be outermost when the project is complete.

Round/s The term used to describe a row in circular knitting.

Row/s The lines of *stitches* running hrizontally across a piece of *knitted fabric*.

Row end/s The edges of a piece of *knitted fabric* that are made up of the beginnings and ends of *rows*.

Running unravelled stitch A dropped stitch that has unravelled, or run, down into the *rows* below the one on the *knitting needle*.

S

Selvedge An edge on the *row ends* of a piece of *knitted fabric* that is created by working the first and last one or two *stitches* in a different *stitch pattern* to the rest of the *row*.

Set-in sleeve A sleeve with a shaped *sleeve cap* that has the underarm seam sewn up before the sleeve is sewn into the armhole.

Sewing in ends The process of stitching any loose ends of *yarn* into the back of the *knitted fabric* to secure and neaten them.

Shaping The widening or narrowing of *knitted fabric* by *increasing* or *decreasing* the number of stitches.

Short-row shaping A technique for shaping *knitted fabric* without *increasing*, *decreasing* or *casting (binding) off*.

Sleeve cap/head/top The top part of a sleeve where it attaches to the body of a garment.

Slip knot The knot used to start almost every piece of *knitting*.

Slipped stitch A *stitch* that is transferred from the *left-hand needle* to the *right-hand needle* without being *knitted* or *purled*.

Smocking A process of binding together *stitches* within a *stitch pattern* to create a bunched effect.

Snag A loop of *yarn* accidentally pulled out of a piece of *knitted fabric*.

Stitch/es The individual loops of *yarn* that make up the *rows* of a piece of *knitted fabric*.

Stitch pattern The design made by a combination of *knit* and *purl* stitches.

Stocking (stockinette) stitch A *knitted fabric* made by working alternate rows of *knit* and *purl* stitches.

Stranding yarn In *colour knitting*, the process of looping and anchoring a colour of *yarn* not in use across the back of a piece of *knitted fabric*.

Substituting yarn Swapping the *yarn* specified in a *pattern* for another *yarn*.

Swatch A small knitted-up sample of a piece of *knitted fabric*; to make such a sample.

Swiss darning An embroidery stitch that duplicates the look of *knitted stitches*.

T

Tension (gauge) The tightness or looseness of the *stitches* in a piece of *knitted fabric*.

Through the back loop Through the loop of a *stitch* that lies behind the *knitting needle* as you look at it.

Tubular cast on A *cast on* technique that creates a soft, rolled edge.

Tucks Pleats that run horizontally across a *knitted fabric*.

Turning Swapping the *knitting needles* in your hands to turn the work around so that the other side is facing you.

Twist stitches A type of *Aran* stitch made by crossing individual *stitches* over one another.

Twisted stitch A *stitch* that has become twisted on the *knitting needle* so that the *front loop* is lying over the back of the *knitting needle* as you look at it.

U

Uneven knitting *Knitted fabric* with unintentionally different-sized *stitches* or ridges in it.

W

Weight A term used to describe the thickness of a *yarn*.

Welt The hem, cuffs or pocket borders on a knitted project.

Wool *Yarn* made from the fleece of sheep primarily, though some breeds of goats, llamas, camels and rabbits have hair that is spun into *yarn* that can be described as wool; a term used generically (and inaccurately) to describe all *yarns*.

Working end of yarn The end of the *yarn* that is coming from the ball.

Working from a chart To *knit* following a *chart* rather than a written *pattern*.

Wrong side The side of a *knitted fabric* that will be innermost when the project is complete.

Y

Yarn The correct term to use to describe knitting material.

Yarnover A technique for creating a hole in a knitted fabric by looping the yarn over the needle before working the next stitch.

resources

The Internet has brought fabulous yarn shops, expert knitting advice and social groups into any home with a computer. Visit the following sites for information and products.

For information on Rowan knitting workshops across the country either visit www.knitrowan.com or call on 44 (0)1484 681881.

www. knitrowan.com

www.bhkc.co.uk

www.da-handknits.demon.co.uk

www.duppdupp.com

www.englishyarns.co.uk

www.getknitted.com

www.glasspens.com/circular-knitting-needles

www.goosepond.com

www.handpaintedyarn.com

www.kangaroo.uk.com

www.kimhargreaves.co.uk

www.knitcafe.com

www.knitcases.com

www.knitknack.co.uk

www.knittinghelp.com

www.knitty.com

www.magknits.com

www.masondixonknitting.com

www.peacefleece.com

www.purlescence.co.uk

www.purlsoho.com

www.ravelry.com

www.stitchnbitch.co.uk

www.techknitting.blogspot.com

www.theknittingparlour.co.uk

www.tillitomas.com

www.vam.ac.uk/collections/fashion/features/knitting/index.html

www.wensleydalelongwoolsheepshop.co.uk

www.winghamwoolwork.co.uk

index

acknowledgments

This book has been quite a challenge, mainly due to its size and the quantity of information I have tried to give you. You can't do a book like this without a huge amount of support, especially as I also work full-time as the Retail Manager for Rowan. I would like to thank everyone that has supported me through this, namely: Kate Haxell, who when she was brought on board as project manager made me feel as though all my Christmases had come at once. I have to thank her for her patience, understanding and support when I was loosing it.Kuo Kang Chen for his wonderful illustrations. Louise Leffler for designing the book so beautifully. Katie Cowan and Michelle Lo for giving me the opportunity to do the book, and all the team at Anova Books. Kate Buller for taking me on as a Retail Manager 12 years ago and making these opportunities possible for me. Rowan Yarns for the support with yarn and patterns. Jane Crowfoot and Penny Hill for helping with the making of swatches and technical support and thanks to Jane for lending samples of her lovely work. Michael Wicks for his patience during photography and the great images he produced. My son, Darren, for his support with research and images for illustration. And finally, to all of my family who have had to endure me being tucked away in the office for weekend after weekend; thanks for all the cups of tea I received in the process.

credits

Photography credits:
istockphoto: 21, 62, 87, 125, 207, 258, 262, 276, 279.
All other photography by Michael Wicks.

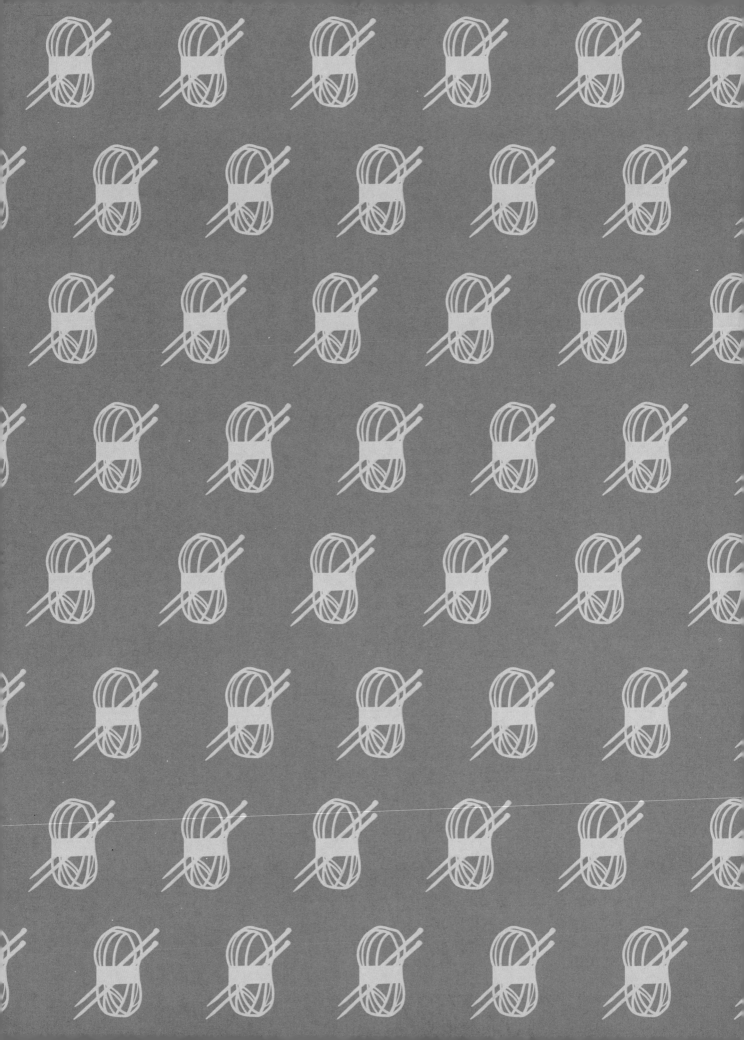